NEW PENGUIN SHAKESPEARE
GENERAL EDITOR: T. J. B. SPENCER
ASSOCIATE EDITOR: STANLEY WELLS

WILLIAM SHAKESPEARE

*

TROILUS
AND
CRESSIDA

EDITED BY
R. A. FOAKES

PENGUIN BOOKS

PENGUIN BOOKS

Published by the Penguin Group
Penguin Books Ltd, 27 Wrights Lane, London W8 5TZ, England
Penguin Putnam Inc., 375 Hudson Street, New York, New York 10014, USA
Penguin Books Australia Ltd, Ringwood, Victoria, Australia
Penguin Books Canada Ltd, 10 Alcorn Avenue, Toronto, Ontario, Canada M4V 3B2
Penguin Books (NZ) Ltd, 182–190 Wairau Road, Auckland 10, New Zealand

Penguin Books Ltd, Registered Offices: Harmondsworth, Middlesex, England

This edition first published 1987
10

Printed in England by Clays Ltd, St Ives plc
Set in Linotron Ehrhardt

CONTENTS

INTRODUCTION

Troilus and Cressida has come into its own as a play for the twentieth century. It was written probably in 1602, soon after *Hamlet*, and is first recorded in an entry for copyright purposes in the Stationers' Register on 7 February 1603. Nothing is known of performances in Shakespeare's lifetime, and the play's history is a blank until John Dryden reworked it, simplified the language, and streamlined the action, especially as it concerns the Trojan War; he also added a notable quarrel scene between Hector and Troilus, and drastically changed the last act by adding a scene in which Cressida commits suicide. This version, better thought of perhaps as an independent treatment of the theme rather than as an adaptation of Shakespeare's play, was seen on the stage in a number of productions between 1679 and 1734. Apart from these, the first full-scale production of the play was that by William Poel in London in December 1912. Poel, a pacifist, cut the text severely, and made the play seem rather absurd to the audience by his treatment of it, which included casting women in the roles of Aeneas, Paris, and Thersites. Nevertheless, the timing of this production, not long before the outbreak of the First World War, was significant, for *Troilus and Cressida* has perhaps made its greatest impact on the stage as a play that casts a cold eye on the realities of war.

It was revived successfully in Cambridge and London in 1922 as an expression of disgust and weariness with the war, but seemed a 'museum piece' to reviewers of a 1936 production. The threat of the Second World War, however, gave a modern dress production in 1938 an immediate relevance; the Trojans wore khaki, and the

Greeks blue uniforms, and Thersites was characterized as an intellectual of the extreme left. As the Second World War receded in memory, other aspects of the play were given more prominence on the stage, especially the theme of wantonness in love, as depicted in Pandarus, Cressida, Paris, and Helen. By 1960, when a notable production was staged by the Royal Shakespeare Company at Stratford, audiences beginning to be familiar with the theatre of the absurd and the work of Bertolt Brecht found no difficulty in responding to the shifting moods of *Troilus and Cressida*, and its combination of heroism with farce, idealism with cynicism. In more recent times audiences who live in an anxious world troubled by the possibility of ever more terrible global conflict have readily appreciated Shakespeare's brilliant dramatization of the futility of the Trojan War.

*

The play has become a focus of critical attention in recent years, and has generated a continuing and lively debate about its nature and significance. Most of Shakespeare's plays fit pretty well into the categories of comedies, histories, and tragedies into which the compilers of the first collected edition, the first Folio of 1623, divided them. *Troilus and Cressida*, however, is an exception; the Folio editors intended initially to place it among the tragedies, but in the end fitted it in between the histories and tragedies. The publishers of the first edition, the Quarto of 1609, seem to have regarded it as a comedy (for fuller comment, see the Account of the Text, page 229). The uncertainty of the earliest editors of the play about its genre has continued to affect modern commentary on it. Although it is still often grouped with *All's Well That Ends Well* (?1602–3) and *Measure for Measure* (?1604) as a 'dark' or 'problem' comedy, it differs markedly from these later plays in a number of ways, notably in dealing with a classical theme, the

8

Trojan War. Many critics have attempted to prove that it belongs to their chosen category, within a range extending from comedy through comical satire, play of ideas, and tragical satire to tragedy.

The problem of establishing the play's genre is further complicated by the difference between the two early texts, as printed in 1609 (the Quarto) and 1623 (the first Folio). It appears that Shakespeare at some point revised the text, and the later version, that printed in the Folio, includes two final exits for Pandarus, one at the end of V.3 and the other, repeating lines from V.3, at the end of the play in V.10. If the first of these is omitted (it is not printed in the Quarto), the play ends on a comic note with Pandarus addressing the audience; but if the second is left out, the play ends with Troilus crying for revenge on Achilles for the death of Hector, and can be seen more plausibly as a tragedy, or at least as having a tragic ending.

One or other of these two passages must be cut in performance, and the textual evidence is inconclusive. It seems to me that the sourly comic ending with Pandarus complaining to the audience is much the more appropriate to the general tone of the play, and the nature of its action; and the play falls naturally into two halves, one predominantly comic, and culminating in Pandarus's address to the audience at the end of III.2, the other harsher, and ending on a more bitter note, but also with Pandarus addressing the audience, so paralleling the first part. Nothing is known about pauses or intervals in early performances, but the end of III.2 seems an obvious place for one. The conventional act and scene divisions are not marked in the early printings of the play, and were first introduced in the eighteenth century; though a great convenience for references to the text, they have no necessary connexion with the treatment of the play on the stage.

The question of the genre of *Troilus and Cressida* has probably taken on much more importance than it deserves. It is satisfying to be able to label a play as a comedy or tragedy, but this one resists easy classification. In recent times dramatists have broken away from traditional categories; Brechtian drama, the theatre of the absurd, and post-absurdist plays have taught us to appreciate tragic farces, farcical tragedies, and dramas of alienation. *Troilus and Cressida* mixes comedy and heroism, farcical satire and revenge, parody and tragedy, so that it relates well to modern modes of drama. Partly because of this, and partly because it affords a mirror to an age which can find in it a reflection of its own doubts about traditional values, as well as its anxieties about war, the play has proved fascinating to the later twentieth century. Another reason for this appeal is that the play is still so fresh to us, as a work virtually rediscovered since the two world wars; because it is not locked into the assumptions and prejudices of a long critical and theatrical history, it can take on several kinds of reflective coloration, according to the reader's or viewer's attitude to the world.

*

In *Troilus and Cressida* Shakespeare seems deliberately to open up conflicting or contradictory perspectives on the main characters and themes of the play. The title promises a play about the most famous medieval addition to the story of Troy, celebrated in two great English versions, Chaucer's *Troilus and Criseyde* and Robert Henryson's *The Testament of Cresseid*, both of which Shakespeare knew. The Prologue, in full armour, announces a stirring play about the Trojan War, beginning in the middle of 'those broils' (line 27) in good epic fashion, as recommended by Horace. The action begins, it is true, with Trojan warriors returning from battle in I.2, and ends with a renewal of fighting in V.4, but mostly takes place during what Aeneas calls 'this dull and long-continued truce' (I.3.262). Moreover, the great cause for which kings and princes, 'their high blood chafed' (Prologue, line 2), have clashed in the siege of Troy turns out to be of less immediate concern than private quarrels and political intrigue.

These clashes of perspective on one level provide matter for comedy and satire; on another level they bring out disturbingly the instability of even the best of men, and the private corruption of public values. The opening scenes lead us into the action involving Pandarus, Troilus, and Cressida. After the Prologue's promises of war, we pass immediately to Troilus removing his armour and refusing to fight, putting the 'cruel battle' (I.1.3) of emotions in his heart above his duty to Troy. Troilus's youth is emphasized in the play – he is 'very young' (I.2.116), beardless (I.2.142), a 'brave boy' (V.3.35) – and his language in the first scene suggests he has an adolescent infatuation with Cressida, in the extravagance of his imagery – 'her hand, | In whose comparison all whites are ink' (I.1.56–7) – and his self-dramatization, recalling himself to the correct stance of the conventional lover, wholly devoted to his mistress,

> And when fair Cressid comes into my thoughts –
> So, traitor! – 'when she comes'? – when is she thence?
>
> I.1.32–3

He is in love with love, turning Cressida into an impossible ideal of beauty; but at the same time he has in her uncle Pandarus a means to press his suit, so that he also sees her, in another perspective, as a prize to be taken, a pearl to be ventured for, a piece of merchandise. The gap between his idealization of Cressida and his matter-of-fact aim to find his way to her bed, reinforced by Pandarus's image of this process as baking a cake, is comic in effect here, especially as Troilus forgets about love when Aeneas calls him, and ends the scene by going off to fight after all.

This scene is brilliantly complemented by the long scene that follows between Pandarus and Cressida. This establishes Pandarus as a gossipy, affectionate uncle, enjoying for its own sake the play of wit, as Cressida skilfully parries his praise of Troilus, and deflects his varied attempts to make her acknowledge an interest in him. Cressida, too, is presumably very young, alone in Troy since her father Calchas, foreseeing the eventual defeat of the Trojans, has gone over to the Greeks, and having no one but Pandarus to 'defend' her honour and beauty (I.2.260–64). Since he has become an enemy to her 'honesty' as agent for Troilus, she relies, cleverly and successfully in this delightful scene, on her wit to avoid his pressure, aided by Pandarus's comic mistaking of Troilus for Deiphobus as the Trojan warriors return in procession from the day's fighting.

Shakespeare does not show us how Pandarus gets through Cressida's defences; the function of her rhyming soliloquy at the end of I.2, in which she confesses her love for Troilus, is to prepare us for her surrender when she appears again in III.2. There is a considerable lapse of narrative time between I.2 and I.3; in I.2 we watch Trojan warriors return from battle, but in I.3 we learn that a truce has been in effect for a long period. In terms of the action of the play, however, events seem to move swiftly, and Pandarus brings about the encounter in III.2 between Troilus and Cressida as if it happened within the next day or two. The one scene in which Helen appears, III.1, provides a central image of love in the world of the play. It is sometimes taken as confirming Thersites' cynical view that 'All the argument is a whore and a cuckold' (II.3.71–2), but there is much more to the scene than this. It is true that, on the one hand, the dialogue of this scene moves through bawdy jokes to Pandarus's song on lovers 'dying' in the act, thence to a definition of love as 'hot deeds', or lechery in Thersites' language, and so finally to Pandarus's allusion to the Gospels, 'is love a generation of vipers?' (III.1.129–30), recalling (anachronistically) Christ's words of scorn to hypocrites, 'ye generation of vipers, how will ye escape the damnation of hell' (Matthew 23.33). On the other hand, the scene is light-hearted, witty, and warm; the affectionate intimacy between Pandarus, Helen, and Paris contrasts with the pompousness of the politicians and the brutalities of the battlefield.

Moreover, this scene sharply focuses the place of women in the male-dominated world of the Greeks and Trojans. They are articles of trade; as Troilus likens winning Cressida to buying or stealing a pearl (I.1.102), so Helen has been stolen from Menelaus in retaliation for the capture by the Greeks of Hesione, Priam's sister (II.2.78). She has evidently adapted to Troy and become an accepted member of the royal family, even to helping to remove Hector's armour (III.1.147), and we have no reason to doubt that Paris means it when he goes off saying 'Sweet, above thought I love thee.' It is in this context that the fulfilment of Troilus's passion is shown in III.2. If Cressida has hitherto defended her 'honesty', her love has grown too 'headstrong' (III.2.121), and she goes to bed with Troilus consciously dedicating her 'folly' to her uncle Pandarus, and unable to stop herself from blabbing about her delight. She is taken up with the 'rapture' of the moment, but Troilus urges another dimension, seeking the maximum intensity of pleasure in the moment, together with eternal constancy. Perhaps Cressida's greater folly is to try to match Troilus's demand. The scene ends with Pandarus holding their hands in a kind of parody of a marriage ceremony as he ushers them off to bed. This ending, like the matter-of-fact activity of Pandarus early in the scene while he goes about his business as a bawd, exposes the radical disconnexion between Troilus's desire for immediate gratification and demand for eternal constancy.

*

In this first part of the play, up to III.2, Troilus's aim is to
seduce Cressida, to 'wallow in the lily-beds' (III.2.11) of
lust, and his passionate verse speeches are comically
distanced by Pandarus's prosaic concern for practical
details. The comic note culminates in the last lines of
III.2, when Pandarus, alone, addresses the audience
directly, wishing all 'tongue-tied maidens' present a
pander to help them. This marks an appropriate point for
a break in performance: the action shifts to the Greek
camp in III.3, to initiate the process which leads to the
exchange of Cressida for Antenor, and the tone alters as
the comic element diminishes in the second half of the
play. Now Troilus insists upon that constancy he had
demanded in III.2, repeatedly urging 'be thou true' to
Cressida (IV.4.57, 61, 64, 65, 73) as if he has no trust in
her anyway, and making demands appropriate only between husband and wife. His 'godly jealousy' (IV.4.79)
echoes St Paul's Second Epistle to the Corinthians 11.2,
'I am jealous over you with godly jealousy; for I have
coupled you to one man'. Again in V.2, when Troilus has
watched Cressida teasing Diomedes, and heard her
confess her 'turpitude' (V.2.114) in taking Diomedes as a
lover, he still cries out, as if she were married to him,

Cressid is mine, tied with the bonds of heaven.

V.2.157

These allusions to marriage are ironic in relation to
Troilus's earlier defence of keeping Helen in Troy:

I take today a wife, and my election
Is led on in the conduct of my will,
My will enkindled by mine eyes and ears,
Two traded pilots 'twixt the dangerous shores
Of will and judgement: how may I avoid,
Although my will distaste what it elected,
The wife I chose? There can be no evasion
To blench from this, and to stand firm by honour.

II.2.62–9

In this scene Troilus does not make a connexion between standing firm on honour and the fact that Helen is the chosen wife of Menelaus, not Paris; equally, later on, he demands from Cressida the loyalty of a wife, although he has treated her as the object of his lust, lamenting that his will, or desire, is 'boundless, and the act a slave to limit' (III.2.81). Hector had reminded Troilus that 'value dwells not in particular will' (II.2.54), but the lesson was wasted on him, if not on the audience, who may see how Troilus exemplifies Hector's argument:

> 'Tis mad idolatry
> To make the service greater than the god;
> And the will dotes that is inclinable
> To what infectiously itself affects,
> Without some image of th'affected merit.
>
> II.2.57–61

Troilus's desire (will) is caught like a disease from Cressida, without reference to her own intrinsic worth; in other words, Troilus sees in her an image corresponding to his desire, and assumes she will conform to that image, without consideration for Cressida as she is.

So he cannot at first credit what he is seeing when he observes Cressida with Diomedes: 'This is, and is not, Cressid' (V.2.149); as he emerges from his confusion of mind, his resentment is channelled into revenge, and his one thought is to seek out and punish Diomedes in battle. The conflict of feelings in the deeply hurt Troilus is superbly dramatized in his long speech at V.2.140–63; at the same time, this scene reveals the essentially self-centred nature of his love for Cressida, which is not, in William Blake's terms, like that of the clod, caring for others, not itself, but is rather that of the pebble:

> Love seeketh only self to please,
> To bind another to its delight,

> *Joys in another's loss of ease,*
> *And builds a Hell in Heaven's despite.*
>
> 'The Clod and the Pebble'

The play gives us more than one perspective on Cressida. Troilus's disgust at her switch to Diomedes is understandable:

> *The fractions of her faith, orts of her love,*
> *The fragments, scraps, the bits, and greasy relics*
> *Of her o'er-eaten faith, are bound to Diomed.*
>
> V.2.161–3

But these lines recall the image of achieving Cressida as baking a cake in the opening scene, and reflect Troilus's basic attitude to love as gratification of the senses. There is another Cressida, a girl cast adrift in Troy with only her uncle, a humorous and immoral old bawd, for protection, a girl who becomes a piece of merchandise in the barter of war, to be traded for Antenor. She is brought to the Greeks in IV.5 at a moment when all the princes and generals are assembled to see Ajax and Hector fight, and each of them, following the lead of Agamemnon, that 'god in office, guiding men' (I.3.231), offers to kiss her in turn. The scornful comments by Ulysses, setting her down as a wanton slut (IV.5.61–3), are sometimes taken as literally true, or as placed to guide audience response. Cressida's initial silence, however, suggests she is overwhelmed, and when she does speak, it is in the witty bantering tone of her dialogue with Pandarus in I.2, as she avoids being kissed by Menelaus and Ulysses. This scene also dramatizes the extent to which women are the playthings of warrior princes.

The world of this play is not one for figures like Lucrece, who committed suicide after being raped, choosing to die rather than live polluted, and with the stain on her husband's name. In his poem on this theme, Shakespeare wrote

For men have marble, women waxen minds,
And therefore are they formed as marble will;
The weak oppressed, the impression of strange kinds
Is formed in them by force, or fraud, or skill.
Then call them not the authors of their ill,
No more than wax shall be accounted evil
Wherein is stamped the semblance of a devil.

The Rape of Lucrece, 1240–46

In *Troilus and Cressida*, women are weak and oppressed, and, like wax, take on the impression of other natures ('strange kinds') who can use force or fraud or skill; the role-model is Helen, forcibly abducted, and making the best of it by taking on the impression of her captor, Paris, and adapting to the court of the Trojans. Cressida parallels Helen, as she is taken by force from the Trojans and handed over to Diomedes, the 'guardian' (V.2.8) whose impression she takes on. Her uncle skilfully man-oeuvres her into bed with Troilus, and her father sends her to Diomedes in V.2; no one except Ulysses dis-approves, and the greatest of the Greek warriors, Achil-les, keeps both a mistress, Polyxena, and, if we can believe Thersites, a 'masculine whore' (V.1.17) in Pat-roclus. Troilus first seduces, and then demands eternal constancy from Cressida, expecting of her a standard of moral behaviour neither he nor the Greek and Trojan generals practise.

*

If there is an exception, it is Hector, whose wise, fair, and true wife (I.3.275) Andromache appears in Act V, but as we hear of him in Act I venting his spleen on her after he has been struck down in battle (I.2.6), so in V.3 he rejects her anxious 'admonishment' not to fight, because his 'honour' demands that he fulfil pledges to fight various Greeks, and because he is 'i'the vein of chivalry' (V.3.32). This recalls Pandarus's praise of Troilus as 'the prince of chivalry' (I.2.229), suggesting the code of medieval knights-at-arms. This image of chivalrous gallantry is maintained in the references to the Greek and Trojan warriors as 'knights', as by Achilles (II. 1.123), Ulysses (II.3.260), Aeneas (IV.5.86), Agamemnon (IV.5.88), and Hector (IV.5.158). Welcomed in the Greek camp after his inconclusive fight with Ajax, Hector is praised by Nestor as a model of gallantry on the battlefield, and is established as the role-model for a warrior.

Yet this image is countered by others. Bored with the truce, Hector sends a challenge to the Greeks in the form of a boast that his lady is fairer and truer than 'ever Greek did compass in his arms', and if the challenge is not met, he can say

> *The Grecian dames are sunburnt, and not worth*
> *The splinter of a lance.*

I.3.282–3

Shakespeare seems here to have had in mind combat in the lists between knights on horseback armed with lances; but this challenge, which wittily confounds the arms of a lover's embrace with the arms of battle, arises from selfish motives. Hector's aim is to stir Achilles to fight again, and to gratify his whim, he risks his own life in single combat, although he is the mainstay of the Trojan army.

The glory, honour, and renown (II.2.200–201) sought by the Trojans in magnanimous deeds in battle refers, as Hector admits, to the 'joint and several dignities' of the Trojan princes, to their personal reputations as well as their joint worthiness. As has often been noted, in the Trojan council scene (II.2) Hector rebukes Paris and Troilus for persisting in keeping Helen against the law of nature and of nations, but has already repudiated his own arguments by sending his challenge, all in the interests of a dubious code of honour that has more to do with reputation than morality. As the play opens up conflicting perspectives on love, so it reveals varying perspectives on codes of heroism and chivalry, as at once noble, generous, and magnanimous and, at the same time, like Troilus's love, self-centred. This is brought out most poignantly in the death of Hector, who, having pursued and killed a Greek for his splendid armour, rests and takes off his armour on the battlefield, leaving himself defenceless before Achilles' Myrmidons.

In V.3 Hector demands King Priam's permission to go to battle, saying 'You know me dutiful' (V.3.72), but this is the duty Hector owes his father, and there is no sense of a larger allegiance to Troy, any more than the Greeks have a commitment to their cause. In the opening scene, Troilus's passion for Cressida prevents him from fighting when he should be on the battlefield; Paris stays behind at the whim of Helen, 'I would fain have armed today, but my Nell would not have it so' (III.1.133–4); and even after he has told Hector he will meet him on the battlefield, Achilles breaks his promise because his 'major vow' is to his mistress Polyxena (V.1.41). It is ironic that Hector rejects the pleading of Andromache and Cassandra, and goes into battle to keep his personal engagement 'to many Greeks' (V.3.68).

These gallant knights seeking glory in magnanimous deeds, meeting each other in single combat under chivalric rules, as when Ajax and Hector fight, are, from another perspective, engaged in a war that will end with the destruction of Troy. In this context, to refuse to fight because of a promise to a mistress and to be concerned for personal glory above all else seem irresponsible stances, and the mercy practised by Hector becomes a vice (V.3.37). In the opening scene Aeneas speaks of the battle as 'good sport' (I.1.115), but Hector finds too late that war cannot be treated as a game played by sporting rules, when, unarmed, he is ruthlessly butchered at the command of Achilles.

*

The Greek and Trojan leaders are also shown as politicians. The Greeks have a special problem in that Achilles, their best warrior, and Ajax, resentful of the general authority ceded to Agamemnon and Ulysses, keep their tents, refuse to fight, and mock the general councils of war. This is the state of affairs in I.3, the Greek council scene, which takes place, as noted earlier, some time after the previous scene, and during a long truce. Probably no one any longer thinks of the long speech of Ulysses (I.3.75–137) as a key statement of Shakespeare's own belief in order and degree. It is indeed a magnificent rhetorical appeal from the disorder among the Greeks to 'degree, priority, and place' in the universe in order to explain what has gone wrong with Greek affairs; and it offers a vision of a hierarchical world harmoniously ordered ('untune that string, | And hark what discord follows!') to set against the possibility of chaos that lies in the wilfulness of Achilles and Ajax. The speech is undercut, however, both by the mocking intervention of Aeneas bringing Hector's challenge and by the device of ballot-rigging resorted to by Ulysses in order to ensure that Ajax rather than Achilles meets Hector's challenge. The whole scene, indeed, has a significant comic thread; the overblown rhetoric of Nestor and Ulysses addressing Agamemnon as godlike (I.3.31), as if he were, in Ulysses' terms, like the sun,

> the glorious planet Sol
> In noble eminence enthroned and sphered
> Amidst the other . . .
>
> I.3.89–91

is effectively mocked by the inability of Aeneas to distinguish the general's 'imperial looks', to pick out 'that god in office, guiding men' (I.3.224, 231) from ordinary mortals.

The 'wisdom' of Ulysses and Nestor as applied to affairs of state has little to do with grand visions of order in the world, and they operate as practical politicians, using devious means to bring Achilles back to the battle-field. Their device for ensuring that Ajax meets Hector's challenge backfires, and merely makes Ajax more proud than ever, as he struts about absurdly in II.3. The meeting with Achilles carefully staged by Ulysses in III.3 shows him appealing to reputation, and the need to stay in the rat-race, as a means of persuading Achilles to fight. This attempt also fails, and 'the policy of those crafty-swearing rascals ... is not proved worth a blackberry' (V.4.9–12), as Thersites observes. So again there are clashing perspectives; the political wisdom orchestrated in Ulysses' abstract conception of an ordered universe is very different from political wisdom as involved in the practical expediency of human affairs.

In the Trojan debate in II.2 on whether to return Helen to the Greeks, Shakespeare puts into Hector's mouth an argument for sending her back chiefly in terms of the 'moral laws | Of nature and of nations', as derived by reason from divine law in Book I of Richard Hooker's *The Laws of Ecclesiastical Polity* (1594; see II.2.185–6 and the Commentary). These abstract principles, however, are at odds with the demands of honour and the chivalry that Hector professes, which requires a war for its expression in magnanimous deeds. Paris also has a point in urging that it would be contemptible to return Helen now as soiled goods, a 'ransacked queen' (II.2.151), to her husband, Menelaus. Paris and Troilus speak in this scene out of passion, but Hector coolly outlines why it is wrong to keep Helen, and then in making up what he calls a 'free determination | 'Twixt right and wrong', he decides to maintain the wrong. His free choice, however, is not governed simply by moral principles; he chooses a life of war, in the hope of gaining honour and fame, and this means holding on to Helen. The fall of Troy has been prophesied, so that both we in the audience and Hector himself have heard Cassandra foretell destruction (II.2.110), and later Ulysses does so too (IV.5.219–

21); nevertheless Hector chooses not to believe them, but rather to play out his life according to values which have meaning for him: it is nobler to die in battle than live in peace won with shame.

*

Hector earns our respect for this. Indeed, there are no simple and clear choices to be made between the varying or conflicting perspectives the play opens up on love, chivalry, honour, order, and policy. As if to emphasize this, Shakespeare gave a prominent role to Thersites, who hangs about the Greek camp continually reducing the Trojan War to simplistic moral judgements: 'Here is such patchery, such juggling, and such knavery! All the argument is a whore and a cuckold' (II.3.70–72). The action of the play shows this is not true, and in any case the unprincipled Thersites speaks out of envy and malice, and the audience sees that his perspective on people and events is cynical and not to be trusted. Shakespeare may have developed this role from Ben Jonson's Carlo Buffone in *Every Man out of his Humour* (1599; a play performed by Shakespeare's company and one in which he may have acted a part), a character well described as one who 'bites at all, but eats on those that feed him' (I.2.203). Thersites also bites those who feed him, taking pleasure in the weaknesses and miseries of others; and, evil himself (when he prays, it is to the 'devil Envy', II.3.20), he aims to stir up discord with his 'spiteful execrations' (II.3.7).

Here in Act II, when we first see Thersites, he is presented to some extent in the role of a professional fool; Achilles says to Ajax 'Will you set your wit to a fool's?' (II.1.85), and later prevents Patroclus from silencing Thersites with the words 'He is a privileged man. – Proceed, Thersites' (II.3.56). In these scenes, and in the later part of III.3, where Thersites plays the role of Achilles' fool, he can be very amusing, as in II.3, where he 'proves' Achilles and Patroclus are fools, or in his parody of Ajax (III.3.270–99); but he announces his allegiance to the devil in his 'prayer' at the beginning of II.3, which, as a kind of soliloquy, gives us an insight into his true character early on. When Shakespeare brings back Thersites in Act V, the good humour has largely gone, and he is more evidently a 'damnable box of envy', as Patroclus calls him (V.1.22); there is something obscene about the relish with which he watches Diomedes, Cressida, and Troilus in V.2, and once battle is joined he becomes merely contemptible, appropriately dismissed from the field and from the play with Margarelon's line 'The devil take thee, coward' (V.7.23).

Thersites is an observer, provoking mischief when he can but avoiding involvement, who degenerates into a voyeur in Act V, his moral denunciations undercut by the lascivious pleasure he takes in the lechery of Diomedes. The play has a number of scenes in which others also act as observers: in I.2, Cressida and Pandarus watch the Trojan heroes returning from battle; in II.3, Ajax is watched and commented on by Agamemnon, Ulysses, and Nestor; Pandarus hovers over Troilus and Cressida as he pushes them together in III.2; in III.3 Achilles observes all the Greek commanders go by his tent and then watches Thersites imitate Ajax; the Greek generals inspect Cressida as she is brought to their camp in IV.5, and then the Greeks and Trojans watch Hector and Ajax fight in single combat; later in this scene Achilles and Hector look one another over, the first time they have met face to face unarmed; and in the most complex of all the scenes of observing, V.2, Ulysses watches Troilus looking at the encounter of Cressida and Diomedes, while Thersites lurks on stage taking note of all of them.

This emphasis on observing relates to the peculiar nature of this play as concerned with characters who exist primarily as public figures. For the Trojans, the idea of chivalry or heroism is bound up with the value they put on honour in the sense of fame or renown. For the Greeks, the idea of order and good policy turns out, in the important scene in which Ulysses advises Achilles (III.3), to be bound up with the value they put on reputation. After Cressida's acknowledgement to the audience at the end of I.2 of the love for Troilus she has concealed from Pandarus, the major characters do not reveal themselves in soliloquy. Some critics complain about this lack of inner life in the characters as a deficiency in the play, and certainly *Troilus and Cressida* is very different in this respect from *Hamlet*, the play Shakespeare was working on a year or two earlier. Shakespeare deliberately avoided soliloquy in a play that is primarily comic in the first three acts, and maintains a satiric detachment throughout. At the same time, he created public figures trying to fulfil the roles expected of them, concerned, as we would now say, with their image, and this is one reason why the play has seemed so startlingly modern to directors and reviewers in recent times. For we live in a world in which it surprises no one that an actor becomes president of a powerful country, and when vast organizations exist to create the images politicians and generals present to the public.

Shakespeare took as his subject for *Troilus and Cressida* the matter of Troy, the most famous legend of antiquity, and his major characters in it already possessed, as they still do, a mythical status as archetypes of heroism (Hector, Achilles), beauty (Helen), or statesmanship (Ulysses). This is to say that in contrast to Hamlet or Othello, for example, we inevitably measure Shakespeare's characterizations of them against the Homeric legend that has for all time established a particular idea of them. Shakespeare was aware of this; he did not need to exhibit Helen as a model of beauty, since he could take it for granted that his audience would think of her so, but he ends the first half of the play in III.2 with a tableau of

Troilus, Cressida, and Pandarus dramatizing themselves as archetypes: 'Let all constant men be Troiluses, all false women Cressids, and all brokers-between Pandars!' (III.2.200–202). So these three, who derive from medieval accretions to the Homeric story, are given a legendary status too.

The action takes place, according to Agamemnon at I.3.12, in the eighth year of the siege of Troy, at a particular moment in time, and is centred on the death of Hector. But this is not a moment in historical time, and Shakespeare gave the play a medieval colouring, by treating the Greek and Trojan heroes as knights, attributing to the Trojans chivalric ideals, and presenting Troilus as a courtly lover. As Troilus appeals to an idea of love as fixed and timeless in constancy, so Ulysses in his long speech on order in I.3 appeals to a concept of order as fixed in a universe of spatial relations, a system of degree in the arrangement of the planets and of society; and Hector, in the Trojan council scene (II.2), also appeals to a fixed system of values, the laws of nature and of nations as supposedly derived from divine law. The events of the play thus take place against these absolutes, of love, order, and value, and also in the context of the qualities permanently attributed to the legendary figures of the Trojan War.

*

It is in this context that the play's preoccupation with time needs to be understood. Elsewhere, most notably in the *Sonnets*, with their plangent sense of love being 'With Time's injurious hand crushed and o'erworn' (Sonnet 63), Shakespeare movingly dwells on mutability; he could also treat the subject satirically, as in Jaques' speech on the seven ages of man in *As You Like It*, II.7, but in no other play is this so prominent a theme as in *Troilus and Cressida*. On the one hand, the action is very specifically related to the passage of a few days. The opening scene is set in daytime, early enough for warriors to be going to fight in battle; I.2 marks their return the same day; the challenge Aeneas brings to the Greeks in I.3 is for a fight to take place 'Tomorrow morning' (II. 1. 123). In III.1 Pandarus is establishing Troilus's excuse for being absent from Priam's supper-table, and he spends that night bringing Troilus and Cressida together. Cressida is traded for Antenor the next morning (IV.1–5). Later that same morning the fight between Hector and Ajax takes place. The Trojan visitors are entertained until night falls by the Greeks, and torches are much in evidence to signify the lateness of the hour in V.1 and V.2. The final action in which Hector is killed follows on the next day.

On the other hand, the sense of swift change and instant reversal of fortunes generated in the narrative action is set against a longer time-scale. In the implied gap of time between I.2 and I.3, a long truce takes effect, the war drags on 'After so many hours, lives, speeches spent' (II.2.1) indefinitely, and Cressida has loved Troilus for 'many weary months' (III.2.113). This larger sense of the passage of months or years in the Trojan War is in turn set against Time itself, personified in a number of notable passages as an active agent in human affairs. Time is most vividly presented as a destroyer (*Tempus edax rerum*, Time the consumer of all things), bringing all to 'blind oblivion' (III.2.185) in a world in which for everyone, however infinite the desire, 'the act' is 'a slave to limit' (III.2.81). This is that 'Injurious Time' robbing Troilus and Cressida of their love in a single night (IV.4.41), and Time as depicted by Ulysses, devouring good deeds, and bringing all things, all values, to destruction:

> *For beauty, wit,*
> *High birth, vigour of bone, desert in service,*

Love, friendship, charity, are subjects all
To envious and calumniating time.

III.3.171–4

Ulysses is here structuring an argument designed to stir the idle Achilles, but his image of time as swiftly passing, bringing all to oblivion, carries a proverbial weight, as embodied in the familiar figure of Time with his scythe, the reaper, associated with change and death. Time is the 'fashionable host' (III.3.165), for ever grasping in the new, and dismissing the old.

Time is also seen in another perspective, as a preserver, and if this image is less resonant in the language of the play, it is no less forceful in the total effect. The play contains its own embodiment of historical time in Nestor, 'Instructed by the antiquary times' (II.3.248), the repository of memory, who proves that time does not necessarily calumniate (as Ulysses argues); indeed, he can, as a 'good old chronicle, | That hast so long walked hand in hand with time' (IV.5.202–3), praise Hector as a greater warrior than his grandfather. In III.2 Troilus, Cressida, and Pandarus envisage their story as outlasting time's powers of destruction, and Troilus argues in II.2 for continuing the war on the grounds that 'fame in time to come' will celebrate their heroic deeds (II.2.203). This perspective on time also is valid, as the continuing life of the legend of Troy shows.

For the most part the Greeks lay emphasis, as Ulysses does in his advice to Achilles in III.3, on the immediate moment, Time the destroyer, while the Trojans are more concerned with time to come, time the preserver. The Greeks are concerned to win the war, knowing Troy is doomed; the Trojans are concerned to win fame, and Hector in particular refuses to accept that Troy is doomed. This is brought out in IV.5, when Agamemnon welcomes Hector to the Greek camp for 'this extant moment' (IV.5.168), and Hector, rejecting prophecies of doom, puts himself in the hands, so to speak, of 'that old common arbitrator, Time' (IV.5.225). The end of the play brings the death of Hector, and we know that the fall of Troy is to come. However, the play finishes not on this note, or with Troilus's desperate cry for revenge, but with Pandarus, bringing the play into the present time for the audience, and looking to his own future in terms of dying from disease: 'Some two months hence my will shall here be made' (V.10.53). This last indication of time in a play so full of markers does not, I think, refer to some particular time or event connected with the first performance, but rounds off the action by adding the impending 'fall' of Pandarus (V.10.49) to the impending fall of Troy.

Once before, at the end of III.2, Pandarus stepped out of his individual part to address the audience in his symbolic role as pander. Then, flushed with success, he gleefully wished all maidens in the audience a pander's help; but now, in his epilogue in Act V, he appears as an ailing old bawd, riddled with the diseases of the profession, sardonically appealing to panders in the audience for sympathy. The effect is to project a play based on ancient legend startlingly into the audience's own world. If the action of the play at first offers us comic perspectives in the posturing of Troilus and Ajax, as also in the presentation of Pandarus as a genial straight man for first Cressida, later Paris and Helen, and even shows Thersites as more of a professional fool than a cynic; and if the later part stresses more the 'bitter disposition of the time' that separates Cressida from Troilus, brings the brutal death of Hector, and turns Troilus into a terrifying, if rather absurd, revenger, more concerned with the loss of his horse to Diomedes than with the loss of Cressida (V.6.7), there is yet a further dimension in Shakespeare's use of Pandarus as mediator between the play and the audience. For whatever the limitations of the Greek and Trojan warriors, they are capable of grand aspirations and noble ideals, whereas the audience Pandarus appeals to in a final sardonic joke is one consisting of 'traders in the flesh' rather than heroes.

It is easier to say what kind of play *Troilus and Cressida* is not than what it is. The conflicting perspectives noted above and the shift in emphasis between the first and second halves of the play create a mixed effect, neither simply comic nor tragic, and not fitting any category very readily. If the play gives little sense of the inner life of the characters, or of a religious dimension, it brilliantly creates a range of characters on the one hand engaged in public business, concerned with major issues, and seeing how they should behave in terms of ideals of order or of value or of law, and on the other hand satirically exposed by the gap between what they say and the way they act. No one character has a commanding role, and if we can identify in some measure with Troilus, Hector, and Ulysses, we are made aware how all of them might join Troilus in crying 'How my achievements mock me!' (IV.2.69), as each in turn is undercut and mocked by events. The exigencies of the moment do not allow politics to be practised in the lofty terms envisaged by Ulysses, or war to be fought in the chivalric terms envisaged by Hector, or love to be enjoyed in perpetuity, as Troilus desires. This does not mean that the play is disillusioned, even nihilistic, as some critics argue; it is, however, notably realistic in the sense that it portrays men and women in society trying in their muddled way to cope with public demands that clash with private desires, and always with the pressure of time upon them. This is why the play seems so relevant still, and why Pandarus ends with his outcry 'O world, world, world! Thus is the poor agent despised!' This is the world of the audience, whose social and political reality, as he implies, relates richly to that portrayed in *Troilus and Cressida*.

*

One other striking feature of the play deserves attention, its range of vocabulary and style. Shakespeare fills the mouths of the Greek and Trojan generals, especially in the debate scenes, with high-sounding terms and a markedly Latinate vocabulary. This has led some to think that he had in mind an especially sophisticated private audience, perhaps the lawyers at one of the Inns of Court, where plays were sometimes staged in connexion with various annual festivities, such as All Saints' Day or Christmas. Attractive as this hypothesis may seem, there is no external evidence to support it, other than some ambiguous sentences in the epistle added to the Quarto in 1609 (see page 161 for further comment on this). In any case, the language of the council scenes, as indeed of the whole play, with its remarkable stylistic variety, is entirely appropriate to the scenes as they unfold, and can be related to the new wave of drama that achieved a marked success on the London stages after 1598 or so. Shakespeare was evidently very much aware of this wave of satirical plays that drew audiences to the new small indoor or 'private' theatres where professional children's companies composed of boy actors or adolescents performed. These companies, the 'little eyases' complained of by Hamlet, commenced playing in 1599 or 1600 at St Paul's and Blackfriars. By this time, Shakespeare's own company were presenting at the Globe satirical comedies by Ben Jonson, and Shakespeare himself probably acted parts in these (the 1616 edition of Ben Jonson's plays lists him as one of the principal actors in *Every Man in his Humour*, 1598). When the Prologue in *Troilus and Cressida* calls attention to the fact that he is 'armed' (line 23), this may be a witty allusion to Ben Jonson's *Poetaster*, staged by the children's company at Blackfriars in 1601, which has an armed Prologue who defends the author against his critics.

The language and styles of *Troilus and Cressida* relate to the development of satirical comedy during the period from 1598 to 1605, but Shakespeare responded and adapted in his own unique way to what was happening in the theatre. In *Troilus and Cressida* the elaborate Latinate style and vocabulary of the Prologue and the debate scenes, especially the Greek council scene in I.3, and elsewhere have a double purpose. On the one hand, their magniloquence establishes something of an epic tone for the Greek and Trojan heroes, befitting these legendary figures as larger than life, and aggrandizing them. On the other hand, their dialogue is at times so inflated as to render them slightly absurd, drawing attention to the gap between their words and their deeds. This is especially noticeable in the Greek council scene, where the grandeur of a vocabulary that is full of coinages like 'conflux', 'protractive', 'persistive', 'importless', 'insisture', 'oppugnancy', 'neglection', 'scaffoldage', and 'exposure', is scarcely matched by an equal grandeur of thought (except perhaps in the fine speech of Ulysses on degree) or grandeur of action. In this scene we certainly encounter a sophisticated use of language, and the emptiness of, for example, Agamemnon's opening speech may not be at once evident to every viewer or reader:

> *Princes,*
> *What grief hath set the jaundice on your cheeks?*
> *The ample proposition that hope makes*
> *In all designs begun on earth below*
> *Fails in the promised largeness: checks and disasters*
> *Grow in the veins of actions highest reared,*
> *As knots, by the conflux of meeting sap,*
> *Infect the sound pine, and divert his grain*
> *Tortive and errant from his course of growth.*
> *Nor, princes, is it matter new to us*
> *That we come short of our suppose so far*
> *That, after seven years' siege, yet Troy walls stand;*
> *Sith every action that hath gone before*
> *Whereof we have record, trial did draw*

> *Bias and thwart, not answering the aim*
> *And that unbodied figure of the thought*
> *That gave't surmisèd shape . . .*
>
> I.3.1–17

Agamemnon continues in a similar vein for a total of thirty lines, which, shorn of similes, circumlocutions, and generalities, provide information that the Trojan War has lasted seven years, but otherwise can be summed up briefly as to their meaning: 'The war has reached stalemate. Why? The gods are against us.' Such speeches may be delivered seriously, of course, as they are daily in parliaments and assemblies around the world, and the hollowness of Agamemnon's grandiloquence in making a simple point is brought home to us gradually as the scene develops – first in the excessive flattery with which the other Greek generals address Agamemnon as godlike; then in the arrival of Aeneas, whose inability to identify the 'god in office', Agamemnon, is comic; and finally in the pettiness of the outcome of the debate, the intrigue of Ulysses and Nestor against Achilles.

The shifting styles of the play are brilliantly varied to suit the occasion and the speakers. The pomp and circumstance of the Greek council scene contrast with the witty prose repartee of Cressida, fencing in words with Pandarus in I.2. These two scenes in turn are set off against the coarse squabbling dialogue of Ajax and Thersites in Act II, the prose of insult and abuse. A quite different prose style and vocabulary mark III.1, creating the cloying atmosphere of Helen's boudoir, echoing with the words 'sweet' and 'love'. The range of styles is extraordinary, as is the apparent effortlessness with which Shakespeare changes tone and mood, to set up the stylistic contrasts which are so effective in creating the play's clash of perspectives. This brilliant use of stylistic variation is nowhere more marked than in the crucial scene for Troilus, V.2, the scene that destroys his illusions about Cressida. The scene begins with short exchanges, mingling prose and verse, between Cressida and Diomedes, punctuated by the anxious cries of Troilus and Ulysses, and the coarse prose interjections of Thersites. As the scene moves to its climax, all the characters in the scene speak in verse, in a sequence culminating, as the emotional temperature rises, in Cressida's lyrical rhymed farewell to Troilus and admission of her guilt (V.2.109–14). This moving moment is at once capped by a parodic couplet given to Thersites, and this leads into the tortured blank verse expressing Troilus's anguish at being forced to face the truth about Cressida. The scene ends with a passage of Thersites' scornful prose on the theme of lechery – a speech which in its turn is at once countered by the entry of the true wife Andromache, gently admonishing her husband Hector in blank verse. But every turn, every change of scene or shift of mood in the play is stunningly created by Shakespeare's mastery of a wide range of styles. *Troilus and Cressida* is a demanding play, certainly, for actors, audiences, and readers, and the complexities of language and imagery provide a rich pattern of resonances for the student and commentator to explore; but at the same time, as is characteristic of Shakespeare's mature plays, these complexities in no way prevent the ordinary reader or viewer from enjoying the vigorous narrative action, the clashes of personality, and the subtle characterizations that make *Troilus and Cressida* one of the dramatist's most fascinating plays.

FURTHER READING

Textual Studies

Debate continues about the relation between the Quarto (1609) and the first Folio (1623) texts, which have about five hundred verbal differences, and more in matters such as punctuation. Until recently major editions of the play, such as those of Alice Walker (New Cambridge, 1957), Kenneth Palmer (new Arden, 1982), and Kenneth Muir (Oxford, 1984), have been eclectic, with a bias towards the Quarto. Muir took the Quarto as his control text, even though he was aware of the convincing reasons presented by Gary Taylor for regarding the Folio text as incorporating substantive revisions by Shakespeare. Some of Taylor's detailed claims are open to challenge, but his main argument in '*Troilus and Cressida*: Bibliography, Performance, and Interpretation' (*Shakespeare Studies* XV, 1982) is persuasive. This essay reviews previous discussions of textual problems in the play. E. A. J. Honigmann's paper, 'The Date and Revision of *Troilus and Cressida*', in *Textual Criticism and Literary Interpretation*, edited by Jerome J. McGann (Chicago, 1985), in which he attempts to restore the authority of the Quarto text, deserves attention.

Background

Much has been written on the question of Shakespeare's knowledge of Chaucer's *Troilus and Criseyde*; the best and fullest account is Ann Thompson's *Shakespeare's Chaucer: A Study in Literary Origins* (London, 1978). Shakespeare's other sources are discussed in Kenneth Muir's *The Sources of Shakespeare's Plays* (London, 1977) and in Geoffrey Bullough's *Narrative and Dramatic Sources of Shakespeare*, Volume VI (London, 1966), which reprints substantial excerpts from William Caxton's translation of Raoul Lefevre's *The Recuyell of the Historyes of Troye* (printed about 1474); from John Lydgate's *The Hystorye, Sege and Dystruccyon of Troye* (1513), also known as *The Troy Book*; from Robert Henryson's *The Testament of*

Cresseid (printed 1532); and from George Chapman's *The Seven Books of Homer's Iliads* (1598). The more general literary and theatrical background of the play is described in Robert K. Presson's *Shakespeare's 'Troilus and Cressida' and the Legends of Troy* (Madison, Wisconsin, 1953) and further explored in Robert Kimbrough's *Shakespeare's 'Troilus and Cressida' and its Setting* (Cambridge, Massachusetts, 1964). In his essay 'The Lost *Troilus and Cressida*' (*Essays and Studies* 17, 1964) Geoffrey Bullough analyses the relationship of Shakespeare's play to the earlier play on the same theme written by Thomas Dekker and Henry Chettle in about 1599. In 'Shakespeare's *Troilus and Cressida* and the Monumental Tradition in Tapestries and Literature' (*Renaissance Drama* 7, 1976), Jill Levenson interestingly argues that Shakespeare was debunking a tradition of respectful treatment of the Troy legends.

The play has also been studied in relation to the drama of the period, and Oscar J. Campbell was perhaps the first to illustrate the formal connexions between Shakespeare's play and the experiments of John Marston and Ben Jonson in writing what Jonson called comical satire round about 1600. Campbell argued crudely and overstated his case in *'Comicall Satyre' and Shakespeare's 'Troilus and Cressida'* (San Marino, 1938), but his work deserves attention. The links with Marston and Jonson are also discussed in R. A. Foakes, *Shakespeare, the Dark Comedies to the Last Plays. From Satire to Celebration* (London, 1971), and these connexions have also been explored from a Marxist point of view by Jonathan Dollimore, who argues in 'Marston's "Antonio" plays and Shakespeare's "Troilus and Cressida": The Birth of a Radical Drama' (*Essays and Studies* 33, 1980) that both Marston and Shakespeare were in effect illustrating the ways in which individuals become alienated from their society. The early staging of *Troilus and Cressida* is considered by George F. Reynolds in an essay in *Joseph Quincy Adams Memorial Studies*, edited by J. G. McManaway, G. E. Dawson and E. E. Willoughby (Washington, D.C., 1948); and some of Shakespeare's specific dramatic techniques are explored by R. Stamm in 'The Glass of Pandar's Praise' (*Essays and Studies* 17, 1964).

Criticism

The New Variorum edition of the play by H. N. Hillebrand
(Philadelphia, 1953) provides a useful perspective on early
critical accounts of the play. G. Wilson Knight's essay on the
'philosophy' of the play (*The Wheel of Fire*, London, 1930) and
W. W. Lawrence's account of it as a 'searching analysis of a
reflective criticism of life' (*Shakespeare's Problem Comedies*, New
York, 1931) were both influential. Knight's preference for
'romance', for the love and heroism he saw in the Trojans
rather than the craft and cunning he detected in the Greeks, has
given way to a general recognition that the play is critical of both
Trojans and Greeks, a point well established by S. L. Bethell in
Shakespeare and the Popular Dramatic Tradition (London, 1944).
The dramatization of conflicting values on both sides in the
Trojan War has been analysed more fully in terms of what he
calls 'complementarity' by Norman Rabkin in *Shakespeare and
the Common Understanding* (Berkeley, 1967). Others have con-
tinued to treat *Troilus and Cressida* as a play of ideas, notably
Winifred Nowottny, in '"Opinion" and "Value" in *Troilus and
Cressida*' (*Essays in Criticism* 4, 1954; Frank Kermode's re-
sponse in the same journal in 1955 is worth noting); W. R.
Elton in 'Shakespeare's Ulysses and the Problem of Value'
(*Shakespeare Studies* II, 1967); and Gayle Greene, writing on
'Language and Value in Shakespeare's *Troilus and Cressida*'
(*Studies in English Literature* 21, 1981).

Some critics treat the play primarily as a philosophical
debate, focusing especially on the Greek and Trojan council
scenes and the values at issue in these, and often such critics
write without any sense of the play as theatre, or of its comic
elements. Some see it in pessimistic terms, as a vision of chaos
or incoherence; the best of such accounts are those by Una
Ellis-Fermor in *The Frontiers of Drama* (London, 1945), Philip
Edwards in *Shakespeare and the Confines of Art* (London, 1968),
and Richard D. Fly, 'Cassandra and the Language of Prophecy
in *Troilus and Cressida*' (*Shakespeare Quarterly* XXVI, 1975).
John Bayley goes further to find incoherence in the play itself,
'scraps of idiotic dialogue and meaningless exclamation'
('Shakespeare's Only Play', *Stratford Papers on Shakespeare*,
Toronto, 1963). It is helpful to set against such a nihilistic view
the argument of Terry Eagleton in *Shakespeare and Society*

(London, 1967), who sees Shakespeare as siding in this play with 'social responsibility', even at the cost of a 'damaging loss of authenticity'. R. A. Yoder, on the other hand, stresses the absurdity of a collective order operating 'at the expense of privacy' (*Shakespeare Survey 25*, 1972).

Responding in a different way to what they see as elements of disillusion or pessimism in the play, others, more concerned with its nature as drama, have argued that it should be viewed as a tragedy, with the focus on either Troilus or Hector as tragic protagonist; the most notable of such accounts are those by Nevill Coghill in *Shakespeare's Professional Skills* (London, 1964), Northrop Frye in *Fools of Time* (London, 1968), and Brian Morris, in 'The Tragic Structure of *Troilus and Cressida*' (*Shakespeare Quarterly* 10, 1959). More persuasive is G. K. Hunter's modified view of the play as '*Troilus and Cressida*: a tragic satire' (*Shakespeare Studies* 13, Tokyo, 1977). An important essay on a related theme is T. McAlindon's exploration of dissonance, incongruity, and breaches of decorum in 'Language, Style and Meaning in *Troilus and Cressida*' (*PMLA* 84, 1969). Juliet Dusinberre also writes on what she sees as the disintegration of language in the play in '*Troilus and Cressida* and the Definition of Beauty' (*Shakespeare Survey 36*, 1983). The play has also drawn J. Hillis Miller to attempt a deconstructionist analysis of its language systems in 'Ariachne's broken Woof' (*Georgia Review* XXXI, 1977). It is worth setting against these rather solemn accounts of the play's language the valuable essay by Patricia Thomson, 'Rant and Cant in *Troilus and Cressida*' (*Essays and Studies* 22, 1969), in which she links the use of hyperbole with the rhetoric of other plays of the period to argue that the effect of Shakespeare's language is comic and deflationary.

The play has inevitably attracted the attention of moralist critics, who tend to emphasize modes of corruption in it. The most interesting essays of this kind are those by A. P. Rossiter in *Angel with Horns* (London, 1961), who sees the play as sceptical and preoccupied with a questioning of values, and by L. C. Knights, '*Troilus and Cressida* Again' (*Scrutiny* 18, 1951). Knights is also concerned to some extent with the theme of time in the play, and this has been studied, again largely in moral terms, by Frederick Turner in *Shakespeare and the Nature of*

Time (London, 1971). Wylie Sypher's more subtle essay in *The Ethic of Time* (New York, 1976) is especially interesting on the role of Hector in relation to the pressures of time. The double time-scale in the play has been analysed by Zdeněk Stříbrný in 'Time in *Troilus and Cressida*' (*Shakespeare-Jahrbuch* 112, 1976). Two essays that deal more specifically with the play's relation to the myth of Troy and treatment of time are R. A. Foakes, '*Troilus and Cressida* Reconsidered' (*University of Toronto Quarterly* 32, 1963), and Douglas Cole, 'Myth and Anti-Myth' (*Shakespeare Quarterly* 31, 1980). Reuben Brower's treatment of Troilus and Hector in terms of both classical and Renaissance traditions of heroism in *Hero and Saint* (Oxford, 1971), is also worth attention.

A notable feature of the play is the extent to which characters consciously perform or assume roles for others to observe, and both Harry Berger Jr, in '*Troilus and Cressida*: The Observer as Basilisk' (*Comparative Drama* 2, 1968–9), and Carolyn Asp, in 'Transcendence Denied: The Failure of Role Assumption in *Troilus and Cressida*' (*Studies in English Literature* 18, 1978), have shown the importance of attending to the attitudinizing of characters. Two important essays for understanding the impact of the play on the modern stage are those by Jeanne T. Newlin on 'The Modernity of *Troilus and Cressida*' (*Harvard Library Bulletin* 17, 1969) and by Joseph Papp on directing a production, in the edition published as the 'Festival Shakespeare' (New York, 1967). Papp sees Cressida as a victim of forces outside her, and his engaging account has been extended by Gayle Greene in 'Shakespeare's Cressida, "A Kind of Self"' (*The Woman's Part. Feminist Criticism of Shakespeare*, edited by Carolyn Lenz, Gayle Greene and Carol Nealy, Urbana, Illinois, 1980). On the other hand, Arnold Stein presents Cressida as a manipulator, like Ulysses, in '*Troilus and Cressida*: The Disjunctive Imagination' (*ELH* 36, 1969); Carolyn Asp has replied to this attack in 'In Defense of Cressida' (*Studies in Philology* 74, 1977). The list could easily be extended, and this selective account of critical perspectives on the play illustrates the somewhat bewildering array of responses it has elicited, reflecting the complexity of a work that seems inexhaustible.

TROILUS AND CRESSIDA

THE CHARACTERS IN THE PLAY

The Trojans

PRIAM, King of Troy
HECTOR
PARIS
DEIPHOBUS
HELENUS, a priest   } sons of Priam
TROILUS
MARGARELON, a bastard
AENEAS
ANTENOR   } Trojan leaders
PANDARUS, a lord, Cressida's uncle
CALCHAS, Cressida's father, a defector to the Greeks
ALEXANDER, Cressida's servant
ANDROMACHE, Hector's wife
CRESSIDA
CASSANDRA, Priam's daughter, a prophetess
Troilus's servants, a BOY and a MAN
Paris's SERVANT
Soldiers, attendants

The Greeks

AGAMEMNON, general commander of the Greeks
MENELAUS, King of Sparta, Agamemnon's brother
ULYSSES
ACHILLES
AJAX   } Greek leaders
NESTOR
DIOMEDES
PATROCLUS, Achilles' companion
THERSITES

THE CHARACTERS IN THE PLAY

HELEN, Menelaus's wife, living with Paris in Troy
Diomedes' SERVANT
Soldiers, Myrmidons, attendants

Speaker of the PROLOGUE

PROLOGUE

PROLOGUE

To what may be inferred in a play.
Like her self . . . . ever
Now goes on bad, In both the causes of war.

Enter Prologue in armour

PROLOGUE

In Troy there lies the scene. From isles of Greece
The princes orgulous, their high blood chafed,
Have to the port of Athens sent their ships
Fraught with the ministers and instruments
Of cruel war. Sixty and nine that wore
Their crownets regal from th'Athenian bay
Put forth toward Phrygia, and their vow is made
To ransack Troy, within whose strong immures
The ravished Helen, Menelaus' queen,
With wanton Paris sleeps – and that's the quarrel. 10
To Tenedos they come,
And the deep-drawing barks do there disgcrge
Their warlike fraughtage; now on Dardan plains
The fresh and yet unbruisèd Greeks do pitch
Their brave pavilions. Priam's six-gated city,
Dardan and Timbria, Helias, Chetas, Troien,
And Antenorides, with massy staples
And corresponsive and fulfilling bolts,
Stir up the sons of Troy.
Now expectation, tickling skittish spirits 20
On one and other side, Trojan and Greek,
Sets all on hazard. And hither am I come,
A Prologue armed, but not in confidence
Of author's pen or actor's voice, but suited
In like conditions as our argument,
To tell you, fair beholders, that our play
Leaps o'er the vaunt and firstlings of those broils,
Beginning in the middle; starting thence away

45

To what may be digested in a play.

30 Like or find fault; do as your pleasures are;
Now good or bad, 'tis but the chance of war.

Exit

TROILUS
>   Call here my varlet, I'll unarm again.
>   Why should I war without the walls of Troy,
>   That find such cruel battle here within?
>   Each Trojan that is master of his heart,
>   Let him to field; Troilus, alas, hath none.

PANDARUS Will this gear ne'er be mended?

TROILUS
>   The Greeks are strong, and skilful to their strength,
>   Fierce to their skill, and to their fierceness valiant;
>   But I am weaker than a woman's tear,
>   Tamer than sleep, fonder than ignorance,   10
>   Less valiant than the virgin in the night,
>   And skilless as unpractised infancy.

PANDARUS Well, I have told you enough of this; for my
   part, I'll not meddle nor make no farther. He that will
   have a cake out of the wheat must needs tarry the
   grinding.

TROILUS Have I not tarried?

PANDARUS Ay, the grinding; but you must tarry the
   bolting.

TROILUS Have I not tarried?   20

PANDARUS Ay, the bolting; but you must tarry the
   leavening.

TROILUS Still have I tarried.

PANDARUS Ay, to the leavening; but here's yet in the
   word hereafter the kneading, the making of the cake,
   the heating of the oven, and the baking. Nay, you must
   stay the cooling too, or you may chance to burn your
   lips.

TROILUS

> Patience herself, what goddess e'er she be,
30 > Doth lesser blench at sufferance than I do.
> At Priam's royal table do I sit,
> And when fair Cressid comes into my thoughts –
> So, traitor! – 'when she comes'? – when is she
>> thence?

PANDARUS Well, she looked yesternight fairer than ever
> I saw her look, or any woman else.

TROILUS

> I was about to tell thee – when my heart,
> As wedgèd with a sigh, would rive in twain,
> Lest Hector or my father should perceive me,
> I have, as when the sun doth light a storm,
40 > Buried this sigh in wrinkle of a smile;
> But sorrow that is couched in seeming gladness
> Is like that mirth fate turns to sudden sadness.

PANDARUS An her hair were not somewhat darker than
> Helen's – well, go to, there were no more comparison
> between the women. But, for my part, she is my kins-
> woman; I would not, as they term it, praise her, but I
> would somebody had heard her talk yesterday, as I did;
> I will not dispraise your sister Cassandra's wit, but –

TROILUS

> O Pandarus! I tell thee, Pandarus –
50 > When I do tell thee, there my hopes lie drowned,
> Reply not in how many fathoms deep
> They lie indrenched. I tell thee I am mad
> In Cressid's love: thou answer'st 'She is fair',
> Pour'st in the open ulcer of my heart
> Her eyes, her hair, her cheek, her gait, her voice;
> Handlest in thy discourse, O, that her hand,
> In whose comparison all whites are ink
> Writing their own reproach; to whose soft seizure
> The cygnet's down is harsh, and spirit of sense
60 > Hard as the palm of ploughman! This thou tell'st me,
> As 'true' thou tell'st me, when I say I love her;

48

But, saying thus, instead of oil and balm,
Thou lay'st in every gash that love hath given me
The knife that made it.

PANDARUS I speak no more than truth.

TROILUS Thou dost not speak so much.

PANDARUS Faith, I'll not meddle in't. Let her be as she
is: if she be fair, 'tis the better for her; an she be not,
she has the mends in her own hands.

TROILUS Good Pandarus – how now, Pandarus?   70

PANDARUS I have had my labour for my travail, ill-
thought-on of her, and ill-thought-on of you; gone
between and between, but small thanks for my labour.

TROILUS What, art thou angry, Pandarus? What, with
me?

PANDARUS Because she's kin to me, therefore she's not
so fair as Helen; an she were not kin to me, she would
be as fair on Friday as Helen is on Sunday, but what
care I? I care not an she were a blackamoor; 'tis all one
to me.   80

TROILUS Say I she is not fair?

PANDARUS I do not care whether you do or no. She's a
fool to stay behind her father; let her to the Greeks,
and so I'll tell her the next time I see her. For my part,
I'll meddle nor make no more i'th'matter.

TROILUS Pandarus –

PANDARUS Not I.

TROILUS Sweet Pandarus –

PANDARUS Pray you, speak no more to me; I will leave
all as I found it, and there an end.   90

Exit. Sound alarum

TROILUS
Peace, you ungracious clamours! Peace, rude sounds!
Fools on both sides! Helen must needs be fair,
When with your blood you daily paint her thus.
I cannot fight upon this argument;
It is too starved a subject for my sword.
But Pandarus – O gods, how do you plague me!

I.1

I cannot come to Cressid but by Pandar,
And he's as tetchy to be wooed to woo
As she is stubborn-chaste against all suit.
100 Tell me, Apollo, for thy Daphne's love,
What Cressid is, what Pandar, and what we –
Her bed is India; there she lies, a pearl:
Between our Ilium and where she resides,
Let it be called the wild and wandering flood,
Ourself the merchant, and this sailing Pandar
Our doubtful hope, our convoy, and our bark.
        Alarum. Enter Aeneas

AENEAS
        How now, Prince Troilus, wherefore not a-field?
TROILUS
        Because not there. This woman's answer sorts,
        For womanish it is to be from thence.
110 What news, Aeneas, from the field today?
AENEAS
        That Paris is returnèd home, and hurt.
TROILUS
        By whom, Aeneas?
AENEAS   Troilus, by Menelaus.
TROILUS
        Let Paris bleed, 'tis but a scar to scorn;
        Paris is gored with Menelaus' horn.
                Alarum
AENEAS
        Hark what good sport is out of town today!
TROILUS
        Better at home, if 'would I might' were 'may' –
        But to the sport abroad, are you bound thither?
AENEAS
        In all swift haste.
TROILUS   Come, go we then together.
                                        Exeunt

50

CRESSIDA

Who were those went by?

ALEXANDER   Queen Hecuba and Helen.

CRESSIDA

And whither go they?

ALEXANDER   Up to the eastern tower,
Whose height commands as subject all the vale,
To see the battle. Hector, whose patience
Is as a virtue fixed, today was moved:
He chid Andromache, and struck his armourer;
And, like as there were husbandry in war,
Before the sun rose he was harnessed light,
And to the field goes he; where every flower
Did as a prophet weep what it foresaw   10
In Hector's wrath.

CRESSIDA   What was his cause of anger?

ALEXANDER

The noise goes, this: there is among the Greeks
A lord of Trojan blood, nephew to Hector;
They call him Ajax.

CRESSIDA   Good, and what of him?

ALEXANDER

They say he is a very man *per se*,
And stands alone.

CRESSIDA So do all men, unless they are drunk, sick, or
have no legs.

ALEXANDER This man, lady, hath robbed many beasts
of their particular additions: he is as valiant as the lion,   20
churlish as the bear, slow as the elephant; a man into
whom nature hath so crowded humours that his valour
is crushed into folly, his folly sauced with discretion.
There is no man hath a virtue that he hath not a
glimpse of, nor any man an attaint but he carries some
stain of it. He is melancholy without cause, and merry
against the hair; he hath the joints of everything, but
everything so out of joint that he is a gouty Briareus,

many hands and no use, or purblind Argus, all eyes
30 and no sight.

CRESSIDA But how should this man, that makes me
smile, make Hector angry?

ALEXANDER They say he yesterday coped Hector in the
battle and struck him down, the disdain and shame
whereof hath ever since kept Hector fasting and wak-
ing.

CRESSIDA Who comes here?

ALEXANDER Madam, your uncle Pandarus.

Enter Pandarus

CRESSIDA Hector's a gallant man.

40 ALEXANDER As may be in the world, lady.

PANDARUS What's that? What's that?

CRESSIDA Good morrow, uncle Pandarus.

PANDARUS Good morrow, cousin Cressid. What do you
talk of? – Good morrow, Alexander. – How do you,
cousin? When were you at Ilium?

CRESSIDA This morning, uncle.

PANDARUS What were you talking of when I came? Was
Hector armed and gone ere ye came to Ilium? Helen
was not up, was she?

50 CRESSIDA Hector was gone, but Helen was not up.

PANDARUS E'en so, Hector was stirring early.

CRESSIDA That were we talking of, and of his anger.

PANDARUS Was he angry?

CRESSIDA So he says here.   *Exit Alexander*

PANDARUS True, he was so. I know the cause too. He'll
lay about him today, I can tell them that, and there's
Troilus will not come far behind him; let them take
heed of Troilus, I can tell them that too.

CRESSIDA What, is he angry too?

60 PANDARUS Who, Troilus? Troilus is the better man of
the two.

CRESSIDA O Jupiter, there's no comparison.

PANDARUS What, not between Troilus and Hector? Do
you know a man if you see him?

CRESSIDA Ay, if I ever saw him before and knew him.

PANDARUS Well, I say Troilus is Troilus.

CRESSIDA Then you say as I say, for I am sure he is not Hector.

PANDARUS No, nor Hector is not Troilus in some degrees. 70

CRESSIDA 'Tis just to each of them; he is himself.

PANDARUS Himself? Alas, poor Troilus, I would he were.

CRESSIDA So he is.

PANDARUS Condition, I had gone barefoot to India.

CRESSIDA He is not Hector.

PANDARUS Himself? No, he's not himself, would 'a were himself! Well, the gods are above; time must friend or end. Well, Troilus, well, I would my heart were in her body. No, Hector is not a better man than 80 Troilus.

CRESSIDA Excuse me.

PANDARUS He is elder.

CRESSIDA Pardon me, pardon me.

PANDARUS Th'other's not come to't; you shall tell me another tale when th'other's come to't. Hector shall not have his wit this year.

CRESSIDA He shall not need it, if he have his own.

PANDARUS Nor his qualities.

CRESSIDA No matter. 90

PANDARUS Nor his beauty.

CRESSIDA 'Twould not become him; his own's better.

PANDARUS You have no judgement, niece. Helen herself swore th'other day that Troilus, for a brown favour – for so 'tis, I must confess – not brown neither –

CRESSIDA No, but brown.

PANDARUS Faith, to say truth, brown and not brown.

CRESSIDA To say the truth, true and not true.

PANDARUS She praised his complexion above Paris.

CRESSIDA Why, Paris hath colour enough. 100

PANDARUS So he has.

CRESSIDA Then Troilus should have too much. If she praised him above, his complexion is higher than his; he having colour enough, and the other higher, is too flaming a praise for a good complexion. I had as lief Helen's golden tongue had commended Troilus for a copper nose.

PANDARUS I swear to you, I think Helen loves him better than Paris.

110 CRESSIDA Then she's a merry Greek indeed.

PANDARUS Nay, I am sure she does. She came to him th'other day into the compassed window – and you know he has not past three or four hairs on his chin –

CRESSIDA Indeed, a tapster's arithmetic may soon bring his particulars therein to a total.

PANDARUS Why, he is very young, and yet will he within three pound lift as much as his brother Hector.

CRESSIDA Is he so young a man, and so old a lifter?

PANDARUS But to prove to you that Helen loves him, she 120 came and puts me her white hand to his cloven chin –

CRESSIDA Juno have mercy, how came it cloven?

PANDARUS Why, you know 'tis dimpled – I think his smiling becomes him better than any man in all Phrygia.

CRESSIDA O, he smiles valiantly.

PANDARUS Does he not?

CRESSIDA O, yes, an 'twere a cloud in autumn.

PANDARUS Why, go to, then: but to prove to you that Helen loves Troilus –

130 CRESSIDA Troilus will stand to the proof, if you'll prove it so.

PANDARUS Troilus? Why, he esteems her no more than I esteem an addle egg.

CRESSIDA If you love an addle egg as well as you love an idle head you would eat chickens i'th'shell.

PANDARUS I cannot choose but laugh, to think how she tickled his chin – indeed, she has a marvellous white hand, I must needs confess –

CRESSIDA Without the rack.

PANDARUS And she takes upon her to spy a white hair on 140 his chin.

CRESSIDA Alas, poor chin, many a wart is richer.

PANDARUS But there was such laughing – Queen Hecuba laughed that her eyes ran o'er –

CRESSIDA With millstones.

PANDARUS And Cassandra laughed –

CRESSIDA But there was more temperate fire under the pot of her eyes; did her eyes run o'er too?

PANDARUS And Hector laughed.

CRESSIDA At what was all this laughing? 150

PANDARUS Marry, at the white hair that Helen spied on Troilus' chin.

CRESSIDA An't had been a green hair I should have laughed too.

PANDARUS They laughed not so much at the hair as at his pretty answer.

CRESSIDA What was his answer?

PANDARUS Quoth she: 'Here's but two and fifty hairs on your chin, and one of them is white.'

CRESSIDA This is her question. 160

PANDARUS That's true, make no question of that. 'Two and fifty hairs,' quoth he, 'and one white: that white hair is my father, and all the rest are his sons.' 'Jupiter,' quoth she, 'which of these hairs is Paris, my husband?' 'The forked one,' quoth he; 'pluck't out, and give it him.' But there was such laughing, and Helen so blushed, and Paris so chafed, and all the rest so laughed, that it passed.

CRESSIDA So let it now; for it has been a great while going by. 170

PANDARUS Well, cousin, I told you a thing yesterday; think on't.

CRESSIDA So I do.

PANDARUS I'll be sworn 'tis true; he will weep you an 'twere a man born in April.

CRESSIDA And I'll spring up in his tears, an 'twere a nettle against May.

Sound a retreat

PANDARUS Hark, they are coming from the field. Shall we stand up here, and see them as they pass toward
180   Ilium? Good niece, do, sweet niece Cressida.

CRESSIDA At your pleasure.

PANDARUS Here, here, here's an excellent place; here we may see most bravely. I'll tell you them all by their names as they pass by, but mark Troilus above the rest.

CRESSIDA Speak not so loud.

Aeneas passes across the stage

PANDARUS That's Aeneas; is not that a brave man? He's one of the flowers of Troy, I can tell you, but mark Troilus; you shall see anon.

Antenor passes across the stage

CRESSIDA Who's that?

190   PANDARUS That's Antenor. He has a shrewd wit, I can tell you, and he's a man good enough; he's one o'th'soundest judgements in Troy whosoever, and a proper man of person. When comes Troilus? I'll show you Troilus anon; if he see me, you shall see him nod at me.

CRESSIDA Will he give you the nod?

PANDARUS You shall see.

CRESSIDA If he do, the rich shall have more.

Hector passes across the stage

PANDARUS That's Hector, that, that, look you, that;
200   there's a fellow! – Go thy way, Hector! – There's a brave man, niece. – O brave Hector! Look how he looks! There's a countenance! Is't not a brave man?

CRESSIDA O, a brave man!

PANDARUS Is 'a not? It does a man's heart good. Look you what hacks are on his helmet, look you yonder, do you see? Look you there, there's no jesting; there's laying on, take't off who will, as they say; there be hacks!

CRESSIDA Be those with swords?

PANDARUS Swords, anything, he cares not; an the devil 210
come to him, it's all one. By God's lid, it does one's
heart good. Yonder comes Paris, yonder comes Paris!

Paris passes across the stage

Look ye yonder, niece, is't not a gallant man too, is't
not? Why, this is brave now. Who said he came hurt
home today? He's not hurt. Why, this will do Helen's
heart good now, ha? Would I could see Troilus now.
You shall see Troilus anon.

Helenus passes across the stage

CRESSIDA Who's that?

PANDARUS That's Helenus – I marvel where Troilus is
– that's Helenus – I think he went not forth today – 220
that's Helenus.

CRESSIDA Can Helenus fight, uncle?

PANDARUS Helenus? No – yes, he'll fight indifferent
well – I marvel where Troilus is. Hark, do you not hear
the people cry 'Troilus'? – Helenus is a priest.

CRESSIDA What sneaking fellow comes yonder?

Troilus passes across the stage

PANDARUS Where? Yonder? That's Deiphobus. – 'Tis
Troilus! There's a man, niece, hem! – Brave Troilus,
the prince of chivalry!

CRESSIDA Peace, for shame, peace! 230

PANDARUS Mark him, note him. O brave Troilus! Look
well upon him, niece, look you how his sword is
bloodied, and his helm more hacked than Hector's,
and how he looks, and how he goes! O admirable
youth! He ne'er saw three and twenty. – Go thy way,
Troilus, go thy way! – Had I a sister were a grace, or a
daughter a goddess, he should take his choice. O
admirable man! Paris? – Paris is dirt to him, and I
warrant Helen, to change, would give an eye to boot.

Common soldiers pass across the stage

CRESSIDA Here come more. 240

PANDARUS Asses, fools, dolts; chaff and bran, chaff and

bran; porridge after meat! I could live and die i'the
eyes of Troilus. Ne'er look, ne'er look, the eagles are
gone; crows and daws, crows and daws! – I had rather
be such a man as Troilus than Agamemnon and all
Greece.

CRESSIDA There is among the Greeks Achilles, a better
man than Troilus.

PANDARUS Achilles? A drayman, a porter, a very camel!

250 CRESSIDA Well, well.

PANDARUS Well, well! Why, have you any discretion?
Have you any eyes? Do you know what a man is? Is not
birth, beauty, good shape, discourse, manhood, learn-
ing, gentleness, virtue, youth, liberality, and so forth
the spice and salt that season a man?

CRESSIDA Ay, a minced man; and then to be baked with
no date in the pie, for then the man's date is out.

PANDARUS You are such another woman! One knows
not at what ward you lie.

260 CRESSIDA Upon my back to defend my belly; upon my
wit to defend my wiles; upon my secrecy to defend
mine honesty; my mask to defend my beauty, and you
to defend all these: and at all these wards I lie, at a
thousand watches.

PANDARUS Say one of your watches.

CRESSIDA Nay, I'll watch you for that; and that's one of
the chiefest of them too. If I cannot ward what I would
not have hit, I can watch you for telling how I took the
blow – unless it swell past hiding, and then it's past

270 watching.

PANDARUS You are such another!

Enter Troilus's Boy

BOY Sir, my lord would instantly speak with you.

PANDARUS Where?

BOY At your own house; there he unarms him.

PANDARUS Good boy, tell him I come.   *Exit Boy*

I doubt he be hurt. Fare you well, good niece.

CRESSIDA Adieu, uncle.

PANDARUS I'll be with you, niece, by and by.
CRESSIDA To bring, uncle?
PANDARUS Ay, a token from Troilus.   *Exit* 280
CRESSIDA
  By the same token you are a bawd.
  Words, vows, gifts, tears, and love's full sacrifice
  He offers in another's enterprise;
  But more in Troilus thousandfold I see
  Than in the glass of Pandar's praise may be.
  Yet hold I off. Women are angels, wooing;
  Things won are done; joy's soul lies in the doing.
  That she beloved knows naught that knows not this:
  Men prize the thing ungained more than it is.
  That she was never yet that ever knew   290
  Love got so sweet as when desire did sue;
  Therefore this maxim out of love I teach:
  'Achievement is command; ungained, beseech.'
  Then, though my heart's content firm love doth bear,
  Nothing of that shall from mine eyes appear.   *Exit*

      Sennet. Enter Agamemnon, Nestor, Ulysses,   I.3
      Diomedes, Menelaus, with other Greek leaders
AGAMEMNON
  Princes,
  What grief hath set the jaundice on your cheeks?
  The ample proposition that hope makes
  In all designs begun on earth below
  Fails in the promised largeness: checks and disasters
  Grow in the veins of actions highest reared,
  As knots, by the conflux of meeting sap,
  Infect the sound pine, and divert his grain
  Tortive and errant from his course of growth.
  Nor, princes, is it matter new to us   10
  That we come short of our suppose so far
  That, after seven years' siege, yet Troy walls stand;
  Sith every action that hath gone before

59

Whereof we have record, trial did draw
Bias and thwart, not answering the aim
And that unbodied figure of the thought
That gave't surmisèd shape. Why then, you princes,
Do you with cheeks abashed behold our works,
And think them shame, which are, indeed, naught
    else
20 But the protractive trials of great Jove
To find persistive constancy in men? –
The fineness of which metal is not found
In fortune's love: for then the bold and coward,
The wise and fool, the artist and unread,
The hard and soft, seem all affined and kin;
But in the wind and tempest of her frown,
Distinction, with a broad and powerful fan,
Puffing at all, winnows the light away,
And what hath mass or matter by itself
30 Lies rich in virtue and unminglèd.

NESTOR

With due observance of thy godlike seat,
Great Agamemnon, Nestor shall apply
Thy latest words. In the reproof of chance
Lies the true proof of men. The sea being smooth,
How many shallow bauble boats dare sail
Upon her patient breast, making their way
With those of nobler bulk;
But let the ruffian Boreas once enrage
The gentle Thetis, and anon behold
The strong-ribbed bark through liquid mountains
40   cut,
Bounding between the two moist elements,
Like Perseus' horse. Where's then the saucy boat,
Whose weak untimbered sides but even now
Co-rivalled greatness? – Either to harbour fled
Or made a toast for Neptune. Even so
Doth valour's show and valour's worth divide
In storms of fortune; for in her ray and brightness

The herd hath more annoyance by the breese
Than by the tiger; but when the splitting wind
Makes flexible the knees of knotted oaks, 50
And flies flee under shade, why then the thing of
    courage,
As roused with rage, with rage doth sympathize,
And with an accent tuned in selfsame key
Returns to chiding fortune.

ULYSSES   Agamemnon,
Thou great commander, nerve and bone of Greece,
Heart of our numbers, soul and only spirit,
In whom the tempers and the minds of all
Should be shut up: hear what Ulysses speaks.
Besides the applause and approbation
The which, most mighty for thy place and sway – 60
(*To Nestor*) And thou most reverend for thy
    stretched-out life –
I give to both your speeches, which were such
As, Agamemnon, every hand of Greece
Should hold up high in brass; and such again
As venerable Nestor, hatched in silver,
Should with a bond of air, strong as the axletree
On which the heavens ride, knit all Greeks' ears
To his experienced tongue – yet let it please both,
Thou great, and wise, to hear Ulysses speak.

AGAMEMNON
Speak, Prince of Ithaca; and be't of less expect 70
That matter needless, of importless burden,
Divide thy lips than we are confident
When rank Thersites opes his mastic jaws
We shall hear music, wit, and oracle.

ULYSSES
Troy, yet upon his basis, had been down,
And the great Hector's sword had lacked a master,
But for these instances:
The specialty of rule hath been neglected,
And look how many Grecian tents do stand

80 Hollow upon this plain, so many hollow factions.
When that the general is not like the hive
To whom the foragers shall all repair,
What honey is expected? Degree being vizarded,
Th'unworthiest shows as fairly in the mask.
The heavens themselves, the planets, and this centre
Observe degree, priority, and place,
Insisture, course, proportion, season, form,
Office, and custom, in all line of order.
And therefore is the glorious planet Sol
90 In noble eminence enthroned and sphered
Amidst the other; whose med'cinable eye
Corrects the ill aspects of planets evil,
And posts like the commandment of a king,
Sans check, to good and bad. But when the planets
In evil mixture to disorder wander,
What plagues and what portents, what mutiny,
What raging of the sea, shaking of earth,
Commotion in the winds, frights, changes, horrors,
Divert and crack, rend and deracinate
100 The unity and married calm of states
Quite from their fixure! O, when degree is shaked,
Which is the ladder to all high designs,
The enterprise is sick. How could communities,
Degrees in schools, and brotherhoods in cities,
Peaceful commerce from dividable shores,
The primogenitive and due of birth,
Prerogative of age, crowns, sceptres, laurels,
But by degree, stand in authentic place?
Take but degree away, untune that string,
110 And hark what discord follows! Each thing meets
In mere oppugnancy: the bounded waters
Should lift their bosoms higher than the shores,
And make a sop of all this solid globe;
Strength should be lord of imbecility,
And the rude son should strike his father dead;
Force should be right, or, rather, right and wrong –

Between whose endless jar justice resides –
Should lose their names, and so should justice too.
Then everything includes itself in power,
Power into will, will into appetite;   120
And appetite, an universal wolf,
So doubly seconded with will and power,
Must make perforce an universal prey,
And last eat up himself. Great Agamemnon,
This chaos, when degree is suffocate,
Follows the choking;
And this neglection of degree it is
That by a pace goes backward in a purpose
It hath to climb. The general's disdained
By him one step below, he by the next,   130
That next by him beneath: so every step,
Exampled by the first pace that is sick
Of his superior, grows to an envious fever
Of pale and bloodless emulation,
And 'tis this fever that keeps Troy on foot,
Not her own sinews. To end a tale of length,
Troy in our weakness lives, not in her strength.

NESTOR
Most wisely hath Ulysses here discovered
The fever whereof all our power is sick.

AGAMEMNON
The nature of the sickness found, Ulysses,   140
What is the remedy?

ULYSSES
The great Achilles, whom opinion crowns
The sinew and the forehand of our host,
Having his ear full of his airy fame,
Grows dainty of his worth, and in his tent
Lies mocking our designs. With him Patroclus,
Upon a lazy bed, the livelong day
Breaks scurril jests,
And with ridiculous and awkward action –
Which, slanderer, he imitation calls –   150

He pageants us. Sometime, great Agamemnon,
Thy topless deputation he puts on,
And, like a strutting player whose conceit
Lies in his hamstring, and doth think it rich
To hear the wooden dialogue and sound
'Twixt his stretched footing and the scaffoldage,
Such to-be-pitied and o'er-wrested seeming
He acts thy greatness in; and when he speaks,
'Tis like a chime a-mending, with terms unsquared
Which, from the tongue of roaring Typhon
160   dropped,
Would seem hyperboles. At this fusty stuff
The large Achilles, on his pressed bed lolling,
From his deep chest laughs out a loud applause,
Cries 'Excellent! 'Tis Agamemnon just.
Now play me Nestor; hum, and stroke thy beard,
As he being dressed to some oration.'
That's done, as near as the extremest ends
Of parallels, as like as Vulcan and his wife;
Yet god Achilles still cries 'Excellent!
170 'Tis Nestor right. Now play him me, Patroclus,
Arming to answer in a night-alarm.'
And then, forsooth, the faint defects of age
Must be the scene of mirth; to cough and spit,
And with a palsy fumbling on his gorget
Shake in and out the rivet – and at this sport
Sir Valour dies; cries 'O, enough, Patroclus,
Or give me ribs of steel; I shall split all
In pleasure of my spleen.' And in this fashion,
All our abilities, gifts, natures, shapes,
180 Severals and generals of grace exact,
Achievements, plots, orders, preventions,
Excitements to the field, or speech for truce,
Success or loss, what is or is not, serves
As stuff for these two to make paradoxes.

NESTOR
  And in the imitation of these twain,

Who, as Ulysses says, opinion crowns
With an imperial voice, many are infect.
Ajax is grown self-willed, and bears his head
In such a rein, in full as proud a place
As broad Achilles; keeps his tent like him,   190
Makes factious feasts, rails on our state of war
Bold as an oracle, and sets Thersites –
A slave whose gall coins slanders like a mint –
To match us in comparisons with dirt,
To weaken and discredit our exposure,
How rank soever rounded in with danger.

ULYSSES
They tax our policy, and call it cowardice,
Count wisdom as no member of the war;
Forestall prescience, and esteem no act
But that of hand; the still and mental parts,   200
That do contrive how many hands shall strike,
When fitness calls them on, and know by measure
Of their observant toil the enemies' weight –
Why, this hath not a finger's dignity.
They call this bed-work, mappery, closet-war;
So that the ram that batters down the wall,
For the great swing and rudeness of his poise,
They place before his hand that made the engine,
Or those that with the fineness of their souls
By reason guide his execution.   210

NESTOR
Let this be granted, and Achilles' horse
Makes many Thetis' sons.
         Tucket

AGAMEMNON
What trumpet? Look, Menelaus.

MENELAUS
From Troy.
         Enter Aeneas

AGAMEMNON
What would you 'fore our tent?

AENEAS

Is this great Agamemnon's tent, I pray you?

AGAMEMNON

Even this.

AENEAS

May one that is a herald and a prince
Do a fair message to his kingly ears?

AGAMEMNON

220 With surety stronger than Achilles' arm
'Fore all the Greekish lords, which with one voice
Call Agamemnon head and general.

AENEAS

Fair leave and large security. How may
A stranger to those most imperial looks
Know them from eyes of other mortals?

AGAMEMNON   How?

AENEAS

Ay;
I ask, that I might waken reverence,
And bid the cheek be ready with a blush
Modest as morning when she coldly eyes
230 The youthful Phoebus.
Which is that god in office, guiding men?
Which is the high and mighty Agamemnon?

AGAMEMNON

This Trojan scorns us, or the men of Troy
Are ceremonious courtiers.

AENEAS

Courtiers as free, as debonair, unarmed,
As bending angels, that's their fame in peace;
But when they would seem soldiers, they have
        galls,
Good arms, strong joints, true swords; and – Jove's
        accord –
Nothing so full of heart. But peace, Aeneas,
240 Peace, Trojan, lay thy finger on thy lips.
The worthiness of praise distains his worth

66

If that he praised himself bring the praise forth;
But what the repining enemy commends,
That breath fame blows; that praise, sole pure, transcends.

AGAMEMNON
Sir, you of Troy, call you yourself Aeneas?

AENEAS
Ay, Greek, that is my name.

AGAMEMNON
What's your affair, I pray you?

AENEAS
Sir, pardon, 'tis for Agamemnon's ears.

AGAMEMNON
He hears naught privately that comes from Troy.

AENEAS
Nor I from Troy come not to whisper him;   250
I bring a trumpet to awake his ear,
To set his sense on the attentive bent,
And then to speak.

AGAMEMNON   Speak frankly as the wind;
It is not Agamemnon's sleeping hour.
That thou shalt know, Trojan, he is awake,
He tells thee so himself.

AENEAS   Trumpet, blow loud;
Send thy brass voice through all these lazy tents;
And every Greek of mettle, let him know
What Troy means fairly shall be spoke aloud.

        The trumpets sound

We have, great Agamemnon, here in Troy   260
A prince called Hector – Priam is his father –
Who in this dull and long-continued truce
Is rusty grown. He bade me take a trumpet,
And to this purpose speak: 'Kings, princes, lords,
If there be one amongst the fair'st of Greece
That holds his honour higher than his ease,
That seeks his praise more than he fears his peril,
That knows his valour, and knows not his fear,

That loves his mistress more than in confession
270   With truant vows to her own lips he loves,
And dare avow her beauty and her worth
In other arms than hers; to him this challenge:
Hector, in view of Trojans and of Greeks,
Shall make it good, or do his best to do it,
He hath a lady, wiser, fairer, truer,
Than ever Greek did compass in his arms;
And will tomorrow with his trumpet call,
Midway between your tents and walls of Troy,
To rouse a Grecian that is true in love.
280   If any come, Hector shall honour him;
If none, he'll say in Troy when he retires,
The Grecian dames are sunburnt, and not worth
The splinter of a lance.' Even so much.

AGAMEMNON

This shall be told our lovers, Lord Aeneas.
If none of them have soul in such a kind,
We left them all at home; but we are soldiers,
And may that soldier a mere recreant prove
That means not, hath not, or is not in love.
If then one is, or hath, or means to be,
290   That one meets Hector; if none else, I'll be he.

NESTOR

Tell him of Nestor, one that was a man
When Hector's grandsire sucked: he is old now;
But if there be not in our Grecian mould
One noble man that hath one spark of fire
To answer for his love, tell him from me,
I'll hide my silver beard in a gold beaver,
And in my vantbrace put this withered brawn;
And, meeting him, will tell him that my lady
Was fairer than his grandam, and as chaste
300   As may be in the world – his youth in flood,
I'll pawn this truth with my three drops of blood.

AENEAS

Now heavens forbid such scarcity of youth!

ULYSSES
  Amen.
AGAMEMNON
  Fair Lord Aeneas, let me touch your hand;
  To our pavilion shall I lead you first.
  Achilles shall have word of this intent;
  So shall each lord of Greece, from tent to tent.
  Yourself shall feast with us before you go,
  And find the welcome of a noble foe.

                              Exeunt all but Ulysses and Nestor

ULYSSES Nestor –   310
NESTOR What says Ulysses?
ULYSSES
  I have a young conception in my brain;
  Be you my time to bring it to some shape.
NESTOR What is't?
ULYSSES
  This 'tis:
  Blunt wedges rive hard knots; the seeded pride
  That hath to this maturity blown up
  In rank Achilles must or now be cropped
  Or, shedding, breed a nursery of like evil
  To overbulk us all.
NESTOR   Well, and how?   320
ULYSSES
  This challenge that the gallant Hector sends,
  However it is spread in general name,
  Relates in purpose only to Achilles.
NESTOR
  True. The purpose is perspicuous even as substance
  Whose grossness little characters sum up;
  And in the publication make no strain
  But that Achilles, were his brain as barren
  As banks of Libya – though, Apollo knows,
  'Tis dry enough – will with great speed of judgement,
  Ay, with celerity, find Hector's purpose   330
  Pointing on him.

ULYSSES
And wake him to the answer, think you?

NESTOR   Yes,
It is most meet. Who may you else oppose,
That can from Hector bring his honour off,
If not Achilles? Though't be a sportful combat,
Yet in this trial much opinion dwells;
For here the Trojans taste our dear'st repute
With their fin'st palate; and trust to me, Ulysses,
Our imputation shall be oddly poised
340   In this willed action; for the success,
Although particular, shall give a scantling
Of good or bad unto the general,
And in such indexes, although small pricks
To their subsequent volumes, there is seen
The baby figure of the giant mass
Of things to come at large. It is supposed
He that meets Hector issues from our choice;
And choice, being mutual act of all our souls,
Makes merit her election, and doth boil,
350   As 'twere from forth us all, a man distilled
Out of our virtues; who miscarrying,
What heart from hence receives the conquering part,
To steel a strong opinion to themselves? –
Which entertained, limbs are his instruments,
In no less working than are swords and bows
Directive by the limbs.

ULYSSES
Give pardon to my speech:
Therefore 'tis meet Achilles meet not Hector.
Let us, like merchants, show our foulest wares,
360   And think perchance they'll sell; if not,
The lustre of the better yet to show
Shall show the better. Do not consent
That ever Hector and Achilles meet,
For both our honour and our shame in this
Are dogged with two strange followers.

NESTOR

I see them not with my old eyes: what are they?

ULYSSES

What glory our Achilles shares from Hector,
Were he not proud, we all should wear with him.
But he already is too insolent;
And we were better parch in Afric sun   370
Than in the pride and salt scorn of his eyes
Should he 'scape Hector fair. If he were foiled,
Why then we did our main opinion crush
In taint of our best man. No, make a lottery,
And by device let blockish Ajax draw
The sort to fight with Hector; among ourselves
Give him allowance as the worthier man,
For that will physic the great Myrmidon,
Who broils in loud applause, and make him fall
His crest that prouder than blue Iris bends.   380
If the dull brainless Ajax come safe off,
We'll dress him up in voices; if he fail,
Yet go we under our opinion still
That we have better men. But, hit or miss,
Our project's life this shape of sense assumes:
Ajax employed plucks down Achilles' plumes.

NESTOR

Now, Ulysses, I begin to relish thy advice,
And I will give a taste of it forthwith
To Agamemnon. Go we to him straight.
Two curs shall tame each other; pride alone   390
Must tarre the mastiffs on, as 'twere their bone.

Exeunt

*

Enter Ajax and Thersites   II.1

AJAX Thersites –

THERSITES Agamemnon – how if he had boils, full, all
  over, generally?

AJAX Thersites –

71

THERSITES And those boils did run? – say so – did not the general run then? Were not that a botchy core?

AJAX Dog!

THERSITES Then there would come some matter from him; I see none now.

10 AJAX Thou bitch-wolf's son, canst thou not hear? Feel, then.

He strikes him

THERSITES The plague of Greece upon thee, thou mongrel beef-witted lord!

AJAX Speak, then, you vinewed'st leaven, speak; I will beat thee into handsomeness!

THERSITES I shall sooner rail thee into wit and holiness; but I think thy horse will sooner con an oration than thou learn a prayer without book. Thou canst strike, canst thou? – A red murrain o'thy jade's tricks!

20 AJAX Toadstool, learn me the proclamation.

THERSITES Dost thou think I have no sense, thou strikest me thus?

AJAX The proclamation!

THERSITES Thou art proclaimed a fool, I think.

AJAX Do not, porpentine, do not; my fingers itch.

THERSITES I would thou didst itch from head to foot, and I had the scratching of thee; I would make thee the loathsomest scab in Greece.

AJAX I say, the proclamation!

30 THERSITES Thou grumblest and railest every hour on Achilles, and thou art as full of envy at his greatness as Cerberus is at Proserpina's beauty, ay, that thou bark'st at him.

AJAX Mistress Thersites!

THERSITES Thou shouldst strike him –

AJAX Cobloaf!

THERSITES He would pun thee into shivers with his fist, as a sailor breaks a biscuit.

AJAX (*beating him*) You whoreson cur!

40 THERSITES Do, do.

AJAX Thou stool for a witch!

THERSITES Ay, do, do! Thou sodden-witted lord, thou
    hast no more brain than I have in mine elbows; an
    assinico may tutor thee. Thou scurvy-valiant ass, thou
    art here but to thrash Trojans, and thou art bought and
    sold among those of any wit, like a barbarian slave. If
    thou use to beat me, I will begin at thy heel, and tell
    what thou art by inches, thou thing of no bowels, thou!

AJAX You dog!

THERSITES You scurvy lord!   50

AJAX (beating him) You cur!

THERSITES Mars his idiot! Do, rudeness, do, camel; do,
    do!

Enter Achilles and Patroclus

ACHILLES Why, how now, Ajax! Wherefore do you this?
    How now, Thersites, what's the matter, man?

THERSITES You see him there, do you?

ACHILLES Ay, what's the matter?

THERSITES Nay, look upon him.

ACHILLES So I do; what's the matter?

THERSITES Nay, but regard him well.   60

ACHILLES Well, why, I do so.

THERSITES But yet you look not well upon him; for,
    whomsoever you take him to be, he is Ajax.

ACHILLES I know that, fool.

THERSITES Ay, but that fool knows not himself.

AJAX Therefore I beat thee.

THERSITES Lo, lo, lo, lo, what modicums of wit he
    utters! His evasions have ears thus long. I have bobbed
    his brain more than he has beat my bones. I will buy
    nine sparrows for a penny, and his *pia mater* is not   70
    worth the ninth part of a sparrow. This lord, Achilles –
    Ajax, who wears his wit in his belly, and his guts in his
    head – I'll tell you what I say of him.

ACHILLES What?

THERSITES I say, this Ajax –

Ajax threatens to beat him; Achilles intervenes

ACHILLES Nay, good Ajax.

THERSITES Has not so much wit –

ACHILLES Nay, I must hold you.

THERSITES As will stop the eye of Helen's needle, for
80   whom he comes to fight.

ACHILLES Peace, fool!

THERSITES I would have peace and quietness, but the
   fool will not: he there, that he – look you there.

AJAX O thou damned cur, I shall –

ACHILLES Will you set your wit to a fool's?

THERSITES No, I warrant you, for a fool's will shame
   it.

PATROCLUS Good words, Thersites.

ACHILLES What's the quarrel?

90 AJAX I bade the vile owl go learn me the tenor of the
   proclamation, and he rails upon me.

THERSITES I serve thee not.

AJAX Well, go to, go to.

THERSITES I serve here voluntary.

ACHILLES Your last service was sufferance, 'twas not
   voluntary; no man is beaten voluntary. Ajax was here
   the voluntary, and you as under an impress.

THERSITES E'en so; a great deal of your wit, too, lies in
   your sinews, or else there be liars. Hector shall have a
100   great catch if he knock out either of your brains: he
   were as good crack a fusty nut with no kernel.

ACHILLES What, with me too, Thersites?

THERSITES There's Ulysses and old Nestor – whose wit
   was mouldy ere your grandsires had nails on their toes
   – yoke you like draught-oxen, and make you plough up
   the war.

ACHILLES What? What?

THERSITES Yes, good sooth; to, Achilles! To, Ajax, to!

AJAX I shall cut out your tongue.

110 THERSITES 'Tis no matter; I shall speak as much as thou
   afterwards.

PATROCLUS No more words, Thersites; peace!

THERSITES I will hold my peace when Achilles' brooch
    bids me, shall I?

ACHILLES There's for you, Patroclus.

THERSITES I will see you hanged like clotpolls ere I
    come any more to your tents; I will keep where there is
    wit stirring, and leave the faction of fools.   *Exit*

PATROCLUS A good riddance.

ACHILLES
    Marry, this, sir, is proclaimed through all our host: 120
    That Hector, by the fifth hour of the sun,
    Will with a trumpet 'twixt our tents and Troy
    Tomorrow morning call some knight to arms
    That hath a stomach, and such a one that dare
    Maintain – I know not what: 'tis trash. Farewell.

AJAX
    Farewell. Who shall answer him?

ACHILLES
    I know not – 'tis put to lottery. Otherwise
    He knew his man.

AJAX
    O, meaning you? I will go learn more of it.

                                        Exeunt

            Enter Priam, Hector, Troilus, Paris, and Helenus   II.2

PRIAM
    After so many hours, lives, speeches spent,
    Thus once again says Nestor from the Greeks:
    'Deliver Helen, and all damage else –
    As honour, loss of time, travail, expense,
    Wounds, friends, and what else dear that is
                consumed
    In hot digestion of this cormorant war –
    Shall be struck off.' Hector, what say you to't?

HECTOR
    Though no man lesser fears the Greeks than I
    As far as touches my particular,

                        75

10   Yet, dread Priam,
There is no lady of more softer bowels,
More spongy to suck in the sense of fear,
More ready to cry out 'Who knows what follows?'
Than Hector is. The wound of peace is surety,
Surety secure; but modest doubt is called
The beacon of the wise, the tent that searches
To th'bottom of the worst. Let Helen go:
Since the first sword was drawn about this question,
Every tithe soul 'mongst many thousand dismes

20   Hath been as dear as Helen – I mean, of ours.
If we have lost so many tenths of ours,
To guard a thing not ours nor worth to us –
Had it our name – the value of one ten,
What merit's in that reason which denies
The yielding of her up?

TROILUS   Fie, fie, my brother!
Weigh you the worth and honour of a king
So great as our dread father in a scale
Of common ounces? Will you with counters sum
The past-proportion of his infinite,

30   And buckle in a waist most fathomless
With spans and inches so diminutive
As fears and reasons? Fie, for godly shame!

HELENUS
No marvel though you bite so sharp at reasons,
You are so empty of them. Should not our father
Bear the great sway of his affairs with reasons,
Because your speech hath none that tells him so?

TROILUS
You are for dreams and slumbers, brother priest;
You fur your gloves with reason. Here are your
      reasons:
You know an enemy intends you harm;

40   You know a sword employed is perilous,
And reason flies the object of all harm.
Who marvels, then, when Helenus beholds

A Grecian and his sword, if he do set
The very wings of reason to his heels,
And fly like chidden Mercury from Jove,
Or like a star disorbed? Nay, if we talk of reason,
Let's shut our gates and sleep. Manhood and honour
Should have hare-hearts, would they but fat their
      thoughts
With this crammed reason; reason and respect
Make livers pale and lustihood deject.   50

HECTOR
Brother,
She is not worth what she doth cost the holding.

TROILUS
What's aught but as 'tis valued?

HECTOR
But value dwells not in particular will;
It holds his estimate and dignity
As well wherein 'tis precious of itself
As in the prizer. 'Tis mad idolatry
To make the service greater than the god;
And the will dotes that is inclinable
To what infectiously itself affects,   60
Without some image of th'affected merit.

TROILUS
I take today a wife, and my election
Is led on in the conduct of my will,
My will enkindled by mine eyes and ears,
Two traded pilots 'twixt the dangerous shores
Of will and judgement: how may I avoid,
Although my will distaste what it elected,
The wife I chose? There can be no evasion
To blench from this, and to stand firm by honour.
We turn not back the silks upon the merchant   70
When we have spoiled them; nor the remainder
      viands
We do not throw in unrespective sieve
Because we now are full. It was thought meet

Paris should do some vengeance on the Greeks:
Your breath of full consent bellied his sails;
The seas and winds, old wranglers, took a truce,
And did him service; he touched the ports desired;
And for an old aunt whom the Greeks held captive
He brought a Grecian queen, whose youth and
    freshness
80   Wrinkles Apollo's, and makes stale the morning.
Why keep we her? – The Grecians keep our aunt:
Is she worth keeping? – Why, she is a pearl
Whose price hath launched above a thousand
    ships,
And turned crowned kings to merchants.
If you'll avouch 'twas wisdom Paris went –
As you must needs, for you all cried 'Go, go!';
If you'll confess he brought home noble prize –
As you must needs, for you all clapped your hands
And cried 'Inestimable!' – why do you now
90   The issue of your proper wisdoms rate,
And do a deed that fortune never did –
Beggar the estimation which you prized
Richer than sea and land? O, theft most base,
That we have stolen what we do fear to keep!
But thieves unworthy of a thing so stolen,
That in their country did them that disgrace
We fear to warrant in our native place!

CASSANDRA (*within*)
    Cry, Trojans, cry!
PRIAM   What noise? What shriek is this?
TROILUS
    'Tis our mad sister. I do know her voice.
CASSANDRA (*within*)
100   Cry, Trojans!
HECTOR
    It is Cassandra.
        *Enter Cassandra, raving, with her hair about her
        ears*

78

CASSANDRA
   Cry, Trojans, cry! Lend me ten thousand eyes,
   And I will fill them with prophetic tears.
HECTOR
   Peace, sister, peace!
CASSANDRA
   Virgins and boys, mid-age and wrinkled old,
   Soft infancy, that nothing can but cry,
   Add to my clamour! Let us pay betimes
   A moiety of that mass of moan to come.
   Cry, Trojans, cry! Practise your eyes with tears!
   Troy must not be, nor goodly Ilium stand;   110
   Our firebrand brother Paris burns us all.
   Cry, Trojans, cry! A Helen and a woe!
   Cry, cry! Troy burns, or else let Helen go.

                                                    Exit

HECTOR
   Now, youthful Troilus, do not these high strains
   Of divination in our sister work
   Some touches of remorse? Or is your blood
   So madly hot that no discourse of reason,
   Nor fear of bad success in a bad cause,
   Can qualify the same?
TROILUS   Why, brother Hector,
   We may not think the justness of each act   120
   Such and no other than event doth form it,
   Nor once deject the courage of our minds,
   Because Cassandra's mad. Her brain-sick raptures
   Cannot distaste the goodness of a quarrel
   Which hath our several honours all engaged
   To make it gracious. For my private part,
   I am no more touched than all Priam's sons;
   And Jove forbid there should be done amongst us
   Such things as might offend the weakest spleen
   To fight for and maintain.   130
PARIS
   Else might the world convince of levity

79

As well my undertakings as your counsels;
But I attest the gods, your full consent
Gave wings to my propension, and cut off
All fears attending on so dire a project.
For what, alas, can these my single arms?
What propugnation is in one man's valour
To stand the push and enmity of those
This quarrel would excite? Yet I protest,
140 Were I alone to pass the difficulties,
And had as ample power as I have will,
Paris should ne'er retract what he hath done,
Nor faint in the pursuit.

PRIAM   Paris, you speak
Like one besotted on your sweet delights.
You have the honey still, but these the gall;
So to be valiant is no praise at all.

PARIS
Sir, I propose not merely to myself
The pleasures such a beauty brings with it;
But I would have the soil of her fair rape
150 Wiped off in honourable keeping her.
What treason were it to the ransacked queen,
Disgrace to your great worths, and shame to me,
Now to deliver her possession up
On terms of base compulsion! Can it be
That so degenerate a strain as this
Should once set footing in your generous bosoms?
There's not the meanest spirit on our party
Without a heart to dare, or sword to draw,
When Helen is defended; nor none so noble
160 Whose life were ill bestowed, or death unfamed,
Where Helen is the subject. Then, I say,
Well may we fight for her whom, we know well,
The world's large spaces cannot parallel.

HECTOR
Paris and Troilus, you have both said well,
And on the cause and question now in hand

Have glozed, but superficially – not much
Unlike young men whom Aristotle thought
Unfit to hear moral philosophy.
The reasons you allege do more conduce
To the hot passion of distempered blood   170
Than to make up a free determination
'Twixt right and wrong; for pleasure and revenge
Have ears more deaf than adders to the voice
Of any true decision. Nature craves
All dues be rendered to their owners: now,
What nearer debt in all humanity
Than wife is to the husband? If this law
Of nature be corrupted through affection,
And that great minds, of partial indulgence
To their benumbèd wills, resist the same,   180
There is a law in each well-ordered nation
To curb those raging appetites that are
Most disobedient and refractory.
If Helen then be wife to Sparta's king,
As it is known she is, these moral laws
Of nature and of nations speak aloud
To have her back returned; thus to persist
In doing wrong extenuates not wrong,
But makes it much more heavy. Hector's opinion
Is this in way of truth; yet, ne'ertheless,   190
My sprightly brethren, I propend to you
In resolution to keep Helen still;
For 'tis a cause that hath no mean dependence
Upon our joint and several dignities.

TROILUS

Why, there you touched the life of our design:
Were it not glory that we more affected
Than the performance of our heaving spleens,
I would not wish a drop of Trojan blood
Spent more in her defence. But, worthy Hector,
She is a theme of honour and renown,   200
A spur to valiant and magnanimous deeds,

Whose present courage may beat down our foes,
And fame in time to come canonize us.
For I presume brave Hector would not lose
So rich advantage of a promised glory
As smiles upon the forehead of this action
For the wide world's revenue.

HECTOR   I am yours,
You valiant offspring of great Priamus.
I have a roisting challenge sent amongst
210 The dull and factious nobles of the Greeks
Will strike amazement to their drowsy spirits.
I was advertised their great general slept,
Whilst emulation in the army crept;
This, I presume, will wake him.   *Exeunt*

II.3   *Enter Thersites*

THERSITES How now, Thersites! What, lost in the
labyrinth of thy fury? Shall the elephant Ajax carry it
thus? He beats me, and I rail at him: O, worthy
satisfaction! Would it were otherwise – that I could
beat him whilst he railed at me. 'Sfoot, I'll learn to
conjure and raise devils, but I'll see some issue of my
spiteful execrations. Then there's Achilles – a rare
engineer. If Troy be not taken till these two undermine
it, the walls will stand till they fall of themselves. O
10 thou great thunder-darter of Olympus, forget that
thou art Jove, the king of gods; and Mercury, lose all
the serpentine craft of thy caduceus, if thou take not
that little little, less than little wit from them that they
have! – which short-armed ignorance itself knows is so
abundant scarce it will not in circumvention deliver a
fly from a spider without drawing their massy irons and
cutting the web. After this, the vengeance on the whole
camp – or rather, the Neapolitan bone-ache – for that,
methinks, is the curse dependent on those that war for

a placket. I have said my prayers, and devil Envy say   20
'Amen'. – What, ho! My Lord Achilles!

Enter Patroclus

PATROCLUS Who's there? Thersites! Good Thersites,
come in and rail.

THERSITES If I could have remembered a gilt counterfeit, thou wouldst not have slipped out of my contem-
plation; but it is no matter – thyself upon thyself! The
common curse of mankind, folly and ignorance, be
thine in great revenue! Heaven bless thee from a tutor,
and discipline come not near thee! Let thy blood be thy
direction till thy death; then if she that lays thee out   30
says thou art a fair corpse, I'll be sworn and sworn
upon't, she never shrouded any but lazars. Amen. –
Where's Achilles?

PATROCLUS What, art thou devout? Wast thou in a
prayer?

THERSITES Ay, the heavens hear me!

Enter Achilles

ACHILLES Who's there?

PATROCLUS Thersites, my lord.

ACHILLES Where, where? – Art thou come? Why, my
cheese, my digestion, why hast thou not served thyself   40
in to my table, so many meals? Come, what's
Agamemnon?

THERSITES Thy commander, Achilles. Then tell me,
Patroclus, what's Achilles?

PATROCLUS Thy lord, Thersites. Then tell me, I pray
thee, what's thyself?

THERSITES Thy knower, Patroclus. Then tell me, Patroclus, what art thou?

PATROCLUS Thou mayst tell that knowest.

ACHILLES O, tell, tell.   50

THERSITES I'll decline the whole question.
Agamemnon commands Achilles, Achilles is my lord,
I am Patroclus' knower, and Patroclus is a fool.

PATROCLUS You rascal!

THERSITES Peace, fool, I have not done.

ACHILLES He is a privileged man. – Proceed, Thersites.

THERSITES Agamemnon is a fool, Achilles is a fool,
Thersites is a fool, and, as aforesaid, Patroclus is a
fool.

60 ACHILLES Derive this; come.

THERSITES Agamemnon is a fool to offer to command
Achilles, Achilles is a fool to be commanded of
Agamemnon, Thersites is a fool to serve such a fool,
and Patroclus is a fool positive.

PATROCLUS Why am I a fool?

THERSITES Make that demand to the Creator; it suffices
me thou art. Look you, who comes here?

ACHILLES Patroclus, I'll speak with nobody. – Come in
with me, Thersites.   *Exit*

70 THERSITES Here is such patchery, such juggling, and
such knavery! All the argument is a whore and a
cuckold; a good quarrel to draw emulous factions and
bleed to death upon. Now the dry serpigo on the
subject, and war and lechery confound all!   *Exit*
        *Enter Agamemnon, Ulysses, Nestor, Diomedes, Ajax,
        and Calchas*

AGAMEMNON Where is Achilles?

PATROCLUS Within his tent, but ill-disposed, my lord.

AGAMEMNON
Let it be known to him that we are here.
He shent our messengers, and we lay by
Our appertainments, visiting of him.

80 Let him be told so, lest perchance he think
We dare not move the question of our place,
Or know not what we are.

PATROCLUS I shall so say to him.   *Exit*

ULYSSES
We saw him at the opening of his tent:
He is not sick.

AJAX Yes, lion-sick, sick of proud heart; you may call it
melancholy, if you will favour the man, but, by my

84

head, 'tis pride: but why, why? Let him show us the
cause – a word, my lord.

    He takes Agamemnon aside

NESTOR What moves Ajax thus to bay at him?   90

ULYSSES Achilles hath inveigled his fool from him.

NESTOR Who, Thersites?

ULYSSES He.

NESTOR Then will Ajax lack matter, if he have lost his
argument.

ULYSSES No. You see, he is his argument that has his
argument – Achilles.

NESTOR All the better: their fraction is more our wish
than their faction; but it was a strong composure a fool
could disunite.   100

ULYSSES The amity that wisdom knits not, folly may
easily untie – here comes Patroclus.

    Enter Patroclus

NESTOR No Achilles with him.

ULYSSES The elephant hath joints, but none for courtesy; his legs are legs for necessity, not for flexure.

PATROCLUS
  Achilles bids me say he is much sorry
  If anything more than your sport and pleasure
  Did move your greatness, and this noble state,
  To call upon him; he hopes it is no other
  But for your health and your digestion sake,   110
  An after-dinner's breath.

AGAMEMNON   Hear you, Patroclus:
  We are too well acquainted with these answers;
  But his evasion, winged thus swift with scorn,
  Cannot outfly our apprehensions.
  Much attribute he hath, and much the reason
  Why we ascribe it to him; yet all his virtues,
  Not virtuously of his own part beheld,
  Do in our eyes begin to lose their gloss,
  Yea, like fair fruit in an unwholesome dish,
  Are like to rot untasted. Go and tell him   120

We came to speak with him, and you shall not sin
If you do say we think him over-proud
And under-honest, in self-assumption greater
Than in the note of judgement; and worthier than
       himself
Here tend the savage strangeness he puts on,
Disguise the holy strength of their command,
And underwrite in an observing kind
His humorous predominance – yea, watch
His pettish lunes, his ebbs, his flows, as if
130   The passage and whole carriage of this action
Rode on his tide. Go tell him this; and add
That if he overhold his price so much,
We'll none of him; but let him, like an engine
Not portable, lie under this report:
'Bring action hither; this cannot go to war.
A stirring dwarf we do allowance give
Before a sleeping giant.' Tell him so.

PATROCLUS
I shall, and bring his answer presently.   *Exit*

AGAMEMNON
In second voice we'll not be satisfied;
140   We come to speak with him. Ulysses, enter you.
                                Exit Ulysses

AJAX What is he more than another?

AGAMEMNON No more than what he thinks he is.

AJAX Is he so much? Do you not think he thinks himself a
better man than I am?

AGAMEMNON No question.

AJAX Will you subscribe his thought, and say he is?

AGAMEMNON No, noble Ajax; you are as strong, as
valiant, as wise, no less noble, much more gentle, and
altogether more tractable.

150 AJAX Why should a man be proud? How doth pride
grow? I know not what it is.

AGAMEMNON Your mind is the clearer, Ajax, and your
virtues the fairer. He that is proud eats up himself.

Pride is his own glass, his own trumpet, his own
chronicle; and whatever praises itself but in the deed,
devours the deed in the praise.

Enter Ulysses

AJAX I do hate a proud man as I hate the engendering of
toads.

NESTOR (*aside*) And yet he loves himself; is't not strange?

ULYSSES
Achilles will not to the field tomorrow.   160

AGAMEMNON
What's his excuse?

ULYSSES   He doth rely on none,
But carries on the stream of his dispose,
Without observance or respect of any,
In will peculiar and in self-admission.

AGAMEMNON
Why will he not, upon our fair request,
Untent his person, and share the air with us?

ULYSSES
Things small as nothing, for request's sake only,
He makes important. Possessed he is with greatness,
And speaks not to himself but with a pride
That quarrels at self-breath. Imagined worth   170
Holds in his blood such swollen and hot discourse
That 'twixt his mental and his active parts
Kingdomed Achilles in commotion rages,
And batters down himself. What should I say?
He is so plaguy proud that the death-tokens of it
Cry 'No recovery.'

AGAMEMNON   Let Ajax go to him. –
Dear lord, go you and greet him in his tent;
'Tis said he holds you well, and will be led,
At your request, a little from himself.

ULYSSES
O Agamemnon, let it not be so!   180
We'll consecrate the steps that Ajax makes
When they go from Achilles. Shall the proud lord,

That bastes his arrogance with his own seam,
And never suffers matter of the world
Enter his thoughts, save such as do revolve
And ruminate himself – shall he be worshipped
Of that we hold an idol more than he?
No; this thrice-worthy and right valiant lord
Must not so stale his palm, nobly acquired,
190   Nor, by my will, assubjugate his merit –
As amply titled as Achilles' is –
By going to Achilles:
That were to enlard his fat-already pride,
And add more coals to Cancer when he burns
With entertaining great Hyperion.
This lord go to him? Jupiter forbid,
And say in thunder: 'Achilles go to him.'

NESTOR (*aside*)
O, this is well; he rubs the vein of him.

DIOMEDES (*aside*)
And how his silence drinks up this applause.

AJAX
200   If I go to him, with my armèd fist
I'll pash him o'er the face.

AGAMEMNON
O, no, you shall not go.

AJAX
An 'a be proud with me, I'll pheeze his pride;
Let me go to him.

ULYSSES
Not for the worth that hangs upon our quarrel.

AJAX A paltry, insolent fellow!

NESTOR (*aside*) How he describes himself!

AJAX Can he not be sociable?

ULYSSES (*aside*) The raven chides blackness.

210 AJAX I'll let his humours' blood.

AGAMEMNON (*aside*) He will be the physician that
should be the patient.

AJAX An all men were o'my mind –

ULYSSES (*aside*) Wit would be out of fashion.

AJAX – 'a should not bear it so, 'a should eat swords first;
    shall pride carry it?

NESTOR (*aside*) An 'twould, you'd carry half.

ULYSSES (*aside*) 'A would have ten shares.

AJAX I will knead him; I'll make him supple.

NESTOR (*aside*) He's not yet through warm. Force him 220
    with praises, pour in, pour in; his ambition is dry.

ULYSSES (*to Agamemnon*)
  My lord, you feed too much on this dislike.

NESTOR
  Our noble general, do not do so.

DIOMEDES
  You must prepare to fight without Achilles.

ULYSSES
  Why, 'tis this naming of him doth him harm.
  Here is a man – but 'tis before his face;
  I will be silent.

NESTOR   Wherefore should you so?
  He is not emulous, as Achilles is.

ULYSSES
  Know the whole world, he is as valiant.

AJAX
  A whoreson dog, that shall palter thus with us! 230
  Would he were a Trojan!

NESTOR What a vice were it in Ajax now –

ULYSSES If he were proud –

DIOMEDES Or covetous of praise –

ULYSSES Ay, or surly borne –

DIOMEDES Or strange, or self-affected.

ULYSSES
  Thank the heavens, lord, thou art of sweet
          composure;
  Praise him that got thee, she that gave thee suck.
  Famed be thy tutor, and thy parts of nature
  Thrice-famed beyond, beyond all erudition; 240
  But he that disciplined thine arms to fight,

Let Mars divide eternity in twain,
And give him half; and for thy vigour,
Bull-bearing Milo his addition yield
To sinewy Ajax. I will not praise thy wisdom,
Which, like a bourn, a pale, a shore, confines
Thy spacious and dilated parts. Here's Nestor,
Instructed by the antiquary times;
He must, he is, he cannot but be wise –
250 But pardon, father Nestor, were your days
As green as Ajax', and your brain so tempered,
You should not have the eminence of him,
But be as Ajax.

AJAX (*to Nestor*)   Shall I call you father?

NESTOR
Ay, my good son.

DIOMEDES   Be ruled by him, Lord Ajax.

ULYSSES
There is no tarrying here; the hart Achilles
Keeps thicket. Please it our great general
To call together all his state of war;
Fresh kings are come to Troy. Tomorrow
We must with all our main of power stand fast,
260 And here's a lord – come knights from east to west,
And cull their flower, Ajax shall cope the best.

AGAMEMNON
Go we to council. Let Achilles sleep;
Light boats sail swift, though greater hulks draw
      deep.

Exeunt

*

III.1   *Music sounds within. Enter Pandarus and a Servant*

PANDARUS Friend, you, pray you, a word: do not you
   follow the young Lord Paris?

SERVANT Ay, sir, when he goes before me.

PANDARUS You depend upon him, I mean.

SERVANT Sir, I do depend upon the Lord.

PANDARUS You depend upon a noble gentleman; I must
needs praise him.

SERVANT The Lord be praised!

PANDARUS You know me, do you not?

SERVANT Faith, sir, superficially.   10

PANDARUS Friend, know me better: I am the Lord
Pandarus.

SERVANT I hope I shall know your honour better.

PANDARUS I do desire it.

SERVANT You are in the state of grace?

PANDARUS Grace? Not so, friend; honour and lordship
are my titles. What music is this?

SERVANT I do but partly know, sir: it is music in parts.

PANDARUS Know you the musicians?

SERVANT Wholly, sir.   20

PANDARUS Who play they to?

SERVANT To the hearers, sir.

PANDARUS At whose pleasure, friend?

SERVANT At mine, sir, and theirs that love music.

PANDARUS Command, I mean, friend.

SERVANT Who shall I command, sir?

PANDARUS Friend, we understand not one another: I
am too courtly, and thou art too cunning. At whose
request do these men play?

SERVANT That's to't indeed, sir: marry, sir, at the   30
request of Paris my lord, who's there in person; with
him, the mortal Venus, the heart-blood of beauty,
love's visible soul –

PANDARUS Who, my cousin Cressida?

SERVANT No, sir, Helen; could you not find out that by
her attributes?

PANDARUS It should seem, fellow, that thou hast not
seen the Lady Cressida. I come to speak with Paris
from the Prince Troilus. I will make a complimental
assault upon him, for my business seethes.   40

SERVANT (aside) Sodden business! There's a stewed
phrase indeed.

III.1

Enter Paris and Helen with attendants

PANDARUS Fair be to you, my lord, and to all this fair
company; fair desires, in all fair measure, fairly guide
them! – especially to you, fair queen: fair thoughts be
your fair pillow!

HELEN Dear lord, you are full of fair words.

PANDARUS You speak your fair pleasure, sweet queen. –
Fair prince, here is good broken music.

50 PARIS You have broke it, cousin: and by my life you shall
make it whole again; you shall piece it out with a piece
of your performance. – Nell, he is full of harmony.

PANDARUS Truly, lady, no.

HELEN O sir –

PANDARUS Rude, in sooth; in good sooth, very rude.

PARIS Well said, my lord; well, you say so in fits.

PANDARUS I have business to my lord, dear queen. – My
lord, will you vouchsafe me a word?

HELEN Nay, this shall not hedge us out; we'll hear you
60 sing, certainly.

PANDARUS Well, sweet queen, you are pleasant with me.
– But, marry, thus, my lord: my dear lord, and most
esteemed friend, your brother Troilus –

HELEN My Lord Pandarus, honey-sweet lord –

PANDARUS Go to, sweet queen, go to – commends
himself most affectionately to you –

HELEN You shall not bob us out of our melody; if you do,
our melancholy upon your head!

PANDARUS Sweet queen, sweet queen; that's a sweet
70 queen, i'faith –

HELEN And to make a sweet lady sad is a sour offence.

PANDARUS Nay, that shall not serve your turn, that shall
it not, in truth, la. Nay, I care not for such words; no,
no – and, my lord, he desires you that if the King call
for him at supper, you will make his excuse.

HELEN My Lord Pandarus –

PANDARUS What says my sweet queen, my very very
sweet queen?

PARIS What exploit's in hand? Where sups he tonight?
HELEN Nay, but, my lord –   80
PANDARUS What says my sweet queen? – My cousin will
    fall out with you.
HELEN (*to Paris*) You must not know where he sups.
PARIS I'll lay my life, with my disposer Cressida.
PANDARUS No, no, no such matter, you are wide; come,
    your disposer is sick.
PARIS Well, I'll make excuse.
PANDARUS Ay, good my lord. Why should you say
    Cressida? No, your poor disposer's sick.
PARIS I spy.   90
PANDARUS You spy? What do you spy? – Come, give me
    an instrument. – Now, sweet queen.
HELEN Why, this is kindly done.
PANDARUS My niece is horribly in love with a thing you
    have, sweet queen.
HELEN She shall have it, my lord, if it be not my Lord
    Paris.
PANDARUS He? No, she'll none of him; they two are
    twain.
HELEN Falling in after falling out may make them   100
    three.
PANDARUS Come, come, I'll hear no more of this; I'll
    sing you a song now.
HELEN Ay, ay, prithee now. By my troth, sweet lord, thou
    hast a fine forehead.
PANDARUS Ay, you may, you may.
HELEN Let thy song be love; this love will undo us all. O
    Cupid, Cupid, Cupid!
PANDARUS Love? Ay, that it shall, i'faith.
PARIS Ay, good now, love, love, nothing but love.   110
PANDARUS In good troth, it begins so.
        He sings
    Love, love, nothing but love, still love, still more!
            For, O, love's bow
            Shoots buck and doe;

93

> The shaft confounds,
>   Not that it wounds,
> But tickles still the sore.
> These lovers cry – O ho, they die!
>   Yet that which seems the wound to kill
120 Doth turn O ho to ha, ha, he!
>   So dying love lives still:
> O ho, a while, but ha, ha, ha!
> O ho, groans out for ha, ha, ha! – Heigh ho!

HELEN In love, i'faith, to the very tip of the nose.

PARIS He eats nothing but doves, love, and that breeds hot blood, and hot blood begets hot thoughts, and hot thoughts beget hot deeds, and hot deeds is love.

PANDARUS Is this the generation of love? Hot blood, hot thoughts, and hot deeds? Why, they are vipers: is love
130 a generation of vipers? – Sweet lord, who's a-field today?

PARIS Hector, Deiphobus, Helenus, Antenor, and all the gallantry of Troy. I would fain have armed today, but my Nell would not have it so. How chance my brother Troilus went not?

HELEN He hangs the lip at something – you know all, Lord Pandarus.

PANDARUS Not I, honey-sweet queen; I long to hear how they sped today. – You'll remember your
140 brother's excuse?

PARIS To a hair.

PANDARUS Farewell, sweet queen.

HELEN Commend me to your niece.

PANDARUS I will, sweet queen.   *Exit*

    Sound a retreat

PARIS
> They're come from field; let us to Priam's hall,
> To greet the warriors. Sweet Helen, I must woo you
> To help unarm our Hector; his stubborn buckles,
> With these your white enchanting fingers touched,
> Shall more obey than to the edge of steel

Or force of Greekish sinews. You shall do more   150
Than all the island kings – disarm great Hector.

HELEN
'Twill make us proud to be his servant, Paris;
Yea, what he shall receive of us in duty
Gives us more palm in beauty than we have,
Yea, overshines ourself.

PARIS
Sweet, above thought I love thee.   *Exeunt*

Enter Pandarus and Troilus's Man, meeting   III.2
PANDARUS How now, where's thy master? At my cousin
    Cressida's?
MAN No, sir; he stays for you to conduct him thither.
    Enter Troilus
PANDARUS O, here he comes. How now, how now?
TROILUS Sirrah, walk off.   *Exit Man*
PANDARUS Have you seen my cousin?
TROILUS
    No, Pandarus; I stalk about her door,
    Like a strange soul upon the Stygian banks
    Staying for waftage. O, be thou my Charon,
    And give me swift transportance to those fields   10
    Where I may wallow in the lily-beds
    Proposed for the deserver! O gentle Pandar,
    From Cupid's shoulder pluck his painted wings,
    And fly with me to Cressid!
PANDARUS
    Walk here i'th'orchard; I'll bring her straight.   *Exit*
TROILUS
    I am giddy; expectation whirls me round.
    Th'imaginary relish is so sweet
    That it enchants my sense. What will it be,
    When that the watery palate tastes indeed
    Love's thrice-repurèd nectar? – death, I fear me,   20
    Swooning destruction, or some joy too fine,

95

Too subtle-potent, tuned too sharp in sweetness,
For the capacity of my ruder powers.
I fear it much; and I do fear besides
That I shall lose distinction in my joys,
As doth a battle, when they charge on heaps
The enemy flying.

Enter Pandarus

PANDARUS She's making her ready; she'll come
straight. You must be witty now. She does so blush,
30 and fetches her wind so short, as if she were frayed
with a sprite. I'll fetch her. It is the prettiest villain; she
fetches her breath as short as a new-ta'en sparrow. *Exit*

TROILUS
Even such a passion doth embrace my bosom.
My heart beats thicker than a feverous pulse,
And all my powers do their bestowing lose,
Like vassalage at unawares encountering
The eye of majesty.

Enter Pandarus and Cressida, veiled

PANDARUS Come, come, what need you blush? Shame's
a baby. (*To Troilus*) Here she is now: swear the oaths
40 now to her that you have sworn to me. (*To Cressida*)
What, are you gone again? You must be watched ere
you be made tame, must you? Come your ways, come
your ways; an you draw backward, we'll put you
i'th'fills. (*To Troilus*) Why do you not speak to her? (*To
Cressida*) Come, draw this curtain, and let's see your
picture. Alas the day, how loath you are to offend
daylight! An 'twere dark, you'd close sooner. (*To
Troilus*) So, so, rub on, and kiss the mistress. How
now, a kiss in fee-farm! Build there, carpenter, the air
50 is sweet. – Nay, you shall fight your hearts out ere I part
you: the falcon as the tercel, for all the ducks i'th'river
– go to, go to.

TROILUS You have bereft me of all words, lady.

PANDARUS Words pay no debts, give her deeds: but
she'll bereave you o'th'deeds too, if she call your

96

activity in question. What, billing again? Here's 'In witness whereof the parties interchangeably' – Come in, come in: I'll go get a fire.   *Exit*

CRESSIDA Will you walk in, my lord?

TROILUS O Cressida, how often have I wished me thus! 60

CRESSIDA Wished, my lord! – The gods grant – O my lord!

TROILUS What should they grant? What makes this pretty abruption? What too curious dreg espies my sweet lady in the fountain of our love?

CRESSIDA More dregs than water, if my fears have eyes.

TROILUS Fears make devils of cherubins; they never see truly.

CRESSIDA Blind fear, that seeing reason leads, finds safer footing than blind reason stumbling without fear: 70 to fear the worst oft cures the worst.

TROILUS O, let my lady apprehend no fear; in all Cupid's pageant there is presented no monster.

CRESSIDA Nor nothing monstrous neither?

TROILUS Nothing, but our undertakings, when we vow to weep seas, live in fire, eat rocks, tame tigers; thinking it harder for our mistress to devise imposition enough than for us to undergo any difficulty imposed. This is the monstruosity in love, lady, that the will is infinite, and the execution confined; that the desire is 80 boundless, and the act a slave to limit.

CRESSIDA They say, all lovers swear more performance than they are able, and yet reserve an ability that they never perform; vowing more than the perfection of ten, and discharging less than the tenth part of one. They that have the voice of lions and the act of hares, are they not monsters?

TROILUS Are there such? Such are not we. Praise us as we are tasted, allow us as we prove. Our head shall go bare till merit crown it; no perfection in reversion shall 90 have a praise in present. We will not name desert before his birth, and, being born, his addition shall be

humble: few words to fair faith. Troilus shall be such
to Cressid as what envy can say worst shall be a mock
for his truth, and what truth can speak truest, not truer
than Troilus.

CRESSIDA Will you walk in, my lord?

Enter Pandarus

PANDARUS What, blushing still? Have you not done
talking yet?

100 CRESSIDA Well, uncle, what folly I commit, I dedicate to
you.

PANDARUS I thank you for that. If my lord get a boy of
you, you'll give him me. Be true to my lord; if he flinch,
chide me for it.

TROILUS You know now your hostages; your uncle's
word and my firm faith.

PANDARUS Nay, I'll give my word for her too. Our
kindred, though they be long ere they are wooed, they
are constant being won; they are burs, I can tell you,
110 they'll stick where they are thrown.

CRESSIDA
Boldness comes to me now, and brings me heart:
Prince Troilus, I have loved you night and day
For many weary months.

TROILUS
Why was my Cressid then so hard to win?

CRESSIDA
Hard to seem won; but I was won, my lord,
With the first glance that ever – pardon me;
If I confess much, you will play the tyrant.
I love you now; but not till now so much
But I might master it. In faith, I lie;
120 My thoughts were like unbridled children, grown
Too headstrong for their mother – see, we fools!
Why have I blabbed? Who shall be true to us
When we are so unsecret to ourselves? –
But though I loved you well, I wooed you not;
And yet, good faith, I wished myself a man,

Or that we women had men's privilege
Of speaking first. Sweet, bid me hold my tongue,
For in this rapture I shall surely speak
The thing I shall repent. See, see, your silence,
Cunning in dumbness, from my weakness draws   130
My soul of counsel from me! – Stop my mouth.

TROILUS

And shall, albeit sweet music issues thence.
    He kisses her

PANDARUS Pretty, i'faith.

CRESSIDA

My lord, I do beseech you, pardon me;
'Twas not my purpose thus to beg a kiss.
I am ashamed – O heavens, what have I done?
For this time will I take my leave, my lord.

TROILUS

Your leave, sweet Cressid!

PANDARUS Leave? An you take leave till tomorrow
    morning –   140

CRESSIDA Pray you, content you.

TROILUS What offends you, lady?

CRESSIDA Sir, mine own company.

TROILUS You cannot shun yourself.

CRESSIDA

Let me go and try.
I have a kind of self resides with you;
But an unkind self, that itself will leave
To be another's fool. Where is my wit?
I would be gone; I speak I know not what.

TROILUS

Well know they what they speak that speak so wisely.   150

CRESSIDA

Perchance, my lord, I showed more craft than love,
And fell so roundly to a large confession,
To angle for your thoughts; but you are wise,
Or else you love not; for to be wise and love
Exceeds man's might – that dwells with gods above.

TROILUS

O that I thought it could be in a woman –
As, if it can, I will presume in you –
To feed for aye her lamp and flames of love;
To keep her constancy in plight and youth,
160 Outliving beauty's outward, with a mind
That doth renew swifter than blood decays!
Or that persuasion could but thus convince me,
That my integrity and truth to you
Might be affronted with the match and weight
Of such a winnowed purity in love –
How were I then uplifted! But alas,
I am as true as truth's simplicity,
And simpler than the infancy of truth.

CRESSIDA

In that I'll war with you.

TROILUS   O virtuous fight,
170 When right with right wars who shall be most right!
True swains in love shall in the world to come
Approve their truths by Troilus; when their rhymes,
Full of protest, of oath, and big compare,
Want similes, truth tired with iteration –
As true as steel, as plantage to the moon,
As sun to day, as turtle to her mate,
As iron to adamant, as earth to th'centre –
Yet, after all comparisons of truth,
As truth's authentic author to be cited,
180 'As true as Troilus' shall crown up the verse,
And sanctify the numbers.

CRESSIDA   Prophet may you be!
If I be false, or swerve a hair from truth,
When time is old and hath forgot itself,
When waterdrops have worn the stones of Troy,
And blind oblivion swallowed cities up,
And mighty states characterless are grated
To dusty nothing; yet let memory,
From false to false, among false maids in love,

Upbraid my falsehood! When they've said 'As false
As air, as water, wind, or sandy earth,   190
As fox to lamb, as wolf to heifer's calf,
Pard to the hind, or stepdame to her son' –
Yea, let them say, to stick the heart of falsehood,
'As false as Cressid.'

PANDARUS Go to, a bargain made; seal it, seal it, I'll be
the witness. Here I hold your hand, here my cousin's.
If ever you prove false one to another, since I have
taken such pains to bring you together, let all pitiful
goers-between be called to the world's end after my
name; call them all Pandars. Let all constant men be   200
Troiluses, all false women Cressids, and all brokers-
between Pandars! Say 'Amen.'

TROILUS Amen.

CRESSIDA Amen.

PANDARUS Amen. Whereupon I will show you a chamber with a bed; which bed, because it shall not speak of
your pretty encounters, press it to death: away! –

>   *Exeunt Troilus and Cressida*

And Cupid grant all tongue-tied maidens here
Bed, chamber, and Pandar to provide this gear!   *Exit*

>   *Flourish. Enter Agamemnon, Ulysses, Diomedes,*   III.3
>   *Nestor, Ajax, Menelaus, and Calchas*

CALCHAS
Now, princes, for the service I have done you,
Th'advantage of the time prompts me aloud
To call for recompense. Appear it to your mind
That, through the sight I bear in things to come,
I have abandoned Troy, left my possession,
Incurred a traitor's name, exposed myself,
From certain and possessed conveniences,
To doubtful fortunes; sequest'ring from me all
That time, acquaintance, custom, and condition
Made tame and most familiar to my nature;   10

And here, to do you service, am become
As new into the world, strange, unacquainted.
I do beseech you, as in way of taste,
To give me now a little benefit,
Out of those many registered in promise,
Which, you say, live to come in my behalf.

AGAMEMNON
What wouldst thou of us, Trojan? Make demand.

CALCHAS
You have a Trojan prisoner, called Antenor,
Yesterday took; Troy holds him very dear.
20 Oft have you – often have you thanks therefore –
Desired my Cressid in right great exchange,
Whom Troy hath still denied; but this Antenor,
I know, is such a wrest in their affairs
That their negotiations all must slack,
Wanting his manage; and they will almost
Give us a prince of blood, a son of Priam,
In change of him. Let him be sent, great princes,
And he shall buy my daughter; and her presence
Shall quite strike off all service I have done
In most accepted pain.

30 AGAMEMNON   Let Diomedes bear him,
And bring us Cressid hither; Calchas shall have
What he requests of us. Good Diomed,
Furnish you fairly for this interchange;
Withal, bring word if Hector will tomorrow
Be answered in his challenge. Ajax is ready.

DIOMEDES
This shall I undertake, and 'tis a burden
Which I am proud to bear.

                              Exeunt Diomedes and Calchas
                    Achilles and Patroclus stand in the entrance to their
                    tent

ULYSSES
Achilles stands i'th'entrance of his tent.
Please it our general to pass strangely by him,

As if he were forgot; and, princes all,   40
Lay negligent and loose regard upon him.
I will come last – 'tis like he'll question me
Why such unplausive eyes are bent, why turned on
        him;
If so, I have derision medicinable
To use between your strangeness and his pride,
Which his own will shall have desire to drink.
It may do good: pride hath no other glass
To show itself but pride; for supple knees
Feed arrogance, and are the proud man's fees.

AGAMEMNON
We'll execute your purpose, and put on   50
A form of strangeness as we pass along –
So do each lord, and either greet him not,
Or else disdainfully, which shall shake him more
Than if not looked on. I will lead the way.

ACHILLES
What, comes the general to speak with me?
You know my mind; I'll fight no more 'gainst Troy.

AGAMEMNON
What says Achilles? Would he aught with us?

NESTOR
Would you, my lord, aught with the general?

ACHILLES No.

NESTOR Nothing, my lord.   60

AGAMEMNON The better. *Exeunt Agamemnon and Nestor*

ACHILLES Good day, good day.

MENELAUS How do you? How do you?   *Exit*

ACHILLES What, does the cuckold scorn me?

AJAX How now, Patroclus?

ACHILLES Good morrow, Ajax.

AJAX Ha?

ACHILLES Good morrow.

AJAX Ay, and good next day too.   *Exit*

ACHILLES
What mean these fellows? Know they not Achilles?   70

PATROCLUS
    They pass by strangely. They were used to bend,
    To send their smiles before them to Achilles;
    To come as humbly as they use to creep
    To holy altars.
ACHILLES   What, am I poor of late?
    'Tis certain, greatness, once fallen out with fortune,
    Must fall out with men too. What the declined is,
    He shall as soon read in the eyes of others
    As feel in his own fall; for men, like butterflies,
    Show not their mealy wings but to the summer,
80   And not a man, for being simply man,
    Hath any honour, but honoured for those honours
    That are without him, as place, riches, and favour –
    Prizes of accident as oft as merit –
    Which when they fall, as being slippery standers,
    The love that leaned on them, as slippery too,
    Doth one pluck down another, and together
    Die in the fall. But 'tis not so with me:
    Fortune and I are friends. I do enjoy
    At ample point all that I did possess,
90   Save these men's looks; who do, methinks, find out
    Something not worth in me such rich beholding
    As they have often given. Here is Ulysses:
    I'll interrupt his reading –
    How now, Ulysses!
ULYSSES   Now, great Thetis' son.
ACHILLES
    What are you reading?
ULYSSES   A strange fellow here
    Writes me that man – how dearly ever parted,
    How much in having, or without or in –
    Cannot make boast to have that which he hath,
    Nor feels not what he owes, but by reflection;
100   As when his virtues shining upon others
    Heat them, and they retort that heat again
    To the first giver.

ACHILLES   This is not strange, Ulysses.
The beauty that is borne here in the face
The bearer knows not, but commends itself
To others' eyes; nor doth the eye itself,
That most pure spirit of sense, behold itself,
Not going from itself, but eye to eye opposed
Salutes each other with each other's form.
For speculation turns not to itself
Till it hath travelled, and is mirrored there   110
Where it may see itself. This is not strange at all.

ULYSSES
I do not strain at the position –
It is familiar – but at the author's drift,
Who in his circumstance expressly proves
That no man is the lord of any thing,
Though in and of him there is much consisting,
Till he communicate his parts to others;
Nor doth he of himself know them for aught
Till he behold them formèd in th'applause
Where they're extended; who like an arch reverb'rate 120
The voice again; or, like a gate of steel
Fronting the sun, receives and renders back
His figure and his heat. I was much rapt in this,
And apprehended here immediately
The unknown Ajax. Heavens, what a man is there!
A very horse, that has he knows not what!
Nature, what things there are
Most abject in regard, and dear in use!
What things again most dear in the esteem,
And poor in worth! Now shall we see tomorrow – 130
An act that very chance doth throw upon him –
Ajax renowned. O heavens, what some men do,
While some men leave to do!
How some men creep in skittish Fortune's hall,
Whiles others play the idiots in her eyes!
How one man eats into another's pride,
While pride is fasting in his wantonness!

                    To see these Grecian lords! – Why, even already
                    They clap the lubber Ajax on the shoulder,
140   As if his foot were on brave Hector's breast,
                    And great Troy shrinking.

ACHILLES

                    I do believe it; for they passed by me
                    As misers do by beggars, neither gave to me
                    Good word nor look. What, are my deeds forgot?

ULYSSES

                    Time hath, my lord, a wallet at his back,
                    Wherein he puts alms for oblivion,
                    A great-sized monster of ingratitudes:
                    Those scraps are good deeds past, which are
                              devoured
                    As fast as they are made, forgot as soon
150   As done. Perseverance, dear my lord,
                    Keeps honour bright: to have done is to hang
                    Quite out of fashion, like a rusty mail
                    In monumental mockery. Take the instant way;
                    For honour travels in a strait so narrow,
                    Where one but goes abreast. Keep then the path,
                    For emulation hath a thousand sons,
                    That one by one pursue; if you give way,
                    Or hedge aside from the direct forthright,
                    Like to an entered tide, they all rush by,
160   And leave you hindmost;
                    Or, like a gallant horse fallen in first rank,
                    Lie there for pavement to the abject rear,
                    O'er-run and trampled on. Then what they do in
                              present,
                    Though less than yours in past, must o'ertop yours;
                    For time is like a fashionable host,
                    That slightly shakes his parting guest by th'hand,
                    And with his arms outstretched, as he would fly,
                    Grasps in the comer: the welcome ever smiles,
                    And farewell goes out sighing. O, let not virtue seek
170   Remuneration for the thing it was;

For beauty, wit,
High birth, vigour of bone, desert in service,
Love, friendship, charity, are subjects all
To envious and calumniating time.
One touch of nature makes the whole world kin,
That all, with one consent, praise new-born gauds,
Though they are made and moulded of things past,
And give to dust that is a little gilt
More laud than gilt o'er-dusted.
The present eye praises the present object: 180
Then marvel not, thou great and complete man,
That all the Greeks begin to worship Ajax,
Since things in motion sooner catch the eye
Than what stirs not. The cry went once on thee,
And still it might, and yet it may again,
If thou wouldst not entomb thyself alive,
And case thy reputation in thy tent;
Whose glorious deeds but in these fields of late
Made emulous missions 'mongst the gods
            themselves,
And drave great Mars to faction.

ACHILLES   Of this my privacy   190
I have strong reasons.

ULYSSES   But 'gainst your privacy
The reasons are more potent and heroical.
'Tis known, Achilles, that you are in love
With one of Priam's daughters –

ACHILLES   Ha? Known?

ULYSSES
Is that a wonder?
The providence that's in a watchful state
Knows almost every grain of Pluto's gold,
Finds bottom in th'uncomprehensive deeps,
Keeps place with thought, and almost, like the gods,
Does thoughts unveil in their dumb cradles.   200
There is a mystery – with whom relation
Durst never meddle – in the soul of state,

Which hath an operation more divine
Than breath or pen can give expressure to.
All the commerce that you have had with Troy
As perfectly is ours as yours, my lord;
And better would it fit Achilles much
To throw down Hector than Polyxena.
But it must grieve young Pyrrhus now at home,
210 When fame shall in our islands sound her trump,
And all the Greekish girls shall tripping sing:
'Great Hector's sister did Achilles win,
But our great Ajax bravely beat down him.'
Farewell, my lord: I as your lover speak;
The fool slides o'er the ice that you should break.

Exit

PATROCLUS
To this effect, Achilles, have I moved you.
A woman impudent and mannish grown
Is not more loathed than an effeminate man
In time of action. I stand condemned for this;
220 They think my little stomach to the war,
And your great love to me, restrains you thus.
Sweet, rouse yourself, and the weak wanton Cupid
Shall from your neck unloose his amorous fold,
And, like a dew-drop from the lion's mane,
Be shook to air.

ACHILLES   Shall Ajax fight with Hector?

PATROCLUS
Ay, and perhaps receive much honour by him.

ACHILLES
I see my reputation is at stake.
My fame is shrewdly gored.

PATROCLUS   O, then, beware:
Those wounds heal ill that men do give themselves.
230 Omission to do what is necessary
Seals a commission to a blank of danger,
And danger, like an ague, subtly taints
Even then when we sit idly in the sun.

ACHILLES
  Go call Thersites hither, sweet Patroclus.
  I'll send the fool to Ajax, and desire him
  T'invite the Trojan lords after the combat
  To see us here unarmed. I have a woman's longing,
  An appetite that I am sick withal,
  To see great Hector in his weeds of peace,
    (Enter Thersites)
  To talk with him, and to behold his visage   240
  Even to my full of view. – A labour saved!

THERSITES A wonder!

ACHILLES What?

THERSITES Ajax goes up and down the field, asking for
  himself.

ACHILLES How so?

THERSITES He must fight singly tomorrow with Hector,
  and is so prophetically proud of an heroical cudgelling
  that he raves in saying nothing.

ACHILLES How can that be?   250

THERSITES Why, he stalks up and down like a peacock, a
  stride and a stand; ruminates like an hostess that hath
  no arithmetic but her brain to set down her reckoning;
  bites his lip with a politic regard, as who should say
  there were wit in his head, an 'twould out – and so
  there is; but it lies as coldly in him as fire in a flint,
  which will not show without knocking. The man's
  undone for ever, for if Hector break not his neck
  i'th'combat, he'll break't himself in vainglory. He
  knows not me: I said 'Good morrow, Ajax' and he 260
  replies 'Thanks, Agamemnon.' – What think you of
  this man, that takes me for the general? He's grown a
  very land-fish, languageless, a monster. A plague of
  opinion! A man may wear it on both sides, like a leather
  jerkin.

ACHILLES Thou must be my ambassador to him, Thersites.

THERSITES Who, I? Why, he'll answer nobody, he

professes not answering; speaking is for beggars; he
270   wears his tongue in's arms. I will put on his presence:
let Patroclus make his demands to me, you shall see
the pageant of Ajax.

ACHILLES To him, Patroclus. Tell him I humbly desire
the valiant Ajax to invite the most valorous Hector to
come unarmed to my tent, and to procure safe-
conduct for his person of the magnanimous and most
illustrious six-or-seven-times-honoured captain-
general of the Grecian army, Agamemnon, et cetera.
Do this.

280 PATROCLUS Jove bless great Ajax.

THERSITES Hum!

PATROCLUS I come from the worthy Achilles –

THERSITES Ha?

PATROCLUS Who most humbly desires you to invite
Hector to his tent –

THERSITES Hum!

PATROCLUS And to procure safe-conduct from
Agamemnon.

THERSITES Agamemnon?

290 PATROCLUS Ay, my lord.

THERSITES Ha!

PATROCLUS What say you to't?

THERSITES God buy you, with all my heart.

PATROCLUS Your answer, sir.

THERSITES If tomorrow be a fair day, by eleven o'clock it
will go one way or other; howsoever, he shall pay for
me ere he has me.

PATROCLUS Your answer, sir.

THERSITES Fare you well, with all my heart.

300 ACHILLES Why, but he is not in this tune, is he?

THERSITES No, but he's out o'tune thus. What music
will be in him when Hector has knocked out his brains,
I know not; but I am sure, none, unless the fiddler
Apollo get his sinews to make catlings on.

ACHILLES Come, thou shalt bear a letter to him straight.

THERSITES Let me carry another to his horse, for that's
the more capable creature.

ACHILLES
My mind is troubled, like a fountain stirred,
And I myself see not the bottom of it.

Exeunt Achilles and Patroclus

THERSITES Would the fountain of your mind were clear 310
again, that I might water an ass at it! I had rather be a
tick in a sheep than such a valiant ignorance. *Exit*

*

Enter, at one door, Aeneas and a servant with a torch; IV.1
*at another, Paris, Deiphobus, Antenor, Diomedes the
Grecian, and others with torches*

PARIS
See, ho! Who is that there?

DEIPHOBUS
It is the Lord Aeneas.

AENEAS
Is the prince there in person? –
Had I so good occasion to lie long
As you, Prince Paris, nothing but heavenly business
Should rob my bed-mate of my company.

DIOMEDES
That's my mind too. – Good morrow, Lord Aeneas.

PARIS
A valiant Greek, Aeneas – take his hand –
Witness the process of your speech within;
You told how Diomed a whole week by days   10
Did haunt you in the field.

AENEAS   Health to you, valiant sir,
During all question of the gentle truce;
But when I meet you armed, as black defiance
As heart can think or courage execute.

DIOMEDES
The one and other Diomed embraces.
Our bloods are now in calm; and, so long, health;

But when contention and occasion meet,
By Jove, I'll play the hunter for thy life
With all my force, pursuit, and policy.

AENEAS

20 And thou shalt hunt a lion that will fly
With his face backward. – In humane gentleness,
Welcome to Troy! Now by Anchises' life,
Welcome indeed! By Venus' hand I swear,
No man alive can love in such a sort
The thing he means to kill more excellently.

DIOMEDES

We sympathize. – Jove, let Aeneas live,
If to my sword his fate be not the glory,
A thousand complete courses of the sun!
But in mine emulous honour let him die,
30 With every joint a wound, and that tomorrow!

AENEAS

We know each other well.

DIOMEDES

We do, and long to know each other worse.

PARIS

This is the most despiteful'st gentle greeting,
The noblest hateful love, that e'er I heard of.
(*To Aeneas*) What business, lord, so early?

AENEAS

I was sent for to the King; but why, I know not.

PARIS (*to Aeneas*)

His purpose meets you: it was to bring this Greek
To Calchas' house, and there to render him,
For the enfreed Antenor, the fair Cressid.
40 Let's have your company, or, if you please,
Haste there before us: I constantly do think –
Or, rather, call my thought a certain knowledge –
My brother Troilus lodges there tonight.
Rouse him, and give him note of our approach.
With the whole quality whereof. I fear
We shall be much unwelcome.

AENEAS (*to Paris*)   That I assure you;
 Troilus had rather Troy were borne to Greece
 Than Cressid borne from Troy.

PARIS (*to Aeneas*)   There is no help;
 The bitter disposition of the time
 Will have it so. On, lord; we'll follow you.   50

AENEAS
 Good morrow, all.   *Exit with servant*

PARIS
 And tell me, noble Diomed, faith, tell me true,
 Even in the soul of sound good-fellowship,
 Who, in your thoughts, merits fair Helen most,
 Myself or Menelaus?

DIOMEDES   Both alike:
 He merits well to have her, that doth seek her,
 Not making any scruple of her soilure,
 With such a hell of pain and world of charge;
 And you as well to keep her, that defend her,
 Not palating the taste of her dishonour,   60
 With such a costly loss of wealth and friends.
 He, like a puling cuckold, would drink up
 The lees and dregs of a flat tamed piece;
 You, like a lecher, out of whorish loins
 Are pleased to breed out your inheritors.
 Both merits poised, each weighs nor less nor
    more;
 But he as you, each heavier for a whore.

PARIS
 You are too bitter to your countrywoman.

DIOMEDES
 She's bitter to her country. Hear me, Paris:
 For every false drop in her bawdy veins   70
 A Grecian's life hath sunk; for every scruple
 Of her contaminated carrion weight
 A Trojan hath been slain. Since she could speak,
 She hath not given so many good words breath
 As for her Greeks and Trojans suffered death.

PARIS

Fair Diomed, you do as chapmen do,
Dispraise the thing that you desire to buy;
But we in silence hold this virtue well:
We'll not commend what we intend to sell.

80 Here lies our way.   *Exeunt*

IV.2   *Enter Troilus and Cressida*

TROILUS

Dear, trouble not yourself; the morn is cold.

CRESSIDA

Then, sweet my lord, I'll call mine uncle down;
He shall unbolt the gates.

TROILUS   Trouble him not;
To bed, to bed. Sleep kill those pretty eyes,
And give as soft attachment to thy senses
As infants' empty of all thought!

CRESSIDA   Good morrow, then.

TROILUS

I prithee now, to bed.

CRESSIDA   Are you a-weary of me?

TROILUS

O Cressida! But that the busy day,
Waked by the lark, hath roused the ribald crows,

10 And dreaming night will hide our joys no longer,
I would not from thee.

CRESSIDA   Night hath been too brief.

TROILUS

Beshrew the witch! With venomous wights she
          stays
As hideously as hell, but flies the grasps of love
With wings more momentary-swift than thought.
You will catch cold, and curse me.

CRESSIDA   Prithee, tarry –
You men will never tarry –

O foolish Cressid, I might have still held off,
And then you would have tarried! – Hark, there's one
    up.

PANDARUS (*within*)
What's all the doors open here?

TROILUS
It is your uncle.   20

CRESSIDA
A pestilence on him! Now will he be mocking:
I shall have such a life!
    Enter Pandarus

PANDARUS How now, how now, how go maidenheads? –
Here, you maid! Where's my cousin Cressid?

CRESSIDA
Go hang yourself, you naughty mocking uncle!
You bring me to do – and then you flout me too.

PANDARUS To do what, to do what? – Let her say what:
what have I brought you to do?

CRESSIDA
Come, come, beshrew your heart; you'll ne'er be
    good,
Nor suffer others.   30

PANDARUS Ha, ha! Alas, poor wretch! A poor capocchia, hast not slept tonight? Would he not – a naughty
man – let it sleep? – A bugbear take him!

CRESSIDA
Did not I tell you? – Would he were knocked
    i'th'head!
    Knocking within
Who's that at door? Good uncle, go and see. –
My lord, come you again into my chamber;
You smile and mock me, as if I meant naughtily.

TROILUS
Ha, ha!

CRESSIDA
Come, you are deceived; I think of no such thing. –
    Knocking within

40   How earnestly they knock! – Pray you, come in;
      I would not for half Troy have you seen here.

                      Exeunt Troilus and Cressida

PANDARUS Who's there? What's the matter? Will you
beat down the door? How now! What's the matter?

    Enter Aeneas

AENEAS Good morrow, lord, good morrow.

PANDARUS Who's there? My Lord Aeneas? By my troth,
I knew you not. What news with you so early?

AENEAS Is not Prince Troilus here?

PANDARUS Here? What should he do here?

AENEAS

      Come, he is here, my lord; do not deny him.
50   It doth import him much to speak with me.

PANDARUS Is he here, say you? 'Tis more than I know,
I'll be sworn. For my own part, I came in late. What
should he do here?

AENEAS Whoa! Nay, then! Come, come, you'll do him
wrong ere you are 'ware; you'll be so true to him to be
false to him. Do not you know of him, but yet go fetch
him hither, go.

                             Exit Pandarus

    Enter Troilus

TROILUS How now! What's the matter?

AENEAS

      My lord, I scarce have leisure to salute you,
60   My matter is so rash. There is at hand
      Paris your brother, and Deiphobus,
      The Grecian Diomed, and our Antenor,
      Delivered to us; and for him forthwith,
      Ere the first sacrifice, within this hour,
      We must give up to Diomedes' hand
      The Lady Cressida.

TROILUS   Is it concluded so?

AENEAS

      By Priam and the general state of Troy.
      They are at hand, and ready to effect it.

TROILUS

How my achievements mock me! –
I will go meet them; and, my Lord Aeneas,   70
We met by chance: you did not find me here.

AENEAS

Good, good, my lord; the secrets of nature
Have not more gift in taciturnity.   *Exeunt*
Enter Pandarus and Cressida

PANDARUS Is't possible? No sooner got but lost? The
devil take Antenor! The young prince will go mad: a
plague upon Antenor! I would they had broke's neck!

CRESSIDA How now! What's the matter? Who was here?

PANDARUS Ah, ha!

CRESSIDA Why sigh you so profoundly? Where's my
lord? Gone? Tell me, sweet uncle, what's the matter?   80

PANDARUS Would I were as deep under the earth as I
am above.

CRESSIDA O the gods! What's the matter?

PANDARUS Prithee, get thee in. Would thou hadst ne'er
been born! I knew thou wouldst be his death – O, poor
gentleman! – A plague upon Antenor!

CRESSIDA Good uncle, I beseech you, on my knees I
beseech you, what's the matter?

PANDARUS Thou must be gone, wench, thou must be
gone; thou art changed for Antenor. Thou must to thy   90
father, and be gone from Troilus: 'twill be his death,
'twill be his bane, he cannot bear it.

CRESSIDA

O you immortal gods! – I will not go.

PANDARUS Thou must.

CRESSIDA

I will not, uncle. I have forgot my father;
I know no touch of consanguinity,
No kin, no love, no blood, no soul so near me
As the sweet Troilus. – O you gods divine,
Make Cressid's name the very crown of falsehood
If ever she leave Troilus! Time, force, and death,   100

Do to this body what extremity you can;
But the strong base and building of my love
Is as the very centre of the earth,
Drawing all things to it. I will go in and weep –

PANDARUS Do, do.

CRESSIDA

Tear my bright hair, and scratch my praised cheeks;
Crack my clear voice with sobs, and break my heart
With sounding 'Troilus'. I will not go from Troy.

Exeunt

IV.3   *Enter Paris, Troilus, Aeneas, Deiphobus, Antenor,*
           and Diomedes

PARIS

It is great morning, and the hour prefixed
Of her delivery to this valiant Greek
Comes fast upon. Good my brother Troilus,
Tell you the lady what she is to do,
And haste her to the purpose.

TROILUS   Walk into her house.
I'll bring her to the Grecian presently;
And to his hand when I deliver her,
Think it an altar, and thy brother Troilus
A priest, there offering to it his own heart.

PARIS

10   I know what 'tis to love;
And would, as I shall pity, I could help. –
Please you walk in, my lords.   *Exeunt*

IV.4   *Enter Pandarus and Cressida*

PANDARUS Be moderate, be moderate.

CRESSIDA

Why tell you me of moderation?
The grief is fine, full perfect, that I taste,

And violenteth in a sense as strong
As that which causeth it. How can I moderate it?
If I could temporize with my affection,
Or brew it to a weak and colder palate,
The like allayment could I give my grief.
My love admits no qualifying dross;
No more my grief, in such a precious loss.   10

    Enter Troilus

PANDARUS Here, here, here he comes. Ah, sweet ducks!
CRESSIDA (*embracing Troilus*) O Troilus! Troilus!
PANDARUS What a pair of spectacles is here! Let me
    embrace too. 'O heart,' as the goodly saying is –
      '— O heart, heavy heart,
        Why sigh'st thou without breaking?'
    where he answers again:
      'Because thou canst not ease thy smart
        By friendship nor by speaking.'
    There was never a truer rhyme. Let us cast away   20
    nothing, for we may live to have need of such a verse.
    We see it, we see it, – How now, lambs!
TROILUS
    Cressid, I love thee in so strained a purity
    That the blest gods, as angry with my fancy,
    More bright in zeal than the devotion which
    Cold lips blow to their deities, take thee from me.
CRESSIDA Have the gods envy?
PANDARUS Ay, ay, ay, ay, 'tis too plain a case.
CRESSIDA
    And is it true that I must go from Troy?
TROILUS
    A hateful truth.
CRESSIDA   What, and from Troilus too?   30
TROILUS
    From Troy and Troilus.
CRESSIDA   Is't possible?
TROILUS
    And suddenly; where injury of chance

Puts back leave-taking, jostles roughly by
All time of pause, rudely beguiles our lips
Of all rejoindure, forcibly prevents
Our locked embrasures, strangles our dear vows
Even in the birth of our own labouring breath:
We two, that with so many thousand sighs
Did buy each other, must poorly sell ourselves
40 With the rude brevity and discharge of one.
Injurious Time now, with a robber's haste,
Crams his rich thievery up, he knows not how;
As many farewells as be stars in heaven,
With distinct breath and consigned kisses to them,
He fumbles up into a loose adieu,
And scants us with a single famished kiss,
Distasted with the salt of broken tears.

AENEAS (*within*) My lord, is the lady ready?

TROILUS

Hark, you are called: some say the Genius so
50 Cries 'Come!' to him that instantly must die. –
Bid them have patience; she shall come anon.

PANDARUS Where are my tears? Rain, to lay this wind,
or my heart will be blown up by the root.   *Exit*

CRESSIDA

I must, then, to the Grecians?

TROILUS   No remedy.

CRESSIDA

A woeful Cressid 'mongst the merry Greeks!
When shall we see again?

TROILUS

Hear me, my love: be thou but true of heart –

CRESSIDA

I true? How now, what wicked deem is this?

TROILUS

Nay, we must use expostulation kindly,
60 For it is parting from us.
I speak not 'be thou true' as fearing thee;
For I will throw my glove to Death himself

That there's no maculation in thy heart.
But 'be thou true,' say I, to fashion in
My sequent protestation: be thou true,
And I will see thee.

CRESSIDA
O, you shall be exposed, my lord, to dangers
As infinite as imminent; but I'll be true!

TROILUS
And I'll grow friend with danger. Wear this sleeve.

CRESSIDA
And you this glove. When shall I see you?   70

TROILUS
I will corrupt the Grecian sentinels,
To give thee nightly visitation –
But yet, be true.

CRESSIDA   O heavens! 'Be true' again?

TROILUS
Hear why I speak it, love.
The Grecian youths are full of quality;
Their loving well composed with gifts of nature,
And flowing o'er with arts and exercise.
How novelty may move, and parts with person,
Alas, a kind of godly jealousy –
Which, I beseech you, call a virtuous sin –   80
Makes me afraid.

CRESSIDA   O heavens, you love me not!

TROILUS
Die I a villain then!
In this I do not call your faith in question
So mainly as my merit: I cannot sing,
Nor heel the high lavolt, nor sweeten talk,
Nor play at subtle games – fair virtues all,
To which the Grecians are most prompt and
          pregnant;
But I can tell that in each grace of these
There lurks a still and dumb-discoursive devil
That tempts most cunningly. But be not tempted.   90

IV.4

CRESSIDA

Do you think I will?

TROILUS

No.
But something may be done that we will not;
And sometimes we are devils to ourselves,
When we will tempt the frailty of our powers,
Presuming on their changeful potency.

AENEAS (*within*)

Nay, good my lord –

TROILUS   Come, kiss, and let us part.

PARIS (*within*)

Brother Troilus!

TROILUS   Good brother, come you hither,
And bring Aeneas and the Grecian with you.

CRESSIDA

100   My lord, will you be true?

TROILUS

Who, I? Alas, it is my vice, my fault:
Whiles others fish with craft for great opinion,
I with great truth catch mere simplicity;
Whilst some with cunning gild their copper
          crowns,
With truth and plainness I do wear mine bare.
Fear not my truth: the moral of my wit
Is 'plain and true'; there's all the reach of it.

> *Enter Aeneas, Paris, Antenor, Deiphobus, and
> Diomedes*

Welcome, Sir Diomed; here is the lady
Which for Antenor we deliver you.

110   At the port, lord, I'll give her to thy hand,
And by the way possess thee what she is.
Entreat her fair, and by my soul, fair Greek,
If e'er thou stand at mercy of my sword,
Name Cressid, and thy life shall be as safe
As Priam is in Ilium.

DIOMEDES   Fair Lady Cressid,

122

So please you, save the thanks this prince expects.
The lustre in your eye, heaven in your cheek,
Pleads your fair usage, and to Diomed
You shall be mistress, and command him wholly.

TROILUS
Grecian, thou dost not use me courteously,   120
To shame the zeal of my petition to thee
In praising her. I tell thee, lord of Greece,
She is as far high-soaring o'er thy praises
As thou unworthy to be called her servant.
I charge thee use her well, even for my charge;
For, by the dreadful Pluto, if thou dost not,
Though the great bulk Achilles be thy guard,
I'll cut thy throat.

DIOMEDES   O, be not moved, Prince Troilus;
Let me be privileged by my place and message
To be a speaker free. When I am hence,   130
I'll answer to my lust, and know, my lord,
I'll nothing do on charge. To her own worth
She shall be prized; but that you say 'Be't so,'
I'll speak it in my spirit and honour: 'No.'

TROILUS
Come, to the port. – I'll tell thee, Diomed,
This brave shall oft make thee to hide thy head.
Lady, give me your hand, and, as we walk,
To our own selves bend we our needful talk.
               Exeunt Troilus, Cressida, and Diomedes
        Sound trumpet

PARIS
Hark, Hector's trumpet!

AENEAS   How have we spent this morning!
The prince must think me tardy and remiss,   140
That swore to ride before him in the field.

PARIS
'Tis Troilus' fault; come, come, to field with him.

DEIPHOBUS
Let us make ready straight.

AENEAS

   Yea, with a bridegroom's fresh alacrity,
   Let us address to tend on Hector's heels.
   The glory of our Troy doth this day lie
   On his fair worth and single chivalry.   *Exeunt*

IV.5   *Enter Ajax, armed, Agamemnon, Achilles, Patroclus,*
           Menelaus, Ulysses, Nestor, Calchas, and trumpeter

AGAMEMNON

   Here art thou in appointment fresh and fair,
   Anticipating time. With starting courage,
   Give with thy trumpet a loud note to Troy,
   Thou dreadful Ajax, that the appallèd air
   May pierce the head of the great combatant,
   And hale him hither.

AJAX   Thou, trumpet, there's my purse.
   Now crack thy lungs, and split thy brazen pipe;
   Blow, villain, till thy spherèd bias cheek
   Outswell the colic of puffed Aquilon.
10   Come, stretch thy chest, and let thy eyes spout blood;
   Thou blowest for Hector.
        Trumpet sounds

ULYSSES

   No trumpet answers.

ACHILLES   'Tis but early days.

AGAMEMNON

   Is not yond Diomed, with Calchas' daughter?

ULYSSES

   'Tis he; I ken the manner of his gait.
   He rises on the toe; that spirit of his
   In aspiration lifts him from the earth.
        Enter Diomedes with Cressida

AGAMEMNON

   Is this the Lady Cressid?

DIOMEDES   Even she.

AGAMEMNON (*kissing her*)
    Most dearly welcome to the Greeks, sweet
        lady.
NESTOR
    Our general doth salute you with a kiss.
ULYSSES
    Yet is the kindness but particular;   20
    'Twere better she were kissed in general.
NESTOR
    And very courtly counsel; I'll begin.
        He kisses her
    So much for Nestor.
ACHILLES
    I'll take that winter from your lips, fair lady.
        He kisses her
    Achilles bids you welcome.
MENELAUS
    I had good argument for kissing once.
PATROCLUS
    But that's no argument for kissing now;
    For thus popped Paris in his hardiment,
    And parted thus you and your argument.
        He kisses her
ULYSSES (*aside*)
    O deadly gall, and theme of all our scorns,   30
    For which we lose our heads to gild his horns.
PATROCLUS
    The first was Menelaus' kiss; this, mine –
        He kisses her again
    Patroclus kisses you.
MENELAUS   O, this is trim!
PATROCLUS
    Paris and I kiss evermore for him.
MENELAUS
    I'll have my kiss, sir. – Lady, by your leave.
CRESSIDA
    In kissing, do you render or receive?

IV.5

MENELAUS
Both take and give.

CRESSIDA   I'll make my match to live,
The kiss you take is better than you give;
Therefore no kiss.

MENELAUS
40 I'll give you boot; I'll give you three for one.

CRESSIDA
You are an odd man; give even, or give none.

MENELAUS
An odd man, lady? Every man is odd.

CRESSIDA
No, Paris is not; for you know 'tis true
That you are odd, and he is even with you.

MENELAUS
You fillip me o'the head.

CRESSIDA   No, I'll be sworn.

ULYSSES
It were no match, your nail against his horn.
May I, sweet lady, beg a kiss of you?

CRESSIDA
You may.

ULYSSES I do desire it.

CRESSIDA   Why, beg then.

ULYSSES
Why then, for Venus' sake, give me a kiss –
50 When Helen is a maid again, and his.

CRESSIDA
I am your debtor; claim it when 'tis due.

ULYSSES
Never's my day, and then a kiss of you.

DIOMEDES
Lady, a word; I'll bring you to your father.

Exit with Cressida

NESTOR
A woman of quick sense.

ULYSSES   Fie, fie upon her!

There's a language in her eye, her cheek, her lip,
Nay, her foot speaks; her wanton spirits look out
At every joint and motive of her body.
O, these encounterers, so glib of tongue,
That give accosting welcome ere it comes,
And wide unclasp the tables of their thoughts   60
To every tickling reader! Set them down
For sluttish spoils of opportunity
And daughters of the game.
    Flourish

ALL
  The Trojan's trumpet.
AGAMEMNON   Yonder comes the troop.
    Enter all of Troy: Hector, Paris, Aeneas, Helenus,
    Troilus, and attendants

AENEAS
  Hail, all you state of Greece! What shall be done
To him that victory commands? Or do you purpose
A victor shall be known? Will you the knights
Shall to the edge of all extremity
Pursue each other, or shall be divided
By any voice or order of the field?   70
Hector bade ask.
AGAMEMNON   Which way would Hector have it?
AENEAS
  He cares not; he'll obey conditions.
AGAMEMNON
  'Tis done like Hector –
ACHILLES   But securely done,
A little proudly, and great deal disprizing
The knight opposed.
AENEAS   If not Achilles, sir,
What is your name?
ACHILLES   If not Achilles, nothing.
AENEAS
  Therefore, Achilles, but whate'er, know this:
In the extremity of great and little,

Valour and pride excel themselves in Hector;
80 The one almost as infinite as all,
The other blank as nothing. Weigh him well,
And that which looks like pride is courtesy.
This Ajax is half made of Hector's blood,
In love whereof half Hector stays at home;
Half heart, half hand, half Hector comes to seek
This blended knight, half Trojan and half Greek.

ACHILLES
A maiden battle, then? – O, I perceive you.

Enter Diomedes

AGAMEMNON
Here is Sir Diomed. – Go, gentle knight;
Stand by our Ajax. As you and Lord Aeneas
90 Consent upon the order of their fight,
So be it, either to the uttermost
Or else a breath. The combatants being kin
Half stints their strife before their strokes begin.

Hector and Ajax prepare to fight

ULYSSES
They are opposed already.

AGAMEMNON
What Trojan is that same that looks so heavy?

ULYSSES
The youngest son of Priam, a true knight,
Not yet mature, yet matchless; firm of word,
Speaking in deeds, and deedless in his tongue;
Not soon provoked, nor being provoked soon calmed;
100 His heart and hand both open and both free;
For what he has he gives, what thinks he shows,
Yet gives he not till judgement guide his bounty,
Nor dignifies an impair thought with breath;
Manly as Hector, but more dangerous;
For Hector in his blaze of wrath subscribes
To tender objects, but he in heat of action
Is more vindicative than jealous love.
They call him Troilus, and on him erect

A second hope, as fairly built as Hector.
Thus says Aeneas, one that knows the youth   110
Even to his inches, and with private soul
Did in great Ilium thus translate him to me.
    Alarum. Hector and Ajax fight

AGAMEMNON
  They are in action.

NESTOR
  Now, Ajax, hold thine own!

TROILUS   Hector, thou sleep'st;
  Awake thee!

AGAMEMNON
  His blows are well disposed – there, Ajax!
    Trumpets cease

DIOMEDES
  You must no more.

AENEAS   Princes, enough, so please you.

AJAX
  I am not warm yet; let us fight again.

DIOMEDES
  As Hector pleases.

HECTOR   Why, then will I no more.
Thou art, great lord, my father's sister's son,   120
A cousin-german to great Priam's seed;
The obligation of our blood forbids
A gory emulation 'twixt us twain.
Were thy commixion Greek and Trojan so
That thou couldst say 'This hand is Grecian all,
And this is Trojan; the sinews of this leg
All Greek, and this all Troy; my mother's blood
Runs on the dexter cheek, and this sinister
Bounds in my father's' – by Jove multipotent,
Thou shouldst not bear from me a Greekish member   130
Wherein my sword had not impressure made
Of our rank feud; but the just gods gainsay
That any drop thou borrow'st from thy mother,
My sacred aunt, should by my mortal sword

Be drained! Let me embrace thee, Ajax:
By him that thunders, thou hast lusty arms;
Hector would have them fall upon him thus.
Cousin, all honour to thee!

AJAX   I thank thee, Hector.
Thou art too gentle and too free a man.
140   I came to kill thee, cousin, and bear hence
A great addition earnèd in thy death.

HECTOR
Not Neoptolemus so mirable –
On whose bright crest Fame with her loud'st oyez
Cries 'This is he' – could promise to himself
A thought of added honour torn from Hector.

AENEAS
There is expectance here from both the sides
What further you will do.

HECTOR   We'll answer it;
The issue is embracement. Ajax, farewell.

AJAX
If I might in entreaties find success,
150   As seld I have the chance, I would desire
My famous cousin to our Grecian tents.

DIOMEDES
'Tis Agamemnon's wish; and great Achilles
Doth long to see unarmed the valiant Hector.

HECTOR
Aeneas, call my brother Troilus to me,
And signify this loving interview
To the expecters of our Trojan part;
Desire them home. – Give me thy hand, my cousin;
I will go eat with thee, and see your knights.
        Agamemnon and the rest come forward

AJAX
Great Agamemnon comes to meet us here.

HECTOR
160   The worthiest of them tell me name by name;
But for Achilles, mine own searching eyes

Shall find him by his large and portly size.

AGAMEMNON

Worthy of arms, as welcome as to one
That would be rid of such an enemy! –
But that's no welcome: understand more clear,
What's past and what's to come is strewed with husks
And formless ruin of oblivion;
But in this extant moment, faith and troth,
Strained purely from all hollow bias-drawing,
Bids thee with most divine integrity   170
From heart of very heart, great Hector, welcome.

HECTOR

I thank thee, most imperious Agamemnon.

AGAMEMNON (to Troilus)

My well-famed lord of Troy, no less to you.

MENELAUS

Let me confirm my princely brother's greeting:
You brace of warlike brothers, welcome hither.

HECTOR

Who must we answer?

AENEAS   The noble Menelaus.

HECTOR

O, you, my lord? – By Mars his gauntlet, thanks!
Mock not that I affect th'untraded oath;
Your *quondam* wife swears still by Venus' glove.
She's well, but bade me not commend her to you.   180

MENELAUS

Name her not now, sir; she's a deadly theme.

HECTOR

O, pardon; I offend.

NESTOR

I have, thou gallant Trojan, seen thee oft,
Labouring for destiny, make cruel way
Through ranks of Greekish youth; and I have seen
                    thee,
As hot as Perseus, spur thy Phrygian steed,
And seen thee scorning forfeits and subduements,

When thou hast hung thy advancèd sword i'th'air,
Not letting it decline on the declined,
190 That I have said unto my standers-by:
'Lo, Jupiter is yonder, dealing life!'
And I have seen thee pause and take thy breath,
When that a ring of Greeks have hemmed thee in,
Like an Olympian wrestling. This have I seen;
But this thy countenance, still locked in steel,
I never saw till now. I knew thy grandsire,
And once fought with him: he was a soldier good,
But by great Mars, the captain of us all,
Never like thee. Let an old man embrace thee;
200 And, worthy warrior, welcome to our tents.

AENEAS
'Tis the old Nestor.

HECTOR
Let me embrace thee, good old chronicle,
That hast so long walked hand in hand with time;
Most reverend Nestor, I am glad to clasp thee.

NESTOR
I would my arms could match thee in contention,
As they contend with thee in courtesy.

HECTOR
I would they could.

NESTOR
Ha!
By this white beard, I'd fight with thee tomorrow.
Well, welcome, welcome! – I have seen the
210   time –

ULYSSES
I wonder now how yonder city stands
When we have here her base and pillar by us.

HECTOR
I know your favour, Lord Ulysses, well.
Ah, sir, there's many a Greek and Trojan dead
Since first I saw yourself and Diomed
In Ilium, on your Greekish embassy.

ULYSSES
  Sir, I foretold you then what would ensue.
  My prophecy is but half his journey yet;
  For yonder walls, that pertly front your town,
  Yond towers, whose wanton tops do buss the
      clouds,   220
  Must kiss their own feet.

HECTOR   I must not believe you.
  There they stand yet, and modestly I think
  The fall of every Phrygian stone will cost
  A drop of Grecian blood. The end crowns all;
  And that old common arbitrator, Time,
  Will one day end it.

ULYSSES   So to him we leave it.
  Most gentle and most valiant Hector, welcome.
  After the general, I beseech you next
  To feast with me, and see me at my tent.

ACHILLES
  I shall forestall thee, Lord Ulysses, thou!   230
  Now, Hector, I have fed mine eyes on thee;
  I have with exact view perused thee, Hector,
  And quoted joint by joint.

HECTOR   Is this Achilles?

ACHILLES
  I am Achilles.

HECTOR
  Stand fair, I pray thee; let me look on thee.

ACHILLES
  Behold thy fill.

HECTOR   Nay, I have done already.

ACHILLES
  Thou art too brief; I will the second time,
  As I would buy thee, view thee limb by limb.

HECTOR
  O, like a book of sport thou'lt read me o'er;
  But there's more in me than thou understand'st.   240
  Why dost thou so oppress me with thine eye?

ACHILLES

Tell me, you heavens, in which part of his body
Shall I destroy him? – whether there, or there, or
    there? –
That I may give the local wound a name,
And make distinct the very breach whereout
Hector's great spirit flew: answer me, heavens!

HECTOR

It would discredit the blest gods, proud man,
To answer such a question. Stand again:
Think'st thou to catch my life so pleasantly
250 As to prenominate in nice conjecture
Where thou wilt hit me dead?

ACHILLES   I tell thee, yea.

HECTOR

Wert thou the oracle to tell me so,
I'd not believe thee. Henceforth guard thee well,
For I'll not kill thee there, nor there, nor there;
But, by the forge that stithied Mars his helm,
I'll kill thee everywhere, yea, o'er and o'er. –
You wisest Grecians, pardon me this brag;
His insolence draws folly from my lips,
But I'll endeavour deeds to match these words,
Or may I never –

260 AJAX   Do not chafe thee, cousin –
And you, Achilles, let these threats alone,
Till accident or purpose bring you to't.
You may have every day enough of Hector,
If you have stomach. The general state, I fear,
Can scarce entreat you to be odd with him.

HECTOR

I pray you, let us see you in the field;
We have had pelting wars since you refused
The Grecians' cause.

ACHILLES   Dost thou entreat me, Hector?
Tomorrow do I meet thee, fell as death;
Tonight all friends.

HECTER   Thy hand upon that match.   270

AGAMEMNON
First, all you peers of Greece, go to my tent;
There in the full convive you. Afterwards,
As Hector's leisure and your bounties shall
Concur together, severally entreat him. –
Beat loud the taborins, let the trumpets blow,
That this great soldier may his welcome know.

> *Exeunt all but Troilus and Ulysses*
> *Drums and trumpets sound*

TROILUS
My Lord Ulysses, tell me, I beseech you,
In what place of the field doth Calchas keep?

ULYSSES
At Menelaus' tent, most princely Troilus.
There Diomed doth feast with him tonight,   280
Who neither looks on heaven nor on earth,
But gives all gaze and bent of amorous view
On the fair Cressid.

TROILUS
Shall I, sweet lord, be bound to thee so much,
After we part from Agamemnon's tent,
To bring me thither?

ULYSSES   You shall command me, sir.
As gentle tell me, of what honour was
This Cressida in Troy? Had she no lover there
That wails her absence?

TROILUS
O sir, to such as boasting show their scars   290
A mock is due. Will you walk on, my lord?
She was beloved, she loved, she is, and doth;
But still sweet love is food for fortune's tooth.

> *Exeunt*

*

V.1   *Enter Achilles and Patroclus*

ACHILLES
I'll heat his blood with Greekish wine tonight,
Which with my scimitar I'll cool tomorrow.
Patroclus, let us feast him to the height.

PATROCLUS
Here comes Thersites.

          Enter Thersites

ACHILLES   How now, thou core of envy?
Thou crusty botch of nature, what's the news?

THERSITES Why, thou picture of what thou seemest,
and idol of idiot-worshippers, here's a letter for thee.

ACHILLES From whence, fragment?

THERSITES Why, thou full dish of fool, from Troy.

          Achilles stands aside to read his letter

10 PATROCLUS Who keeps the tent now?

THERSITES The surgeon's box, or the patient's wound.

PATROCLUS Well said, adversity! And what need these
tricks?

THERSITES Prithee, be silent, boy; I profit not by thy
talk. Thou art thought to be Achilles' male varlet.

PATROCLUS Male varlet, you rogue? What's that?

THERSITES Why, his masculine whore. Now, the rotten
diseases of the south, guts-griping ruptures, catarrhs,
loads o'gravel i'th'back, lethargies, cold palsies, and
20 the like, take and take again such preposterous discoveries!

PATROCLUS Why, thou damnable box of envy, thou,
what mean'st thou to curse thus?

THERSITES Do I curse thee?

PATROCLUS Why, no, you ruinous butt, you whoreson
indistinguishable cur.

THERSITES No! Why art thou then exasperate, thou idle
immaterial skein of sleave-silk, thou green sarcenet
flap for a sore eye, thou tassel of a prodigal's purse,
30 thou? Ah, how the poor world is pestered with such
waterflies, diminutives of nature!

136

PATROCLUS Out, gall!

THERSITES Finch-egg!

ACHILLES

> My sweet Patroclus, I am thwarted quite
> From my great purpose in tomorrow's battle.
> Here is a letter from Queen Hecuba,
> A token from her daughter, my fair love,
> Both taxing me and gaging me to keep
> An oath that I have sworn. I will not break it.
> Fall Greeks; fail fame; honour or go or stay;   40
> My major vow lies here; this I'll obey. –
> Come, come, Thersites, help to trim my tent;
> This night in banqueting must all be spent. –
> Away, Patroclus!

> *Exeunt Achilles and Patroclus*

THERSITES With too much blood and too little brain, these two may run mad; but if with too much brain and too little blood they do, I'll be a curer of madmen. Here's Agamemnon, an honest fellow enough, and one that loves quails, but he has not so much brain as ear-wax; and the goodly transformation of Jupiter 50 there, his brother, the bull, the primitive statue and oblique memorial of cuckolds, a thrifty shoeing-horn in a chain, hanging at his brother's leg – to what form but that he is should wit larded with malice, and malice forced with wit, turn him to? To an ass were nothing; he is both ass and ox. To an ox were nothing; he is both ox and ass. To be a dog, a mule, a cat, a fitchew, a toad, a lizard, an owl, a puttock, or a herring without a roe, I would not care; but to be Menelaus I would conspire against destiny. Ask me not what I would be, if I were 60 not Thersites; for I care not to be the louse of a lazar so I were not Menelaus. – Hoyday! Spirits and fires!

> *Enter Hector, Troilus, Ajax, Agamemnon, Ulysses,*
> *Nestor, Menelaus, Diomedes, with lights*

AGAMEMNON

> We go wrong, we go wrong.

AJAX   No, yonder 'tis –
There, where we see the lights.

HECTOR   I trouble you.

AJAX
No, not a whit.

Enter Achilles

ULYSSES   Here comes himself to guide you.

ACHILLES
Welcome, brave Hector; welcome, princes all.

AGAMEMNON
So now, fair prince of Troy, I bid good night.
Ajax commands the guard to tend on you.

HECTOR
Thanks, and good night to the Greeks' general.

MENELAUS
Good night, my lord.

70 HECTOR   Good night, sweet Lord Menelaus.

THERSITES Sweet draught, sweet, quoth 'a! Sweet sink,
sweet sewer!

ACHILLES
Good night and welcome both at once to those
That go or tarry.

AGAMEMNON Good night.

Exeunt Agamemnon and Menelaus

ACHILLES
Old Nestor tarries, and you too, Diomed;
Keep Hector company an hour or two.

DIOMEDES
I cannot, lord; I have important business,
The tide whereof is now. – Good night, great Hector.

HECTOR
Give me your hand.

80 ULYSSES (*aside to Troilus*) Follow his torch; he goes
To Calchas' tent. I'll keep you company.

TROILUS (*aside to Ulysses*)
Sweet sir, you honour me.

HECTOR   And so, good night.

Exit Diomedes, Ulysses and Troilus following
ACHILLES Come, come, enter my tent.
       Exeunt Achilles, Hector, Ajax, and Nestor
THERSITES That same Diomed's a false-hearted rogue,
  a most unjust knave; I will no more trust him when he
  leers than I will a serpent when he hisses. He will
  spend his mouth, and promise, like Brabbler the
  hound; but when he performs, astronomers foretell it,
  that it is prodigious, there will come some change. The
  sun borrows of the moon when Diomed keeps his   90
  word. I will rather leave to see Hector than not to dog
  him: they say he keeps a Trojan drab, and uses the
  traitor Calchas his tent. I'll after. – Nothing but
  lechery! All incontinent varlets!   *Exit*

Enter Diomedes   **V.2**
DIOMEDES What, are you up here, ho? Speak.
CALCHAS (*within*) Who calls?
DIOMEDES Diomed. – Calchas, I think? Where's your
  daughter?
CALCHAS (*within*) She comes to you.
    Enter Troilus and Ulysses at a distance; after them,
    Thersites
ULYSSES Stand where the torch may not discover us.
    Enter Cressida
TROILUS
  Cressid comes forth to him.
DIOMEDES   How now, my charge?
CRESSIDA
  Now, my sweet guardian! – Hark, a word with you.
    She whispers to him
TROILUS Yea, so familiar!
ULYSSES She will sing any man at first sight.   10
THERSITES And any man may sing her, if he can take her
  clef: she's noted.
DIOMEDES Will you remember?

CRESSIDA Remember? Yes.

DIOMEDES
Nay, but do, then,
And let your mind be coupled with your words.

TROILUS What should she remember?

ULYSSES List!

CRESSIDA
Sweet honey Greek, tempt me no more to folly.

20 **THERSITES** Roguery!

DIOMEDES Nay then –

CRESSIDA I'll tell you what –

DIOMEDES
Foh, foh, come, tell a pin! You are forsworn.

CRESSIDA
In faith I cannot; what would you have me do?

THERSITES A juggling trick – to be secretly open.

DIOMEDES
What did you swear you would bestow on me?

CRESSIDA
I prithee, do not hold me to mine oath;
Bid me do anything but that, sweet Greek.

DIOMEDES Good night.

30 **TROILUS** Hold, patience!

ULYSSES How now, Trojan?

CRESSIDA Diomed –

DIOMEDES
No, no, good night; I'll be your fool no more.

TROILUS Thy better must.

CRESSIDA Hark, one word in your ear.

TROILUS O plague and madness!

ULYSSES
You are moved, Prince; let us depart, I pray you,
Lest your displeasure should enlarge itself
To wrathful terms. This place is dangerous,
40 The time right deadly; I beseech you, go.

TROILUS
Behold, I pray you.

ULYSSES   Nay, good my lord, go off.
  You flow to great distraction; come, my lord.
TROILUS
  I pray thee, stay.
ULYSSES   You have not patience; come.
TROILUS
  I pray you, stay; by hell and all hell's torments,
  I will not speak a word.
DIOMEDES   And so, good night.
CRESSIDA
  Nay, but you part in anger.
TROILUS   Doth that grieve thee?
  O withered truth!
ULYSSES   Why, how now, lord?
TROILUS   By Jove,
  I will be patient.
CRESSIDA   Guardian! Why, Greek?
DIOMEDES Foh, foh, adieu; you palter.
CRESSIDA
  In faith, I do not: come hither once again.   50
ULYSSES
  You shake, my lord, at something; will you go?
  You will break out.
TROILUS   She strokes his cheek!
ULYSSES   Come, come.
TROILUS
  Nay, stay; by Jove, I will not speak a word.
  There is between my will and all offences
  A guard of patience; stay a little while.
THERSITES How the devil luxury, with his fat rump and
  potato-finger, tickles these together! Fry, lechery, fry!
DIOMEDES But will you, then?
CRESSIDA
  In faith I will, lo; never trust me else.
DIOMEDES
  Give me some token for the surety of it.   60
CRESSIDA I'll fetch you one.   *Exit*

V.2

ULYSSES
You have sworn patience.

TROILUS   Fear me not, sweet lord;
I will not be myself, nor have cognition
Of what I feel: I am all patience.
Enter Cressida

THERSITES Now the pledge; now, now, now!

CRESSIDA Here, Diomed, keep this sleeve.
She gives him the sleeve

TROILUS O beauty, where is thy faith?

ULYSSES My lord –

TROILUS
I will be patient; outwardly I will.

CRESSIDA
70 You look upon that sleeve; behold it well.
He loved me – O false wench! – Give't me again.
She snatches the sleeve

DIOMEDES Whose was't?

CRESSIDA
It is no matter, now I have't again.
I will not meet with you tomorrow night;
I prithee, Diomed, visit me no more.

THERSITES Now she sharpens – well said, whetstone!

DIOMEDES I shall have it.

CRESSIDA What, this?

DIOMEDES Ay, that.

CRESSIDA
80 O all you gods! – O pretty, pretty pledge!
Thy master now lies thinking in his bed
Of thee and me, and sighs, and takes my glove,
And gives memorial dainty kisses to it
As I kiss thee –
Diomedes takes the sleeve
                                  Nay, do not snatch it from me;
He that takes that doth take my heart withal.

DIOMEDES
I had your heart before; this follows it.

142

TROILUS I did swear patience.

CRESSIDA

You shall not have it, Diomed, faith, you shall
    not;
I'll give you something else.

DIOMEDES I will have this. Whose was it?   90

CRESSIDA

It is no matter.

DIOMEDES   Come, tell me whose it was.

CRESSIDA

'Twas one's that loved me better than you will.
But now you have it, take it.

DIOMEDES   Whose was it?

CRESSIDA

By all Diana's waiting-women yond,
And by herself, I will not tell you whose.

DIOMEDES

Tomorrow will I wear it on my helm;
And grieve his spirit that dares not challenge it.

TROILUS

Wert thou the devil, and wor'st it on thy horn,
It should be challenged.

CRESSIDA

Well, well, 'tis done, 'tis past – and yet it is not;   100
I will not keep my word.

DIOMEDES   Why then, farewell;
Thou never shalt mock Diomed again.

CRESSIDA

You shall not go; one cannot speak a word
But it straight starts you.

DIOMEDES   I do not like this fooling.

TROILUS

Nor I, by Pluto: but that that likes not you
Pleases me best.

DIOMEDES   What, shall I come? The hour?

CRESSIDA

Ay, come – O Jove! – do come: I shall be plagued.

DIOMEDES
  Farewell till then.
CRESSIDA   Good night; I prithee come.

                                    Exit Diomedes

  Troilus, farewell! One eye yet looks on thee,
110 But with my heart the other eye doth see.
  Ah, poor our sex! This fault in us I find,
  The error of our eye directs our mind;
  What error leads must err – O, then conclude,
  Minds swayed by eyes are full of turpitude.   *Exit*
THERSITES
  A proof of strength she could not publish more,
  Unless she say 'My mind is now turned whore.'
ULYSSES
  All's done, my lord.
TROILUS   It is.
ULYSSES   Why stay we then?
TROILUS
  To make a recordation to my soul
  Of every syllable that here was spoke.
120 But if I tell how these two did co-act,
  Shall I not lie in publishing a truth?
  Sith yet there is a credence in my heart,
  An esperance so obstinately strong,
  That doth invert th'attest of eyes and ears,
  As if those organs had deceptious functions,
  Created only to calumniate.
  Was Cressid here?
ULYSSES   I cannot conjure, Trojan.
TROILUS She was not, sure.
ULYSSES Most sure she was.
TROILUS
130 Why, my negation hath no taste of madness.
ULYSSES
  Nor mine, my lord: Cressid was here but now.
TROILUS
  Let it not be believed for womanhood.

Think, we had mothers: do not give advantage
To stubborn critics, apt, without a theme
For depravation, to square the general sex
By Cressid's rule; rather think this not Cressid.

ULYSSES
What hath she done, Prince, that can soil our
    mothers?

TROILUS
Nothing at all, unless that this were she.

THERSITES
Will he swagger himself out on's own eyes?

TROILUS
This she? No, this is Diomed's Cressida.   140
If beauty have a soul, this is not she;
If souls guide vows, if vows are sanctimony,
If sanctimony be the gods' delight,
If there be rule in unity itself,
This is not she. O madness of discourse,
That cause sets up with and against itself!
Bifold authority, where reason can revolt
Without perdition, and loss assume all reason
Without revolt. This is, and is not, Cressid!
Within my soul there doth conduce a fight   150
Of this strange nature, that a thing inseparate
Divides more wider than the sky and earth;
And yet the spacious breadth of this division
Admits no orifex for a point as subtle
As Ariachne's broken woof to enter.
Instance, O instance, strong as Pluto's gates!
Cressid is mine, tied with the bonds of heaven.
Instance, O instance, strong as heaven itself!
The bonds of heaven are slipped, dissolved, and
    loosed;
And with another knot, five-finger-tied,   160
The fractions of her faith, orts of her love,
The fragments, scraps, the bits, and greasy relics
Of her o'er-eaten faith, are bound to Diomed.

ULYSSES

  May worthy Troilus be half attached
  With that which here his passion doth express?

TROILUS

  Ay, Greek, and that shall be divulgèd well
  In characters as red as Mars his heart
  Inflamed with Venus; never did young man fancy
  With so eternal and so fixed a soul.

170   Hark, Greek: as much as I do Cressid love,
  So much by weight hate I her Diomed.
  That sleeve is mine that he'll bear in his helm;
  Were it a casque composed by Vulcan's skill,
  My sword should bite it; not the dreadful spout,
  Which shipmen do the hurricano call,
  Constringed in mass by the almighty sun,
  Shall dizzy with more clamour Neptune's ear
  In his descent than shall my prompted sword
  Falling on Diomed.

180 THERSITES He'll tickle it for his concupy.

TROILUS

  O Cressid! O false Cressid! False, false, false!
  Let all untruths stand by thy stainèd name,
  And they'll seem glorious.

ULYSSES   O, contain yourself;
  Your passion draws ears hither.

     Enter Aeneas

AENEAS

  I have been seeking you this hour, my lord.
  Hector by this is arming him in Troy.
  Ajax, your guard, stays to conduct you home.

TROILUS

  Have with you, Prince. – My courteous lord, adieu. –
  Farewell, revolted fair! – and, Diomed,

190   Stand fast, and wear a castle on thy head!

ULYSSES I'll bring you to the gates.

TROILUS Accept distracted thanks.

     Exeunt Troilus, Aeneas, and Ulysses

THERSITES Would I could meet that rogue Diomed! I
would croak like a raven; I would bode, I would bode.
Patroclus will give me anything for the intelligence of
this whore; the parrot will not do more for an almond
than he for a commodious drab. Lechery, lechery, still
wars and lechery; nothing else holds fashion! A burning devil take them!   *Exit*

Enter Hector and Andromache   V.3

ANDROMACHE
When was my lord so much ungently tempered,
To stop his ears against admonishment?
Unarm, unarm, and do not fight today.

HECTOR
You train me to offend you; get you gone.
By all the everlasting gods, I'll go!

ANDROMACHE
My dreams will sure prove ominous to the day.

HECTOR
No more, I say.
      Enter Cassandra

CASSANDRA   Where is my brother Hector?

ANDROMACHE
Here, sister; armed, and bloody in intent.
Consort with me in loud and dear petition;
Pursue we him on knees; for I have dreamed   10
Of bloody turbulence, and this whole night
Hath nothing been but shapes and forms of
            slaughter.

CASSANDRA
O, 'tis true.

HECTOR   Ho! Bid my trumpet sound!

CASSANDRA
No notes of sally, for the heavens, sweet brother.

HECTOR
Be gone, I say; the gods have heard me swear.

CASSANDRA

    The gods are deaf to hot and peevish vows;
    They are polluted offerings, more abhorred
    Than spotted livers in the sacrifice.

ANDROMACHE

    O, be persuaded! Do not count it holy
20   To hurt by being just; it is as lawful,
    For we would give much, to use violent thefts,
    And rob in the behalf of charity.

CASSANDRA

    It is the purpose that makes strong the vow;
    But vows to every purpose must not hold.
    Unarm, sweet Hector.

HECTOR   Hold you still, I say;
    Mine honour keeps the weather of my fate.
    Life every man holds dear, but the dear man
    Holds honour far more precious-dear than life.
        Enter Troilus
    How now, young man, mean'st thou to fight
        today?

ANDROMACHE

30   Cassandra, call my father to persuade.

                        Exit Cassandra

HECTOR

    No, faith, young Troilus; doff thy harness, youth.
    I am today i'the vein of chivalry.
    Let grow thy sinews till their knots be strong,
    And tempt not yet the brushes of the war.
    Unarm thee, go; and doubt thou not, brave boy,
    I'll stand today for thee, and me, and Troy.

TROILUS

    Brother, you have a vice of mercy in you,
    Which better fits a lion than a man.

HECTOR

    What vice is that? Good Troilus, chide me for it.

TROILUS

40   When many times the captive Grecian falls,

Even in the fan and wind of your fair sword,
You bid them rise and live.

HECTOR

O, 'tis fair play.

TROILUS   Fool's play, by heaven, Hector.

HECTOR

How now, how now?

TROILUS   For th'love of all the gods,
Let's leave the hermit Pity with our mothers;
And when we have our armours buckled on,
The venomed vengeance ride upon our swords,
Spur them to ruthful work, rein them from ruth!

HECTOR

Fie, savage, fie!

TROILUS   Hector, then 'tis wars.

HECTOR

Troilus, I would not have you fight today.   50

TROILUS

Who should withhold me?
Not fate, obedience, nor the hand of Mars
Beckoning with fiery truncheon my retire;
Not Priamus and Hecuba on knees,
Their eyes o'ergallèd with recourse of tears;
Nor you, my brother, with your true sword drawn,
Opposed to hinder me, should stop my way,
But by my ruin.

          Enter Priam and Cassandra

CASSANDRA

Lay hold upon him, Priam, hold him fast;
He is thy crutch. Now if thou lose thy stay,   60
Thou on him leaning, and all Troy on thee,
Fall all together.

PRIAM   Come, Hector, come; go back.
Thy wife hath dreamed, thy mother hath had visions,
Cassandra doth foresee, and I myself
Am like a prophet suddenly enrapt,
To tell thee that this day is ominous.

Therefore, come back.

HECTOR   Aeneas is a-field,
And I do stand engaged to many Greeks,
Even in the faith of valour, to appear
This morning to them.

70 PRIAM   Ay, but thou shalt not go.

HECTOR
I must not break my faith.
You know me dutiful; therefore, dear sir,
Let me not shame respect, but give me leave
To take that course by your consent and voice,
Which you do here forbid me, royal Priam.

CASSANDRA
O Priam, yield not to him!

ANDROMACHE   Do not, dear father.

HECTOR
Andromache, I am offended with you.
Upon the love you bear me, get you in.

Exit Andromache

TROILUS
This foolish, dreaming, superstitious girl
Makes all these bodements.

80 CASSANDRA   O, farewell, dear Hector!
Look how thou diest! Look how thy eye turns pale!
Look how thy wounds do bleed at many vents!
Hark how Troy roars, how Hecuba cries out,
How poor Andromache shrills her dolour forth!
Behold distraction, frenzy, and amazement
Like witless antics one another meet,
And all cry 'Hector! Hector's dead!' – O Hector!

TROILUS
Away! Away!

CASSANDRA
Farewell – yes, soft: Hector, I take my leave.
90 Thou dost thyself and all our Troy deceive.   *Exit*

HECTOR
You are amazed, my liege, at her exclaim.

Go in, and cheer the town. We'll forth, and fight,
Do deeds of praise, and tell you them at night.

PRIAM

Farewell; the gods with safety stand about thee!

Exeunt Priam and Hector by different doors. Alarum

TROILUS

They are at it, hark! – Proud Diomed, believe
I come to lose my arm or win my sleeve.

Enter Pandarus

PANDARUS Do you hear, my lord? Do you hear?

TROILUS What now?

PANDARUS Here's a letter come from yond poor girl.

TROILUS Let me read.   100

PANDARUS A whoreson tisick, a whoreson rascally tisick
so troubles me, and the foolish fortune of this girl; and
what one thing, what another, that I shall leave you one
o'these days; and I have rheum in mine eyes too, and
such an ache in my bones that unless a man were curst
I cannot tell what to think on't. – What says she there?

TROILUS

Words, words, mere words, no matter from the heart;
Th'effect doth operate another way.

He tears the letter

Go, wind, to wind, there turn and change together.
My love with words and errors still she feeds,   110
But edifies another with her deeds.   *Exeunt*

Alarum; excursions. Enter Thersites   V.4

THERSITES Now they are clapper-clawing one another;
I'll go look on. That dissembling abominable varlet
Diomed has got that same scurvy doting foolish young
knave's sleeve of Troy there in his helm. I would fain
see them meet, that that same young Trojan ass, that
loves the whore there, might send that Greekish
whore-masterly villain with the sleeve back to the
dissembling luxurious drab of a sleeveless errand.

O'th't'other side, the policy of those crafty-swearing
10 rascals – that stale old mouse-eaten dry cheese, Nestor, and that same dog-fox, Ulysses – is not proved
worth a blackberry. They set me up in policy that
mongrel cur, Ajax, against that dog of as bad a kind,
Achilles; and now is the cur Ajax prouder than the cur
Achilles, and will not arm today; whereupon the Grecians begin to proclaim barbarism, and policy grows
into an ill opinion.

> *Enter Diomedes and Troilus*

Soft! Here comes sleeve, and t'other.

TROILUS
Fly not, for shouldst thou take the river Styx,
I would swim after.

20 DIOMEDES   Thou dost miscall retire;
I do not fly, but advantageous care
Withdrew me from the odds of multitude.
Have at thee.

THERSITES Hold thy whore, Grecian! Now for thy
whore, Trojan! Now the sleeve, now the sleeve!

> *Exeunt Troilus and Diomedes, fighting*
> *Enter Hector*

HECTOR
What art thou, Greek? Art thou for Hector's match?
Art thou of blood and honour?

THERSITES No, no, I am a rascal, a scurvy railing knave,
a very filthy rogue.

HECTOR
30 I do believe thee – live.   *Exit*

THERSITES God-a-mercy that thou wilt believe me; but
a plague break thy neck – for frighting me! What's
become of the wenching rogues? I think they have
swallowed one another. I would laugh at that miracle –
yet, in a sort, lechery eats itself. I'll seek them.   *Exit*

DIOMEDES

Go, go, my servant, take thou Troilus' horse;
Present the fair steed to my Lady Cressid.
Fellow, commend my service to her beauty;
Tell her I have chastised the amorous Trojan,
And am her knight by proof.

SERVANT   I go, my lord.   *Exit*

> *Enter Agamemnon*

AGAMEMNON

Renew, renew! The fierce Polydamas
Hath beat down Menon; bastard Margarelon
Hath Doreus prisoner,
And stands colossus-wise, waving his beam,
Upon the pashèd corpses of the kings   10
Epistrophus and Cedius. Polyxenes is slain,
Amphimachus and Thoas deadly hurt,
Patroclus ta'en or slain, and Palamedes
Sore hurt and bruised; the dreadful Sagittary
Appals our numbers. Haste we, Diomed,
To reinforcement, or we perish all.

> *Enter Nestor with soldiers*

NESTOR

Go, bear Patroclus' body to Achilles,
And bid the snail-paced Ajax arm for shame. –
There is a thousand Hectors in the field;
Now here he fights on Galathe his horse,   20
And there lacks work; anon he's there afoot,
And there they fly or die, like scalèd schools
Before the belching whale; then is he yonder,
And there the strawy Greeks, ripe for his edge,
Fall down before him, like the mower's swath:
Here, there, and everywhere, he leaves and takes,
Dexterity so obeying appetite
That what he will he does; and does so much
That proof is called impossibility.

> *Enter Ulysses*

ULYSSES

30 O, courage, courage, princes! Great Achilles
Is arming, weeping, cursing, vowing vengeance;
Patroclus' wounds have roused his drowsy blood,
Together with his mangled Myrmidons,
That noseless, handless, hacked and chipped, come
   to him,
Crying on Hector. Ajax hath lost a friend,
And foams at mouth, and he is armed and at it,
Roaring for Troilus, who hath done today
Mad and fantastic execution,
Engaging and redeeming of himself
40 With such a careless force and forceless care
As if that luck, in very spite of cunning,
Bade him win all.

   Enter Ajax

AJAX

Troilus! Thou coward Troilus!   *Exit*

DIOMEDES   Ay, there, there!

NESTOR

So, so, we draw together.   *Exit*

   Enter Achilles

ACHILLES   Where is this Hector? –
Come, come, thou boy-queller, show thy face;
Know what it is to meet Achilles angry –
Hector! Where's Hector? I will none but Hector.

             Exeunt

V.6   *Enter Ajax*

AJAX

Troilus, thou coward Troilus, show thy head!
   Enter Diomedes

DIOMEDES

Troilus, I say! Where's Troilus?

AJAX   What wouldst thou?

DIOMEDES

I would correct him.

AJAX

Were I the general, thou shouldst have my office
Ere that correction. – Troilus, I say! What, Troilus!
Enter Troilus

TROILUS

O traitor Diomed! Turn thy false face, thou traitor,
And pay thy life thou owest me for my horse!

DIOMEDES

Ha, art thou there?

AJAX

I'll fight with him alone; stand, Diomed.

DIOMEDES

He is my prize; I will not look upon.   10

TROILUS

Come, both you cogging Greeks; have at you both!
Exeunt, fighting

Enter Hector

HECTOR

Yea, Troilus? O, well fought, my youngest
    brother!
Enter Achilles

ACHILLES

Now do I see thee, ha? Have at thee, Hector!
They fight

HECTOR

Pause, if thou wilt.

ACHILLES

I do disdain thy courtesy, proud Trojan;
Be happy that my arms are out of use.
My rest and negligence befriends thee now,
But thou anon shalt hear of me again;
Till when, go seek thy fortune.   *Exit*

HECTOR   Fare thee well:

I would have been much more a fresher man,   20
Had I expected thee.

Enter Troilus

How now, my brother!

TROILUS

Ajax hath ta'en Aeneas. Shall it be?
No, by the flame of yonder glorious heaven,
He shall not carry him! I'll be ta'en too
Or bring him off. Fate, hear me what I say!
I reck not though thou end my life today.   *Exit*

Enter one in sumptuous armour

HECTOR

Stand, stand, thou Greek; thou art a goodly mark –
No? Wilt thou not? – I like thy armour well;
I'll frush it, and unlock the rivets all,
30   But I'll be master of it. Wilt thou not, beast, abide?
Why then, fly on; I'll hunt thee for thy hide.

Exeunt

V.7   *Enter Achilles with Myrmidons*

ACHILLES

Come here about me, you my Myrmidons;
Mark what I say. Attend me where I wheel;
Strike not a stroke, but keep yourselves in breath,
And when I have the bloody Hector found,
Impale him with your weapons round about;
In fellest manner execute your arms.
Follow me, sirs, and my proceedings eye.
It is decreed Hector the great must die.   *Exeunt*

Enter Menelaus and Paris, fighting; then Thersites

THERSITES The cuckold and the cuckold-maker are at
10   it. Now, bull! Now, dog! 'Loo, Paris, 'loo! Now, my
double-horned Spartan! 'Loo, Paris, 'loo! – The bull
has the game; 'ware horns, ho!

Exeunt Paris and Menelaus

Enter Margarelon

MARGARELON Turn, slave, and fight.
THERSITES What art thou?

MARGARELON A bastard son of Priam's.

THERSITES I am a bastard too; I love bastards. I am a
bastard begot, bastard instructed, bastard in mind,
bastard in valour, in everything illegitimate. One bear
will not bite another, and wherefore should one bastard? Take heed, the quarrel's most ominous to us – if   20
the son of a whore fight for a whore, he tempts
judgement. Farewell, bastard.   *Exit*

MARGARELON The devil take thee, coward!   *Exit*

Enter Hector, carrying a suit of armour   V.8

HECTOR

Most putrefièd core, so fair without,
Thy goodly armour thus hath cost thy life.
Now is my day's work done; I'll take good breath.
Rest, sword; thou hast thy fill of blood and death.
    Enter Achilles and his Myrmidons

ACHILLES

Look, Hector, how the sun begins to set,
How ugly night comes breathing at his heels;
Even with the vail and dark'ning of the sun
To close the day up, Hector's life is done.

HECTOR

I am unarmed; forgo this vantage, Greek.

ACHILLES

Strike, fellows, strike; this is the man I seek.   10
    Hector falls
So, Ilium, fall thou; now, Troy, sink down!
Here lies thy heart, thy sinews, and thy bone. –
On, Myrmidons; and cry you all amain:
'Achilles hath the mighty Hector slain.'
    A retreat sounded
Hark, a retreat upon our Grecian part.

MYRMIDONS

The Trojan trumpets sound the like, my lord.

ACHILLES

The dragon wing of night o'erspreads the earth,
And, stickler-like, the armies separates.
My half-supped sword, that frankly would have fed,

20 Pleased with this dainty bait, thus goes to bed.
Come, tie his body to my horse's tail;
Along the field I will the Trojan trail.   *Exeunt*

V.9   *Enter Agamemnon, Ajax, Menelaus, Nestor,
             Diomedes, and the rest, marching to drumbeats.
             Shouts within*

AGAMEMNON

Hark, hark, what shout is that?

NESTOR   Peace, drums!

SOLDIERS (*shouting within*) Achilles! Achilles! Hector's
slain! Achilles!

DIOMEDES

The bruit is Hector's slain, and by Achilles.

AJAX

If it be so, yet bragless let it be;
Great Hector was a man as good as he.

AGAMEMNON

March patiently along. Let one be sent
To pray Achilles see us at our tent. –
If in his death the gods have us befriended,

10 Great Troy is ours, and our sharp wars are ended.

                                            Exeunt

V.10   *Enter Aeneas, Paris, Antenor, Deiphobus, and sol-
              diers with drums*

AENEAS

Stand, ho! Yet are we masters of the field.
Never go home; here starve we out the night.
          Enter Troilus

158

TROILUS
  Hector is slain.
ALL   Hector? The gods forbid!
TROILUS
  He's dead; and at the murderer's horse's tail,
  In beastly sort, dragged through the shameful field.
  Frown on, you heavens, effect your rage with speed!
  Sit, gods, upon your thrones, and smile at Troy!
  I say, at once let your brief plagues be mercy,
  And linger not our sure destructions on!
AENEAS
  My lord, you do discomfort all the host.   10
TROILUS
  You understand me not that tell me so.
  I do not speak of flight, of fear, of death,
  But dare all imminence that gods and men
  Address their dangers in. Hector is gone;
  Who shall tell Priam so, or Hecuba?
  Let him that will a screech-owl aye be called
  Go into Troy, and say there 'Hector's dead' –
  There is a word will Priam turn to stone,
  Make wells and Niobes of the maids and wives,
  Cold statues of the youth, and, in a word,   20
  Scare Troy out of itself. But march away;
  Hector is dead; there is no more to say –
  Stay yet. You vile abominable tents,
  Thus proudly pight upon our Phrygian plains,
  Let Titan rise as early as he dare,
  I'll through and through you! – And, thou great-sized
          coward,
  No space of earth shall sunder our two hates;
  I'll haunt thee like a wicked conscience still,
  That mouldeth goblins swift as frenzy's thoughts. –
  Strike a free march to Troy! With comfort go;   30
  Hope of revenge shall hide our inward woe.
    Enter Pandarus
PANDARUS But hear you, hear you!

TROILUS

    Hence, broker-lackey! Ignomy and shame
    Pursue thy life, and live aye with thy name!

                   Exeunt all but Pandarus

PANDARUS A goodly medicine for mine aching bones! –
    O world, world, world! Thus is the poor agent de-
    spised! O traitors and bawds, how earnestly are you
    set a-work, and how ill requited! Why should our
    endeavour be so desired, and the performance so
40   loathed? What verse for it? What instance for it? – Let
    me see:

        Full merrily the humble-bee doth sing,
        Till he hath lost his honey and his sting;
        And being once subdued in armèd tail,
        Sweet honey and sweet notes together fail.
    Good traders in the flesh, set this in your painted
    cloths:
    As many as be here of Pandar's hall,
    Your eyes, half out, weep out at Pandar's fall;
50   Or if you cannot weep, yet give some groans,
    Though not for me, yet for your aching bones.
    Brethren and sisters of the hold-door trade,
    Some two months hence my will shall here be made;
    It should be now, but that my fear is this:
    Some gallèd goose of Winchester would hiss.
    Till then I'll sweat, and seek about for eases,
    And at that time bequeath you my diseases.   *Exit*

THE PREFATORY LETTER IN THE
QUARTO (SECOND STATE)

The authorship of this epistle is unknown, and its date remains uncertain. There is no external evidence to support the often proposed theory that it was written in connexion with a performance of *Troilus and Cressida* at an Inn of Court in 1602 or 1603; but it refers to the play as *new*, and this was not true in 1609 when the Quarto with the epistle was published (see the Account of the Text, page 229). Advertisements, however, frequently have little respect for the truth, and the letter could have been a publisher's blurb, written by someone with a legal turn of mind to present a play not seen for some years, and newly published. It remains a mystery. If it was written in 1602 or 1603, then it is difficult to explain why, or for whom, or how it survived to be associated with Shakespeare's manuscript in 1609; if it was written for the publisher, it is not clear why he went to such trouble to present *Troilus and Cressida* as a new play in 1609. The text of the letter is as follows:

A never writer to an ever reader. News
Eternal reader, you have here a new play, never staled with the stage, never clapper-clawed with the palms of the vulgar, and yet passing full of the palm comical; for it is a birth of your brain that never undertook anything comical vainly. And were but the vain names of comedies changed for the titles of commodities, or of plays for pleas, you should see all those grand censors, that now style them such vanities, flock to them for the main grace of their gravities; especially this author's comedies, that 10
are so framed to the life that they serve for the most common commentaries of all the actions of our lives, showing such a dexterity, and power of wit, that the most displeased with plays are pleased with his comedies. And all such dull and heavy-witted worldlings as were never

capable of the wit of a comedy, coming by report of them
to his representations, have found that wit there that they
never found in themselves, and have parted better-witted
than they came, feeling an edge of wit set upon them
20 more than ever they dreamed they had brain to grind it
on. So much and such savoured salt of wit is in his
comedies that they seem, for their height of pleasure, to
be born in that sea that brought forth Venus. Amongst all
there is none more witty than this; and had I time I would
comment upon it, though I know it needs not for so much
as will make you think your testern well bestowed – but
for so much worth as even poor I know to be stuffed in it.
It deserves such a labour as well as the best comedy in
Terence or Plautus. And believe this, that when he is
30 gone, and his comedies out of sale, you will scramble for
them, and set up a new English inquisition. Take this for
a warning, and at the peril of your pleasure's loss, and
judgements, refuse not, nor like this the less, for not
being sullied with the smoky breath of the multitude, but
thank fortune for the 'scape it hath made amongst you;
since by the grand possessors' wills I believe you should
have prayed for them rather than been prayed. And so I
leave all such to be prayed for (for the states of their wits'
healths) that will not praise it. *Vale.*

COMMENTARY

In the Commentary and the Account of the Text the Quarto (1609) is referred to as 'Q' and the first Folio (1623) as 'F'. 'Bullough' refers to *Narrative and Dramatic Sources of Shakespeare*, compiled by Geoffrey Bullough, Volume VI (1966); 'Caxton' refers to William Caxton, *The Recuyell of the Historyes of Troye*, as reprinted in Bullough; and 'Golding's Ovid' refers to Arthur Golding's translation of Ovid's *Metamorphoses* (1567), edited by W. H. D. Rouse (1961). Biblical quotations are given, with modernized spelling and punctuation, from the Bishops' Bible (1568 etc.), the version probably most familiar to Shakespeare.

Prologue

The armed Prologue (see line 23) is ironically appropriate to a play which, ostensibly about war, turns out to be largely concerned with sex and politics, but may also glance at Ben Jonson's play *Poetaster* (1601), in which an armed Prologue does verbal battle on behalf of the author. See the Introduction, page 30.

2 *orgulous* haughty
   high blood chafed strong passion roused
4 *Fraught* laden
6 *crownets* coronets
7 *Phrygia* (the area of Asia Minor where Troy was located, in the north-west of what is now Turkey)
8 *immures* walls
9 *ravished* carried off by force
11 *Tenedos* (an island near Troy)
13 *fraughtage* cargo
   Dardan Trojan. (Dardanus was the legendary ancestor of Priam and founder of Troy.)

16–17   *Dardan . . . Antenorides*. Shakespeare took the names of the gates from William Caxton's *Recuyell of the Historyes of Troye*, one of his main sources for the play; see Bullough, VI.188.

18   *corresponsive and fulfilling* answering and fitting exactly

19   *Stir up the sons of Troy* (that is, the sons of Troy stir up the six-gated city to warlike preparations). Many editors emend *Stir* ('Stirre' F) to 'Sperr', an obsolete variant of 'spar', to fasten securely. This makes good sense, but does nothing to improve the awkward syntax.

25   *In like conditions as* in a manner corresponding to (that is, armed and prepared for war)
      our argument the theme of our play (but see also I.1.94 and the note)

27   *vaunt* beginning. (Compare the French *avant*.)

I.1   The setting is Ilium (line 103), the palace of King Priam of Troy. Shakespeare creates settings and atmosphere largely through dialogue and action, and no attempt at scenic illusion was made on the Elizabethan stage.

1   *varlet* servant
      unarm again. Troilus has just put on his armour; this is ironic in contrast to Prologue's high talk of war.

5   *field* battlefield
      Troilus (pronounced as two syllables)
      none (that is, for fighting)

6   *gear* affair, business (referring to the Trojan War, or to Troilus's doting on Cressida, or both)

7, 8   *to* in addition to

10   *fonder* more foolishly doting

14   *I'll not meddle nor make no farther*. The double negative intensifies Pandarus's meaning, 'I'll have nothing more to do with it'.

15   *tarry* wait for

19   *bolting* sifting (of flour)

24–25   *the word* (that is, the word *tarry*)

27   *stay* wait for

30   *Doth lesser blench at sufferance* flinches less at suffering (but Troilus seems to mean 'flinches more')

33   *So ... thence.* Rowe first suggested emending this line, which in Q (and F substantially) reads 'So traitor then she comes when she is thence'.

37   *wedgèd* split
         rive split

39   *a storm.* Another widely accepted emendation by Rowe; the Q (and F) reading is 'a scorne'. *Storm* gives the line an appropriate contrast to line 41, and in the secretary hand of Shakespeare's time confusions of 'c' and 't' and of 'n' and 'm' were common.

43   *An* if

52   *indrenched* drowned
         mad. Robert Burton devoted Part 3 of *The Anatomy of Melancholy* (1621) to love, saying that men possessed by love become insensible and insane, and advising his readers to go to Bedlam, the hospital for the mad, to study examples; see especially Section 2, Member 4, Subsection 1.

53   *fair* beautiful

54   *ulcer.* Love poetry conventionally imaged the lover as 'wounded' by his mistress's 'cruelty', or gashed (compare line 63) by Cupid's arrows; but Shakespeare here ironically suggests that Troilus's heart is diseased or morally corrupt.

56   *that her hand* that hand of hers

58   *to* compared with
         seizure grasp

59   *spirit of sense* the very essence of the feeling of touch (the spirit as immaterial opposed to the body as material)

62   *balm* ointment

69   *has the mends* (that is, by using cosmetics)

71   *have had my labour for my travail* (that is, have taken all this trouble for nothing)

77   *an* even if

78   *Friday ... Sunday* (contrasting a fast-day with a feast-day, when Helen would dress in finery. The image is one of numerous anachronisms in the play.)

83   *stay behind her father*. Cressida's father, Calchas,
      foreseeing the fall of Troy, has gone over to the
      Greeks; this passage foreshadows her transfer to the
      Greeks in Act IV.

90   (stage direction) *alarum* (a call to arms, sounded on
      trumpets or drums)

93   *paint* (as with rouge)

94   *argument* theme of contention; quarrel

97   *I cannot ... Pandar.* Cressida is evidently in the
      protection of her uncle Pandarus; but she lives, it
      seems, in her own house (see III.2.1–2).

100   *Apollo, for thy Daphne's love.* The story, told in Gold-
      ing's Ovid, I.545–700, is relevant to Troilus's desire
      for Cressida. The maid Daphne, fleeing the hot love
      of Apollo, was transformed into a laurel bush to
      preserve her virginity. Apollo, patron of medicine,
      could not find a herb to heal the hurt of love.

102   *India* (as remote, and symbolizing fabulous wealth)

103   *Ilium*. Priam's palace, imagined, following Caxton's
      Recuyell, as the citadel of the city of Troy; Caxton says
      it was built upon a rock (Bullough, VI.188).
      Shakespeare's spelling of the name varies, and else-
      where, as at IV.4.115 and IV.5.112, Q and F have
      'Ilion', following Chapman's *Seven Books of the Iliads*
      or Caxton (who prints 'Ylyon'); see Bullough, VI.129,
      188. In this edition the form *Ilium* is used throughout.

105   *merchant* (one of a series of images that undermine
      the idealism of Troilus's love; see the Introduction,
      page 11)

107   *a-field* on the battlefield

108   *sorts* is fitting

111   *hurt*. It turns out at I.2.214–15 that Paris is not
      wounded after all.

114   *Menelaus' horn*. The image is of Menelaus as both
      bull and wearing cuckold's horns (see also V.7.10 and
      the note).

115, 117 *sport* (treating war as a game: see the Introduction,
      pages 18–19, Troilus quibbles also on the *sport* of
      love-making.)

I.2   The setting is ambiguous; the scene appears to be a domestic one, and to take place in Cressida's house (as Pandarus is summoned to his *own house* at line 274). At the same time, Hecuba and Helen have passed by (line 1), and later the Trojan warriors pass across the stage, as returning from battle, when the stage turns into a street; Cressida and Pandarus *stand up* (line 179) to watch them, and may be imagined as looking out from a window, or as out of doors.

5   *moved* angry. This anecdote about Hector being struck down by Ajax in battle (see lines 33–6) and venting his anger on Andromache relates to the ceremonious fight between Hector and Ajax in IV.5 and to Hector's annoyance with Andromache in V.3.

7   *husbandry* careful management. (Like a good farmer (husbandman), Hector was in the field (of battle) early.)

8   *harnessed light* in light armour

10   *weep* (being wet with dew)

12   *noise* rumour

13   *nephew* (used loosely; Ajax is Hector's *father's sister's son* (IV.5.120), or first cousin)

15, 16   *per se ... alone* by himself (Latin '*per se*'), hence perfect and unique

20   *additions* qualities, what they are known for. (See also IV.5.141 and the note.)

22   *humours* qualities of mind or temperament (originally the four principal fluids of the body, blood, phlegm, choler, and bile or melancholy, which were thought to determine each person's mental qualities)

25   *glimpse* trace
      attaint blemish

27   *against the hair* against the natural way an animal's hair lies (or, as we now say, against the grain)

28   *Briareus* (a legendary monster with a hundred arms and fifty heads)

29   *Argus.* To protect Io, who had been ravished and transformed to a cow by Jupiter, Juno put her in the care of Argus, who had a hundred eyes, only two of

which slept at any time. The story is told in Golding's Ovid, I.775 ff.

33   *coped* fought with

34   *disdain* vexation

43   *cousin* (used loosely between any relatives and between friends not related by blood)

54   (stage direction) No separate exit is marked for Alexander in Q or F, but since he says nothing after line 40, I follow the Arden editor and some directors in making him leave so that he does not hear Pandarus talking about Troilus.

66   *is Troilus* (that is, is his own man, and perfect in himself. These lines, playing upon the idea of identity, relate to Cressida's later concern with herself at III.2.146–8, to Troilus's anguished lines at V.2.132–63, and to the treatment of Ajax in II.3 and Achilles in III.3; see the Introduction, pages 15–16.)

70   *degrees* respects

72–3   *I would he were.* Troilus is not himself because he is 'sick' for love of Cressida.

75   *Condition, I had gone barefoot to India* (that is, 'it is as absurd to say Troilus is himself as to imagine me walking barefoot to India')

77   *'a* he

79   *heart* (affection for Troilus)

85   *come to't* reached maturity. Troilus is *The youngest son of Priam . . . Not yet mature* (IV.5.96–7).

87   *wit* understanding

94   *brown favour* dark or sunburnt complexion

102   *Then Troilus should* in that case Troilus would

105   *as lief* rather

107   *copper nose* (caused by disease or drink)

110   *merry Greek* wanton, loose reveller (a common usage, as at IV.4.55)

112   *compassed* curved, or bay

114   *tapster's* (that is, of the simplest kind)

118   *lifter* (quibbling on the meaning 'thief', as in 'shoplifter')

120   *puts me.* This survival of an old dative construction is common in Shakespeare's works (compare the mod-

ern 'do me a favour'); here *me* emphasizes Pandarus's role as narrator.

123–4   *Phrygia.* See the note to line 7 of the Prologue.

127   *an* as if

       a cloud in autumn (as being dull and disagreeable, the opposite of what Pandarus means)

130   *stand to the proof* (1) abide by the demonstration; (2) have an erection

135   *chickens i'th'shell.* An addled egg is often one in which the chicken dies during hatching.

139   *the rack* (that is, being tortured)

144   *that* so much that

145   *With millstones* (signifying a hard-hearted person who does not weep; Cressida cannot see the joke)

161–3   *Two and fifty . . . his sons.* Priam is supposed to have had fifty sons or 'heires' (the spelling in Q); counting the forked hair as two, and adding the white one, Troilus has fifty-two hairs on his chin.

165   *forked* (suggesting horns and that Paris is a cuckold)

175–7   *April . . . a nettle against May.* April showers proverbially led to May flowers, but Cressida turns aside Pandarus's implied praise of Troilus by converting them to stinging nettles.

182   *an excellent place* (perhaps a bench or rostrum to give them elevation. At the Globe the warriors may simply have entered through one door, processed around the stage past Cressida and Pandarus, and left by another. In Chaucer's *Troilus and Criseyde*, II.610 ff., Criseyde by herself watches Troilus alone return from battle.)

183   *bravely* splendidly

193   *proper* handsome

196   *give you the nod* (that is, make you look a fool or noddy)

198   *the rich shall have more* (that is, you will be even more foolish; perhaps alluding to the parable of the talents, Matthew 25.29)

207   *laying on, take't off who will* dealing blows vigorously, whatever anyone says to deny it

211   *By God's lid* (a common petty oath) by God's eyelid

214   *brave* splendid

214–15   *Who said he came hurt home.* Aeneas said it (I.1.111).

223   *indifferent* tolerably

228   *hem* (acknowledging his mistake)

229   *prince of chivalry.* The suggestion is of a medieval man-at-arms; see I.3.283 and the note.

236   *grace* model of virtue (alluding also to the three Graces, in Greek mythology daughters of Zeus, and givers of beauty and grace)

239   *to change* in exchange
to boot in addition

244   *daws* jackdaws (typifying folly, as crows typified ugliness)

256   *minced* (taking Pandarus's list of qualities as the ingredients for a mince-pie)

257   *the man's date is out* (that is, he is past his best, or 'outdated'. Cressida's play on 'dates' as fruit, used for sweetening pies, recalls Pandarus's image of baking a cake, I.1.14–28.)

258   *such another woman* (that is, no different from other women)

259   *ward* guard (in fencing)

260–70   *Upon my back . . . watching.* Cressida takes up Pandarus's words in terms of the threat he represents to her chastity and reputation, reminding him that, as her uncle, he should defend her, but revealing too her own sexual consciousness.

262   *honesty* chastity
mask. Ladies wore masks out of doors to protect their complexions against the weather.

265   *watches* (quibbling on the meaning 'devotional exercises')

266   *watch you* be on my guard against you

269   *swell past hiding* (revealing that she is pregnant)

276   *doubt* fear

285   *glass* mirror

286   *wooing* while being wooed

287, 289   These lines are marked in Q by inverted commas as 'sententiae' (notable sayings).

288   *That she* that woman

289   *than it is* (that is, than it is worth)

293   *Achievement ... beseech.* Italicized and marked by inverted commas in Q and F, this line sums up Cressida's amoral philosophy; once possessed, a woman is in the man's power; while she holds off, men sue to her.

294   *content* (1) satisfaction; (2) capacity

I.3   This scene takes us to the Greek camp, and a ceremonial council meeting, marked by sounding a *Sennet*, or fanfare on trumpets. Diomedes is present as a Greek commander, but says nothing; Ajax and Achilles are absent, as involved in the issues debated. The extravagant language of the first part of the scene, with its grand generalizations about order, is ironically counter-poised by the pettiness of the actual complaint against Achilles and Ajax, and, even more so, by the cheap trick resorted to finally by Ulysses and Nestor. The mention of a *truce* (line 262) points to a lapse of time between this and the previous scene. See the Introduction, page 26.

    (stage direction) *Sennet.* See the headnote above.

2   *grief* injury or offence
      jaundice (showing as yellow, the colour of envy or jealousy)

3   *proposition* offer

6   *veins* (sap-vessels in plants)

7   *conflux* confluence

8   *his* (still the usual genitive of 'it' as well as 'he' in Shakespeare's time)

9   *Tortive* twisting

11   *suppose* expectation

13   *Sith* since

14   *trial* (the subject of the clause) putting to the proof

15   *Bias and thwart* awry and off course

16   *unbodied figure* abstract conception

18   *works* actions

20   *protractive* delaying

21   *persistive* steadfast

23   *In fortune's love* (that is, in good fortune)

24 *artist* scholar (compare 'Master of Arts')

25 *affined* related

30 *virtue* worth, excellence

31 *observance of* deference to (perhaps making a bow)
      seat throne

33 *reproof* rebuff

35 *bauble* toylike, insignificant

38 *Boreas* the north wind

39 *Thetis* (a sea-nymph, mother of Achilles) the sea

41 *elements* air and water. (The other two, fire and earth,
      were thought of as dry.)

42 *Perseus' horse* (the winged Pegasus, which could fly;
      properly the horse of Bellerophon, but the confusion
      was common, perhaps because the dying Medusa,
      the monster slain by Perseus in rescuing Andromeda,
      was said to have given birth to Pegasus)

43 *untimbered* frail, lacking a strong frame
      but even now just now, this very moment past

44 *Co-rivalled* vied with

45 *toast* sop

47 *her* (commonly used for 'its'; compare *his* in line 8)

48 *breese* gad-fly

54 *Returns* replies. So Q; F reads 'Retyres', which makes
      no sense.

57 *tempers* dispositions

58 *shut up* comprised, summed up

60 *The which* which

61 *stretched-out life.* Nestor is old enough to have fought
      with Hector's grandfather; see IV.5.196-7.

63 *Agamemnon, every hand.* Q and F both read
      'Agamemnon and the hand'; various emendations
      have been suggested, but the simplest is to treat
      Agamemnon as a vocative, taking 'and the' as a mis-
      reading of 'euerye', a possible error in secretary
      hand (Richard Proudfoot's suggestion).

64 *in brass* (that is, inscribed in brass, as on a monument,
      typifying what will not perish)

65 *hatched* (a technical term, meaning inlaid with strips
      of silver for ornamental purposes; so Nestor's silver
      hair seems a metal superior to brass)

66   *axletree* the earth (around which, in Ptolemaic astronomy, all the heavens revolved)

69   *great . . . wise* (Agamemnon as great, Hector as wise)

70–74   These lines are not in Q.

70   *expect* expectation

71   *importless* trivial

73   *rank* foul
     opes opens
     mastic (a resin used in varnish, but the Greek root means to chew (as in 'masticate'), and the suggestion is of jaws chewing and exuding a gummy liquid. There may also be a conscious echo of 'mastix', from the Greek for a scourge, as used, for example, by Thomas Dekker in the title of his play *Satiromastix* (1601).)

75   *his basis* its foundation

77   *instances* causes

78   *specialty of rule* bond of discipline

80   *Hollow . . . hollow* (1) empty; (2) false or unsound

81   *When that* when

83   *Degree being vizarded* the gradation of rank being masked or obscured

85   *this centre* (the earth, as centre of the Ptolemaic universe; compare line 66)

87   *Insisture* (a coinage found nowhere else) steady continuance

88   *in all line* (that is, in a proper canon or rule)

89   *planet Sol* the sun (regarded as a planet in the Ptolemaic system because of its apparent motion in relation to the fixed stars)

90   *sphered* placed in the heavens

91   *other* (the Old and Middle English plural) others
     med'cinable healing

92   *ill aspects* (in astrology, the relative positions of heavenly bodies when their influence is malign)

93   *posts* speeds

94   *Sans check* without pausing

95   *to disorder* (that is, so as to produce disorder on earth)

96   *mutiny* discord

99   *deracinate* uproot

101   *fixure* stability

104   *Degrees in schools* academic rankings (Bachelor, Doctor, etc.) in universities

        brotherhoods guilds or fraternities

105   *dividable shores* (literally, shores that divide, that is, are separated by the sea)

106   *primogenitive* condition of being first-born (and so having rights of succession). This is apparently a coinage, the accepted form being 'primogeniture'.

108   *authentic* authoritative

111   *mere oppugnancy* total conflict

113   *sop* (literally, bread or toast soaked in wine or water; recalling Nestor's image at line 45)

114   *imbecility* physical weakness. The modern sense, weakness of mind, was not current in Shakespeare's time.

115   *rude* violent, brutal

117   *jar* discord

        resides has its place (as weighing the opposing claims of parties in a trial)

120   *Power into will, will into appetite.* The image is of all distinctions of right or wrong, justice or injustice, being lost in mere force, which is an expression of *will* or self-seeking, and hence of greed or lust. This terrible general image relates to the specific instances of *appetite* given rein in the play, from Troilus's desire for Cressida in 1.1 to Thersites' comment *lechery eats itself* (V.4.35).

125   *suffocate* smothered

127   *neglection* neglect

128–9   *goes backward in a purpose | It hath to climb* (that is, aiming to rise in power or rank, each in fact falls back)

132   *Exampled* justified

132–3   *the first pace that is sick | Of his superior* the first sick step his superior takes

138   *discovered* revealed

143   *forehand* mainstay (literally, he who fights in the front of the battle)

145   *dainty* sparing

148   *scurril* scurrilous

151	*pageants* mimics
152	*topless deputation* supreme function (as commander)
153–4	*conceit	Lies in his hamstring* wits (and, perhaps, self-esteem) are in his legs
155	*wooden dialogue and sound* stupid dialogue, and the sound of an actor's tread on boards
156	*stretched footing* long strides
	scaffoldage scaffolding for a stage
157	*o'er-wrested* overstrained
159	*unsquared* unfitting. The image is of stone or wood not cut to a true right angle.
160	*Typhon* (a mythical monster, whose voice was heard in volcanic eruptions, linked by Ovid with Mount Etna: Golding's Ovid, V.408 ff.)
161	*fusty* stale
162	*pressed* (quibbling on the military sense 'forced into service')
166	*being dressed to* preparing for
168	*Vulcan and his wife*. The lame and ugly blacksmith god Vulcan was married to Venus, goddess of love and beauty; Ulysses is stressing how *unlike* they were.
171	*answer* defend himself
174–5	*gorget . . . rivet*. The *gorget* was a kind of collar designed to protect the throat, and was fastened at the side with a bolt or *rivet*.
176	*Sir Valour dies* (that is, Achilles 'dies' of laughter)
178	*spleen* (thought of as the seat of laughter)
180	*Severals and generals of grace exact* individual and general attainments in their consummate excellence. (Ulysses complains that their best qualities are being ridiculed.)
181	*preventions* precautions
182	*Excitements* exhortations
184	*paradoxes* absurdities
187	*imperial* commanding
	infect infected
188–9	*bears his head	In such a rein* (that is, he is just as unbridled as)
189	*place* high rank, dignity
193	*gall* (as the seat of bitterness or envy)

195   *exposure* undefended state

196   *rank* densely

197   *tax* find fault with

199   *Forestall prescience* obstruct foresight or planning

202–3   *know by measure | Of their observant toil the enemies' weight* (that is, know by computing as a result of laboured observation the size of the enemy forces)

205   *mappery* map-making

207   *swing* force
        rudeness of his poise violence of its impact

210   *his execution* its action or operation

211–12   *Achilles' horse | Makes many Thetis' sons* (that is, his horse would be worth many times the value of Achilles. Thetis was his mother; see line 39.)

212   (stage direction) *Tucket* (a flourish sounded on a trumpet)

219   *Do a fair message* present a gentle or peaceful message

225   *Know them from eyes of other mortals.* Both sides were thought of as wearing armour which masked the face (see IV.5.195), but Shakespeare (and Aeneas) seem to be mocking the Greek flattery of Agamemnon and his *godlike seat* (line 31); perhaps he was played by a short actor.

230   *Phoebus* (the sun god)

235   *free* generous, open

236   *bending angels* (an anachronism; the image is of angels bowing in adoration of God)

237   *galls* venom

238–9   *Jove's accord – | Nothing so full of heart* (this is as much as to say 'God willing, no one is as courageous as they are')

241–4   *The worthiness . . . blows* (that is, the honour of praise sullies the merit of that man who speaks his own praise; but fame spreads abroad the commendations of a grudging enemy)

241   *distains* sullies

243   *repining* grudging

252   *set his sense on the attentive bent* (that is, force him to turn and listen)

253   *frankly* freely

263   *rusty* (linking with *mettle* (metal), line 258)

269   *loves his mistress more than in confession* (that is, loves her more than in merely saying so, and will show it by fighting for her)

270   *truant* (as idle, and because in making love the warrior plays truant from the battlefield)

272   *arms.* Love and war merge in this one word.

276   *compass* embrace

282   *sunburnt* ugly. A fair skin was prized for beauty; see I.2.262 and the note.

283   *lance.* With its suggestions of medieval tournaments, this links with the idea of *chivalry*, as at I.2.229 and V.3.32, and with the image of warriors as *knights* (II.1.123, IV.5.86, 88 etc.).
        Even so much this is all I was told to say

285   *soul in such a kind* (that is, enthusiasm for such a business)

287   *recreant* villain, or coward

288   *means not, hath not* (that is, means not to be, has not been)

293   *mould* bodily form

296   *beaver* face-guard (of a helmet)

297   *vantbrace* armour for the fore-arm

301   *pawn* pledge (so F; Q has 'proue')

306–9   Agamemnon's rhymed couplets mark the end of the ceremonial part of the scene.

313   *time* occasion

316   *seeded* run to seed

318   *rank* overgrown, and puffed up
        or either

324–5   *substance* | *Whose grossness little characters sum up.* *Substance* is (1) meaning; (2) wealth. Hector's meaning is as clear as if it had been set out in figures, and just as small figures sum up great wealth, so this general challenge points to the gross Achilles.

326   *make no strain* (that is, have no doubt)

328   *Apollo* (patron of the muses, also the source of oracular wisdom, and so a measure of the dullness of Achilles)

333   *oppose* put forward as antagonist

339   *imputation* reputation
       oddly poised unfairly valued

340   *willed* determined by the will (the warrior who is to
       fight Hector will be chosen, unlike those he encoun-
       ters at random in battle). F has 'wilde', correcting
       'vilde' (Q), so that 'wild' and 'vile' are possible read-
       ings, though neither makes much sense.
       success result

341   *scantling* standard of measurement

342   *general* general public

343   *indexes* (1) signs; (2) summaries of the contents of
       books

343–4 *small pricks | To their subsequent volumes* tiny markings
       in relation to the books that follow, and also small
       pointers to the size (*volume*) of what they imply

344   *subsequent* (accented on the second syllable)

349   *Makes merit her election* (that is, selects the best)

351   *who miscarrying* he being defeated

352–3 *What heart . . . themselves?* The rhetorical question
       spells out what would happen if the Greek champion
       were to lose; how could anyone take heart from this,
       and strengthen his belief in himself? The word *part*
       links with *scantling* (line 341) and *shares* (line 367).

354–6 *Which entertained . . . limbs.* These lines depict the
       effect success will have for the winning side, working
       in the limbs of all, and so in the weapons directed by
       their limbs.

360   *And think . . . not.* This short line remained after the
       revision in F of this passage in Q, which omits lines
       354–6; see the Collations, page 235.

367   *shares from* takes away from (but implying 'shares
       with'; Q has 'share' for *wear* in line 368)

371   *salt* bitter, stinging

373   *opinion* reputation

374   *taint* disgrace

375   *blockish* stupid

376   *sort* lot

377   *allowance* praise

378   *Myrmidon* (Achilles, leader of the Myrmidons; see
       V.7)

379   *broils* grows hot with pleasure
        fall lower

380   *blue Iris bends.* Achilles' crest is curved like a rainbow, which was identified with Iris, messenger of the gods; but Shakespeare was thinking also of the common blue flower.

382   *dress him up in voices* (that is, over-praise him in our reports)

385   *shape of sense* form of interpretation

391   *tarre . . . on* incite

II.1   This scene, which introduces Thersites, whose scurrilous railing is partly licensed by his status as a professional fool (line 85; see the Introduction, page 22), is appropriately in prose. Thersites goes through clown's routines still used in cross-talk acts, as with Achilles (lines 56–60): *You see him . . . Nay, look upon him . . . Nay, but regard him well . . .* etc. Perhaps at the Globe there was some indication of Ajax's 'tent' on stage.

6   *botchy core* (that is, Agamemnon would be like the core of a boil covered with sores or ulcers)

8   *matter* (1) pus; (2) good sense

12   *plague of Greece.* Perhaps suggested by the plague sent upon the Greeks by Apollo in Homer's *Iliad*, Book 1 (Bullough, VI.114); but it is Thersites' habit to find images of disease.

13   *beef-witted* stupid. (Eating beef was thought to dull the wits.)

14   *vinewed'st* mouldiest (perhaps with a biblical echo of *leaven* as the unregenerative part of man: 'Purge out therefore the old leaven', 1 Corinthians 5.7)

15   *handsomeness* graciousness

17   *con* study

18   *learn a prayer without book* memorize a prayer without reference to the Book of Common Prayer (one of several anachronisms in the play)

19   *murrain* pestilence
        jade vicious horse

20   *learn me* tell me about

25   *porpentine* porcupine

28   *Greece.* Q here adds 'when thou art forth in the incursions thou strikest as slow as another'. This passage was omitted from F, I think as a deliberate cut, because it breaks the flow of dialogue with an irrelevant joke.

32   *Cerberus . . . Proserpina's beauty.* Cerberus, the three-headed dog, guarded the gates of Hades, where Proserpina, daughter of Ceres, was taken by Pluto to be his queen.

34   *Mistress* (Ajax's clumsy attempt at insult)

35   *Thou shouldst* (that is, if you were to)

36   AJAX *Cobloaf!* (mistakenly printed in Q as a stage direction, '*Aiax Coblofe*'. The confusion in Q continues with the omission of the next three speech-prefixes. See the Collations, page 236.)
     Cobloaf (a small loaf shaped with a round head)

37   *pun* pound
     shivers fragments

41   *stool* (as something small, like a *Toadstool* or *Cobloaf*, lines 20 and 36; and possibly suggesting a close-stool, or privy, so backfiring upon Ajax, whose name puns on 'a jakes', meaning a privy; see line 63)

44   *assinico* donkey (from the Spanish *asnico*, a little ass)

45–6   *bought and sold* (that is, treated with contempt)

47   *use to beat* make a habit of beating

48   *bowels* feelings

52   *Mars his* Mars's

63   *Ajax* (that is, a jakes; see line 41 and the note)

68   *ears thus long* (miming ass's ears)
     bobbed buffeted

70   *nine sparrows for a penny* (a recollection of passages from the Gospels, Matthew 10.29, 'Are not two little sparrows sold for a farthing?', and Luke 12.6, 'Are not five sparrows sold for two farthings?')
     pia mater brain (strictly, the name given to the innermost membrane covering the brain)

78   *I must hold you.* Ajax struggles to break from Achilles.

85   *set your wit to a fool's* (echoing Proverbs 26.4, 'Give not

the fool an answer after his foolishness, lest thou
become like unto him')

fool. Thersites is a professional; see the headnote to
this scene.

88   *Good words* (that is, 'speak gently')

95   *sufferance* suffering

97   *under an impress* (1) conscripted; (2) marked or
stamped (by Ajax's fists)

108   *to* go to it (like oxen)

110   *as much* (that is, as much sense; usually emended to
'as much wit')

113   *brooch* ornament or trinket (implying his insigni-
ficance; usually emended to 'brach' (bitch), as more
abusive and suggesting effeminacy, but the original is
wittier)

116   *clotpolls* blockheads

121   *the fifth hour* eleven o'clock (according to Thersites,
III.3.295)

124   *stomach* relish (for a fight)

II.2   This council scene in Troy parallels the Greek council in I.3, and as Agamemnon had a *godlike seat*
(I.3.31), so Priam here probably had a throne to sit in
at the Globe; the formality of this scene contrasts with
the two prose scenes of foolery with Thersites set on
either side of it.

2   *Nestor.* This embassy by Nestor, not previously mentioned, is Shakespeare's invention, and helps to bring
home the meaninglessness of the war.

6   *cormorant* (that is, all-devouring, as the cormorant is
noted for its greed)

9   *particular* personal concern

11   *more softer bowels* more tender feelings

14   *The wound of peace is surety* (that is, a sense of safety
hurts or endangers peace)

16   *tent* probe used by surgeons

19   *tithe* tenth

dismes (pronounced 'dimes' and meaning 'tenths', so

equivalent to *tithe*; Hector says that the war has taken one of every ten Trojan warriors, each one as dear as Helen)

23   *Had it our name* (that is, if it were part of us, if Helen were a Trojan)

29   *past-proportion* immensity (*past* means 'beyond reach or measure')

31   *spans* handspans (roughly nine inches measured from the thumb to the little finger of the outstretched hand)

33   *No marvel though* no wonder for all that
       reasons (quibbling on raisins)

34–6   *not . . . none.* The two negatives intensify; Troilus's speech offers no reasons why Priam should not rule with prudence.

38   *fur your gloves with reason* (that is, comfort yourself with arguments for discretion)

41   *object* sight (or object as perceived)

44–5   *wings of reason . . . chidden Mercury.* Mercury, the son of Jupiter, did his bidding as messenger of the gods, and was represented as wearing winged sandals.

46   *star disorbed* star dislodged from its sphere, a falling or shooting star

48   *hare-hearts* (that is, hearts as timid as the hare)

49   *respect* consideration

50   *livers* (as the seat of courage)

54   *in particular will* as determined by an individual

55   *his* its

59–61   *the will dotes . . . merit.* Difficult lines, playing on *affect* as desire and disease; Hector says it is madness when the desire for something is caught like a disease from the object desired, madness to submit to it without some idea of its intrinsic value. The passage is related to Jesus's attack on the scribes and Pharisees in Matthew 23, especially such verses as 17, 'whether is greater, the gold, or the temple that sanctifieth the gold'? For *is inclinable*, Q has 'is attributiue', a reading preferred by many editors, interpreted as 'attributes value'.

62   *I take . . . a wife.* Troilus's example is ironic in relation

to his affair with Cressida, to whom he does not offer marriage.

election choice

63,64, 66,67   *will.* Several meanings are played on here: volition, desire, and also carnal appetite.

65   *traded* experienced

65–6   *the dangerous shores | Of will and judgement.* The danger is that sexual desire, aroused by the senses, may get the better of judgement in making choice of a wife.

66   *avoid* reject (in law, invalidate an agreement)

67   *distaste* dislike

69   *blench* flinch

72   *in unrespective sieve* indiscriminately in a basket

74   *vengeance.* Hesione, Priam's sister, mother of Ajax, the *aunt* of line 78, was, according to Caxton, seized by the Greeks and kept in servitude; in revenge, Paris abducted Helen, causing the Trojan War (Bullough, VI.188–92).

80   *Apollo* (that is, the sun, appearing fresh every morning)

82   *a pearl* (alluding to the image of heaven as 'one precious pearl', Matthew 13.46)

83   *price* value. This line echoes Marlowe's 'Was this the face that launched a thousand ships?' (*Doctor Faustus*, V.1.92).

90   *proper* own

    rate reprove, exclaim against

91   *do a deed that fortune never did* (that is, act with more inconstancy than ever fortune did)

92   *estimation* valued object

96   *in their country* (that is, in Greece)

97   *warrant* answer for, justify

101   (stage direction) *Cassandra.* Priam's daughter, a priestess, who was given the power of prophecy by Apollo; but, because she slighted him, he punished her by ensuring that no one would believe her prophecies.

    raving, with her hair about her ears. Q has '*rauing*', F '*with her haire about her eares*' a conventional mark of

madness; in the first Quarto of *Hamlet* the mad
Ophelia is directed to enter at IV.5.20 with '*her haire
downe*'.

105   *old* old age

107   *betimes* early, in advance

108   *moiety* portion

109   *Practise* make use of

111   *firebrand brother*. Paris's mother, Hecuba, dreamed
when pregnant with him that she was delivered of a
firebrand which burned Troy (Virgil, *Aeneid* VII.320
ff.).

113   *or else* (equivalent to 'if we do not')

114   *strains* impassioned sounds

117   *discourse of reason* rational argument

119   *qualify* moderate, cool

121   *event* the outcome

124   *distaste* make distasteful

125   *honours*. Troilus introduced this term (lines 26, 47,
and 69) and exploits its overlapping meanings of
esteem, fame, reputation, and magnanimity to plead
for retaining Helen; see also lines 150 and 200.

126   *gracious* successful

129   *spleen* (as the seat of courage)

131   *convince* convict

133   *attest* call to witness

134   *propension* inclination

137   *propugnation* defence

138   *push* attack

140   *pass* endure

149   *rape* carrying off by force

151   *ransacked* carried off as plunder

155   *strain* propensity, disposition

156   *generous* noble

157   *party* side

166   *glozed* commented

167–8   *young men whom Aristotle thought | Unfit to hear moral
philosophy*. This refers to a well-known passage in the
Nicomachean Ethics, I.3, in which Aristotle says young
men are too much swayed by their feelings, so that
moral and political issues are not a proper study for

them. The debate between Hector, Paris, and Troilus turns on a number of matters discussed by Aristotle, such as honour, choice (election), and justice, and Shakespeare may have used the *Ethics* consciously here. The reference to Aristotle is, of course, an anachronism.

170   *distempered* disordered

173   *adders* (proverbially deaf; see Psalm 58.4)

178   *affection* passion, lust

179   *that* if

179–80   *of partial indulgence | To their benumbèd wills* out of a prejudiced yielding to their besotted desires

183   *refractory* rebellious

185–6   *moral laws | Of nature and of nations* (that is, laws as implanted by nature in the mind, and the laws which bind nations in a mutual agreement. The best-known discussion of the derivation through reason of the laws of nations from the laws of nature, and their relation to divine law, is in Book I of Richard Hooker's *The Laws of Ecclesiastical Polity* (1594), especially Chapter X.)

188   *extenuates* mitigates

190   *in way of truth* as a point of abstract principle

191   *propend* incline

196   *affected* aspired to

197   *performance of our heaving spleens* discharge of our swelling resentment

203   *canonize* (accented on the second syllable) deify

205   *advantage* favourable chance

207   *revenue* (accented on the second syllable)

209   *roisting* swaggering
        challenge (delivered by Aeneas at I.3.260–83)

212   *advertised* (accented on the second syllable) informed

213   *emulation* rivalry for power or honour

II.3   As II.1 took place at Ajax's tent, so this scene is set outside the *tent* (lines 76 and 84) of Achilles, though a stage-door could have been used for the entrance to this. Thersites seems to carry straight on from II.1 in his fury at Ajax, as though there were almost no time interval between these scenes.

2   *carry it* have the better of it

5   *'Sfoot* (an oath, shortened from 'by God's foot')

6   *but* (meaning 'but in any case')

8   *engineer* (1) designer of military works; (2) plotter or contriver

10   *Olympus* (a mountain in Greece, legendary seat of the gods)

11–12   *Mercury, lose all the serpentine craft of thy caduceus.* Mercury, messenger of the gods, carried a wand entwined by two serpents, the *caduceus*. He typified cunning, and was the god of thieves.

14   *short-armed* (that is, lacking in reach, or understanding)

15   *in circumvention* by craft

16   *irons* swords

18   *Neapolitan bone-ache* syphilis (known as the Neapolitan (or French) disease)

20   *placket* petticoat (that is, woman)

        devil Envy. Envy, one of the seven deadly sins, is invoked appropriately, as the source of much of Thersites' railing.

21   (stage direction) *Enter Patroclus.* This is in F, but not in Q, and is usually moved to follow *Amen* (line 32) on the grounds that it is unlikely that Patroclus would remain silent while Thersites abuses him; but the Greek warriors enjoy his railing, and it is best to follow F here.

24–5   *counterfeit* false coin

25   *slipped* (quibbling on 'slip', a counterfeit coin)

29   *blood* passion (as opposed to reason)

32   *lazars* lepers

40   *cheese* (supposed to promote good digestion)

51   *decline the whole question* recite the whole matter at issue (as one might 'decline' the cases of a Latin noun)

56   *a privileged man* (that is, as licensed fool; see the headnote to II.1)

60   *Derive* explain

64	*positive* absolute
70	*patchery* roguery (from 'patch' meaning fool, from the nickname of Cardinal Wolsey's jester)
72	*draw* bring about
73	*serpigo* (any spreading skin disease, especially ringworm)
74	(stage direction) *Enter . . . Calchas*. Although both Q and F include Calchas here, he says nothing in the scene, and is usually omitted; but perhaps he was visually identifiable as a Trojan among the Greeks, preparing for III.3, where he asks for the return of Cressida.
76	*ill-disposed* unwell
78	*shent* put to shame
79	*appertainments* prerogatives
81	*move the question of our place* raise the issue of my rank (that is, as general in command)
84	*opening of his tent.* A stage-door could have been draped to look like the entrance to a tent; see the headnote to this scene.
95–6	*argument . . . argument* (1) theme; (2) subject of contention (see I.1.94)
98–9	*their fraction is more our wish than their faction* (that is, we would prefer them to quarrel rather than combine to form a party)
99	*composure* combination
104–5	*joints, but none for courtesy.* It was thought that elephants could not bend their knees, hence their proverbial association with pride.
108	*state* council of state
111	*breath* breather, stroll for exercise
114	*apprehensions* grasp (mental and physical)
115	*attribute* distinction
117	*beheld* observed, attended to
123	*under-honest* less than honourable
	self-assumption arrogance, self-importance
124	*note of judgement* sign of good judgement
125	*tend* attend
	strangeness coldness, aloofness
127	*observing kind* compliant manner

128   *humorous predominance* capricious authority (but alluding also to the predominance of 'humours'; see I.2.22 and the note)

129   *pettish lunes* peevish tantrums. *Lune* is from Latin *luna*, the moon, which governs the *ebbs* and *flows* of the sea.

132   *overhold* overvalue

133   *engine* engine of war (such as a battering ram)

134   *Not portable* (1) not easily moved; (2) insufferable

136   *allowance* approval

138   *presently* straightaway

139   *In second voice we'll not be satisfied* (that is, we will not put up with a messenger)

146   *subscribe* assent to

155–6   *whatever praises itself but in the deed, devours the deed in the praise.* Agamemnon says that self-praise destroys the worth of the deed which earns praise (*but* means 'except'); see the similar remark of Aeneas at I.3.241–4 and Proverbs 27.1–2.

162   *dispose* inclination

164   *In will peculiar and in self-admission* independent in his wilfulness and in self-approval

167   *for request's sake only* merely because they are requested

169–70 *a pride | That quarrels at self-breath.* If Achilles is too proud to speak to himself here, the plot of Ulysses only succeeds in producing the same effect on Ajax, as burlesqued by Thersites at III.3.251–65.

173–4   *Kingdomed Achilles . . . batters down himself.* The image of man as a microcosm, state, or kingdom, provided with reason as the king able to govern unruly passions, was commonplace; see Proverbs 25.27, 'He that cannot rule himself is like a city which is broken down, and hath no walls'.

175   *death-tokens* fatal symptoms

178   *holds you well* thinks well of you

183   *seam* grease

185–6   *such as do revolve | And ruminate himself* (that is, his thoughts turn over and over in brooding on himself)

189   *stale his palm* lower his dignity

190 *assubjugate* reduce to submission

194 *Cancer* (the division or sign of the Zodiac entered by the sun on 21 June; hence an emblem of heat)

195 *Hyperion* (god of the sun)

198 *rubs the vein of him* encourages him in his natural inclination

201 *pash* strike, smash

203 *An 'a* if he
   pheeze deal with, do for

210 *let his humours' blood* bleed him to cure his waywardness (on *humours*, see I.2.22 and the note)

218 *ten shares* (that is, the lot; possibly alluding to the usual number of shares in a company of players, though Shakespeare's company seems to have had eight shares at this time; see Andrew Gurr, *The Shakespearean Stage, 1574–1642* (1980), pages 45–6)

220 *through* thoroughly
   Force stuff

230 *that shall palter thus* who thinks he can trifle so

235 *surly borne* behaved in a surly manner

236 *self-affected* self-loving, conceited

238 *got* begot

239 *parts of nature* natural gifts

244 *Bull-bearing Milo.* Milo was a noted athlete of ancient Greece who is said to have carried a bull or heifer along the racing track, killed it with a blow of his fist, and eaten it, all in one day.
   addition title or attribute

246 *bourn* boundary
   pale fence

247 *dilated* spread abroad

248 *antiquary* ancient

251 *green* immature
   tempered composed

252 *eminence of* superiority over

256 *Keeps thicket* (that is, stays in hiding)

257 *state* council

259 *main* full might

261 *cope* be a match for

263 *hulks* large and unwieldy ships

III.1   Returning us to Troy and the lodgings of Paris, Shakespeare brilliantly conveys through the language of this scene a sense of luxury, idleness, and love as *hot thoughts, and hot deeds* (lines 125–9).

4   *depend upon him* serve him as a dependant

5   *Lord* (treating 'Lord' as meaning 'God')

13   *know your honour better* (that is, find you to be a better man than you seem)

15   *in the state of grace* virtuous (as under divine influence; but Pandarus takes *grace* as a title of address to a man of the highest rank, a king or duke)

28   *cunning* clever

32, 33   *mortal Venus . . . visible soul* (examples of oxymoron: as a goddess Venus is immortal; the soul is invisible)

33   *visible.* Q and F both have 'inuisible', which is literally correct, but ruins the Servant's paradoxes.

41   *Sodden* (past participle of 'seethe') boiled

41–2   *stewed phrase* (quibbling on 'stew' meaning 'brothel')

43   *Fair be to you* may good fortune be yours. Pandarus proceeds to play on several senses of *fair*, such as 'beautiful', 'pleasing', 'equitable', 'free from moral stain'.

49   *broken music* (music arranged for a group of instruments of differing kinds, probably including strings and woodwind, such as viols and oboes)

50   *broke* interrupted
    cousin. See the note to I.2.43.

51   *piece it out* complete it, make it whole

55   *Rude* unskilled

56   *fits* (1) strains of music; (2) spasms (alluding to Pandarus's repetitions)

59   *hedge us out* exclude us from your conference. Pandarus tries to take Paris aside, and the text suggests that Helen hangs upon him.

61   *pleasant* merry, joking

67   *bob* cheat

81   *cousin* (meaning Paris (as at line 50), who may be angered by Helen's flirting with Pandarus; but this is also a clue to Paris that Pandarus is thinking of his niece or cousin Cressida (see line 83))

83   HELEN... *You must not know where he sups.* So in Q and F; editors often omit the speech-heading for Helen and give this line to Pandarus, but she is surely picking up from Paris's question *Where sups he tonight?* (line 79) and speaking to him.

84   *my disposer* the one *I* know (hence *my*) can do what she wants with Troilus. Paris and Helen evidently know what Pandarus, Troilus, and Cressida are up to.

85   *wide* (that is, wide of the mark)

91–2   *give me an instrument.* Pandarus consents to sing in order to avoid further exposure of his arrangements for Troilus.

98–9   *are twain* are estranged

100–101   *Falling in after falling out may make them three* (proverbial; reconciliation (making love) after quarrelling may lead to conception)

105   *forehead* impudence, assurance

106   *you may* (that is, you may say what you please)

110   *good now* if you please

115–16   *The shaft confounds, | Not that it wounds* love's arrow (with a bawdy pun on *shaft*) pierces and overthrows the lover without visibly hurting him

117   *sore* (quibbling on *sore* meaning a buck of the fourth year)

119   *the wound to kill.* These lines play on the common image in love poetry of lovers 'dying' in the act of consummation.

125   *doves* (symbolic of tender affection)

130   *generation of vipers.* Shakespeare anachronistically makes Pandarus refer to the Gospels, alluding to a phrase used several times, as at Matthew 23.33, 'ye generation of vipers, how will ye escape the damnation of hell?' Pandarus is not aware of these implications, but Shakespeare's audience would have been.

133   *gallantry* gallants, nobility

136   *hangs the lip* appears vexed

139   *sped* fared

141   *To a hair* exactly

145   *from field* from the battlefield. Compare *to field* (I.1.5, IV.4.142).

149 *edge of steel* sword-edge

151 *the island kings* (the Greek leaders; see the Prologue, lines 1–2)

154 *palm* praise, honour (as at II.3.189)

III.2 This scene takes place in the *orchard* (line 15) or garden outside Cressida's house, into which Pandarus ushers the lovers at the end of the scene; at the Globe a stage-door would have served as the entrance to it.

3 *stays* waits

8–9 *Stygian banks . . . be thou my Charon.* Charon, the ferryman of Hades or the underworld, gave passage (*waftage*) to the souls of the dead over the river Styx to Hades. For the association of love with dying, see III.1.115–19 and the notes.

11 *wallow.* Long associated with gross sensuality, this serves as a reminder of what Troilus is about; see the Introduction, page 11.

13 *painted* coloured

15 *I'll bring her straight.* Pandarus's matter-of-fact attitude nicely contrasts with Troilus's rapturous hyperboles.

19 *watery* salivating

20 *thrice-repurèd* thrice-purified (so Q; F's 'thrice reputed' is probably a compositor's error)

21 *Swooning.* 'Sounding' (Q, F) is a variant form.

25 *distinction* the power to discriminate

26 *battle* army
  on heaps in masses

29 *be witty* have your wits about you

30 *fetches her wind . . . short* (that is, breathes in short pants, from excitement)

30–31 *frayed with a sprite* frightened by a ghost

34 *thicker* faster

35 *bestowing* use

36 *vassalage* humble people

41–2 *watched ere you be made tame* (that is, as hawks were tamed by keeping them awake)

43 *an* if

44 *i'th'fills* in the shafts of a cart (as if to control a mare)

45 *draw this curtain.* Cressida is veiled, like Olivia in
    Twelfth Night, I.5.223.

48 *rub on, and kiss the mistress* (an image from bowls: 'pass
    all impediments (rubs) and hit the jack (mistress)';
    literally, 'make contact (compare "rub shoulders")
    and kiss your love')

49 *in fee-farm* (that is, granted in perpetuity; 'fee-farm' is
    a form of tenure by which land is held in perpetuity
    subject to a fixed rent)
    Build there (metaphorically as if building a house on
    the land held *in fee-farm*)

50 *fight* (that is, in the 'wars' of love)

51 *the falcon . . . i'th'river* (that is, I will bet all the ducks in
    the river that the *falcon*, or female hawk, matches the
    tercel, the male hawk, in eagerness)

54 *Words pay no debts, give her deeds.* The opposition of
    words and deeds is proverbial, but Pandarus is play-
    ing on *deeds* as sexual *activity*.

56–7 *In witness . . . interchangeably* (a legal formula used in
    drawing up reciprocal agreements)

58 *I'll go get a fire.* As Cressida's uncle and guardian,
    Pandarus takes charge of her house, where he has
    arranged for the lovers to meet. At I.2.274 Troilus is
    reported to be at Pandarus's house, but no scene
    takes place there.

59 *Will you walk in, my lord?* The invitation is repeated at
    line 97, and textual corruption has been suspected;
    but it is dramatically appropriate that Troilus should
    hold her in talk here.

64 *abruption* breaking off
    too curious too subtle or minute (to matter, Troilus
    implies)

67 *cherubins* (a common plural form of the singular
    'cherub' or 'cherubin' until the seventeenth century)

69 *seeing reason* (that is, reason that sees)

73 *Cupid's pageant* (perhaps, for the well-read, alluding
    to the pageant of Cupid in Spenser's *Faerie Queene*,
    III.xii, which is altogether monstrous)

193

79   *monstruosity* (a common early form) monstrosity

80–81 *the desire is boundless, and the act a slave to limit* (another version of the contrast between wish and performance, the ideal and the actual, that runs through the action of play; see the Introduction, page 29)

83   *able* able to carry out

86   *the voice of lions and the act of hares* (proverbial for those who have courage in word and not in deed; 'lions in hall, and hares in the field', as a fourteenth-century poem puts it)

88–9 *as we are tasted* (that is, as you have knowledge of us by experience; perhaps with a hint of carnal knowledge, as at *Cymbeline*, II.4.57, 'you have tasted her in bed')
    allow us as we prove commend us for what we show ourselves to be

90   *in reversion* to come in the future

92   *addition* title

93   *few words to fair faith* (proverbial: true loyalty needs few words)

94–5 *what envy can say worst shall be a mock for his truth* (that is, what the malicious will be able to do is to mock him for his faithfulness to her)

100   *folly* (with overtones of wantonness, as in *Othello*, V.2.133, 'She turned to folly; and she was a whore')

102   *get* beget

105   *your hostages* (that is, your security)

131   *My soul of counsel* (that is, the secrets of my heart)

147   *unkind* unnatural

148   *Where is my wit?* Cressida realizes she has made a surrender, forgotten the *wit* she relied on to defend herself (see I.2.260–70 and 293 and the notes), and so become Troilus's *fool* or dupe.

152   *roundly* plainly
    large free

154–5 *to be wise and love | Exceeds man's might* (a commonplace; Troilus responds by claiming only truth or faithfulness, not wisdom)

158   *aye* ever

159   *plight* condition (but suggesting also the verb, and

perhaps the plighting of troth in betrothal or marriage)

160   *outward* appearance

161   *blood* passion

164   *affronted* counterbalanced

165   *winnowed* unadulterated

172   *Approve* confirm

173   *big compare* large comparisons

175   *as plantage to the moon* as the cultivation of plants depends on the waxing moon. *Plantage* is apparently Shakespeare's coinage, and this comparison seems out of place in Troilus's string of proverbial sayings, so that some editors have accepted Pope's emendation to 'planets'.

176   *turtle* turtle-dove (noted for its enduring affection for its mate)

177   *adamant* loadstone or magnet
        centre axis on which it rotates

179   *authentic author* original authority

181   *numbers* lines, verses

186   *characterless are grated* with no mark left are worn away. *Characterless* is accented on the second syllable.

192   *Pard* leopard
        hind female deer
        stepdame stepmother (proverbially unkind to her stepchildren)

193   *stick* pierce

198   *pitiful* compassionate

201-2   *brokers-between.* 'Broker' commonly meant a hired match-maker or bawd.

207   *press it to death* (a joking allusion to execution by pressure of weights on the body, last practised in the eighteenth century)

208-9   *And Cupid . . . gear.* Pandarus turns to the audience, a choric moment that links with his lines which end the play, V.10.35-57; see the Introduction, pages 9, 28-9.

209   *gear* equipment

III.3   This scene in the Greek camp, like II.1 and II.3, again calls for an indication of tents. Possibly a stage-door was draped to suggest a tent, since Achilles is seen at line 37 in the entrance to his tent (here Q has the stage direction 'Achilles *and* Patro *stand in their tent*', changed in F to '*Enter* Achilles *and* Patroclus *in their tent*'); or perhaps a tent stood on stage throughout, symbolizing the Greek camp as opposed to the indoor scenes in Troy. Ulysses has to have a book about him, which he is reading when noticed by Achilles at lines 92–3.

1   This is the first time Calchas speaks, but see the note to the stage direction at II.3.74.

2   *advantage of the time* favourable opportunity (as at II.2.205)

4   *bear* possess
    come. Q and F read 'loue', which makes no sense in a passage about Calchas's foresight as a seer.

5   *possession* property (now only the plural 'possessions' is used)

8   *sequest'ring* separating

9   *condition* position in society

20   *therefore* for that

21   *in right great exchange* (that is, in exchange for an important Trojan)

22   *still* ever

23   *wrest* tuning-key (that is, Antenor harmoniously orders Trojan affairs)

25   *Wanting his manage* lacking his management

27   *change of* exchange for

30   *most accepted pain* hardships I have gladly endured
    bear him escort him, take him along

33   *Furnish you fairly* equip yourself handsomely, in proper form

34–5   *tomorrow . . . Ajax is ready*. Shakespeare does not show us how Ajax was selected to fight Hector. We know from I.3 that Ulysses and Nestor were plotting to rig the lottery, and now we learn that they succeeded, and the time of the encounter is fixed.

39   *strangely* disdainfully

41   *loose* casual, slight

43   *Why ... him.* This line is an alexandrine, and the extra syllables are often dropped by editors who omit *bent, why*. The tautology enacts Ulysses' mood of contempt, and seems rhetorically apt.
    unplausive disapproving

45   *use* (that is, use to make a link)

46   *Which his own will shall have desire to drink* (that is, Ulysses will present his 'medicine' of mockery in such a guise that Achilles will want to drink it)

47   *glass* mirror (the proud can only see themselves for what they are when they are confronted by pride in others)

49   *fees* tribute, homage

73   *use to creep* are in the habit of moving meekly. For *use*, Q and F have 'vs'd', but 'd' and 'e' are easily confused in the secretary hand Shakespeare wrote, and the compositor may have assimilated this to *used* in line 71.

75–6   *fallen out with fortune, | Must fall out with men* out of favour with fortune, must lose men's regard

76   *the declined* the man brought low

79   *mealy* powdery or scaly

82   *without him* external to him

84   *Which when they fall, as being slippery standers* (that is, when *honours* such as high rank, riches, and favour, being slippery supporters, are lost)

85–6   *The love ... another* (that is, the respect that was given on account of the honours, and the honours themselves, being mutually dependent, tumble down together: *pluck down*, meaning to pull down or demolish a building, gives force to the idea of falling)

89   *At ample point* in the fullest measure

91   *beholding* regard

94   *Thetis.* See I.3.39 and the note.

95   *A strange fellow.* The author cannot be identified; Ulysses is reading from a property book, and his speeches develop familiar ideas of Shakespeare's age.

96   *me.* See I.2.120 and the note.

96   *how dearly ever parted* however richly gifted

97   *How much in having, or without or in* however much he
        possesses, either in wealth (outside himself) or in
        talent (inside himself)

        or . . . or either . . . or

99   *owes* owns

101   *retort* reflect, throw back

104   *commends it* commends

105–6   *To others'. . . itself.* These lines were omitted in F, no
        doubt accidentally, as the compositor's eye jumped
        down three lines all ending in *itself.*

106   *spirit of sense.* essence of sensibility. See also I.1.59
        and the note.

107–8   *Not going . . . form* (that is, the eye cannot stand
        outside itself, but sees itself only as reflected in the
        mirror of another's eyes)

109   *speculation* sight, vision

110   *mirrored.* The Q and F reading, 'married', is possible,
        but seems too strong for this context.

112   *strain at the position* (that is, make a difficulty of
        accepting the thesis)

114   *circumstance* detailed arguments

116   *Though in and of him there is much consisting* (that is,
        though great worth resides in him (consists in him)
        and he possesses (consists of) many different valu-
        able qualities)

117   *parts* abilities. See line 96.

118   *know them for aught* recognize their worth

120   *extended* enlarged (or perhaps 'valued', 'assessed', a
        legal sense, used in land valuation)

        who (that is, those who make the *applause*)

123   *figure* shape

        rapt in taken by

128   *abject in regard, and dear in use* despised in reputation,
        and precious in use. This sequence develops further
        the issues raised in the debate on value at II.2.53 ff.

131   *chance.* Ulysses has, of course, ensured that Ajax
        was chosen by a rigged *lottery* (I.3.374–5), not by
        chance.

134   *skittish* fickle

135   *play the idiots* act like fools (by not attending to Fortune)

137   *fasting in his wantonness.* The idea is that in his arrogance he starves his pride, which needs to be sustained. For *fasting*, F has 'feasting', perhaps catching 'ea' from *eats* in the previous line; the context requires the antithesis of *fasting*.

141   *shrinking* recoiling in fear. Q has 'shriking' (perhaps meaning 'shrieking'), which makes sense, but the revision or correction in F is more vivid.

145   *Time ... back.* The image of Time as an old man carrying a satchel was commonplace; see the Introduction, pages 25–9, for the importance of time in the play.

     wallet bag, knapsack

147   *A great-sized monster of ingratitudes.* The *monster* could be Time, as *edax rerum*, the consumer of all things, or *oblivion*, as representing ingratitude for good deeds forgotten: the charity of time is to give to oblivion.

150   *Perseverance* (accented on the second syllable)

152   *mail* coat of mail. In Chaucer's *Troilus and Criseyde*, V.1559, Hector wears medieval armour of chain-mail.

153   *monumental mockery* (that is, a monument to mock the former wearer of it)

     instant quickest

155   *abreast* (literally, side by side, but in this *strait* only a single file is possible)

156   *emulation.* Ulysses appeals here to rivalry and fashion, keeping up with others, not to the higher values of order and degree he canvassed in I.3.

158   *hedge* shift, go

     forthright straight path ahead

161–3   *Or ... trampled on.* These lines from F (omitted in Q) vividly suggest a ruthlessness of competition.

162   *the abject rear* the unregarded who bring up the rear. F has 'the abiect, neere', which looks deliberate because of the comma, but 'nearly over-run' makes poor sense.

166   *slightly* casually

172   *bone* (equivalent to 'body')

173   *Love, friendship, charity*. Charity, or Christian compassion, is the highest form of love, superior to the other terms; they would recall perhaps for Shakespeare's audience St Paul's appeal to faith, hope, and charity in 1 Corinthians 13, and his insistence that 'Charity faileth never away' (verse 8).

175   *nature* (that is, human nature as frail and easily led astray)

176   *gauds* trinkets, ornaments

177   *Though they are made . . . of things past* (that is, though there is really nothing new about them)

179   *laud* praise

181   *complete* (accented on the first syllable) perfectly accomplished

184   *The cry went . . . on thee* (that is, you were talked of by everyone)

187   *case* hide, cover as with a case

189   *Made emulous missions 'mongst the gods* (that is, made the gods go into battle on both sides in the attempt to imitate or rival Achilles)

190   *faction* fighting, dissension

192   *heroical* appropriate to a hero

194   *one of Priam's daughters* (the first allusion to Polyxena, who is named only once, at line 208)

196   *providence* foresight

197   *Pluto's gold*. Pluto, god of the underworld, is here, as often in Shakespeare's age, confused with Plutus, god of wealth.

198   *uncomprehensive* fathomless (what cannot be comprehended)

199–200 *Keeps place . . . cradles* (that is, keeps abreast with what is thought and almost, with godlike prescience, anticipates thoughts before they are uttered)

201   *whom* (rather than 'which' because the *state* is personified as having a *soul*)
        relation report

204   *expressure* expression

205   *commerce* intercourse

206   *As perfectly is ours as yours* is as well-known to us as it is to you

209   *Pyrrhus.* The son of Achilles, he remained at home until after the death of Achilles at the hands of Paris, when he came to Troy to avenge his father.

210   *trump* trumpet (the common attribute of fame)

213   *him* (Hector)

214   *lover* friend

215   *The fool slides o'er the ice that you should break* (that is, the fool Ajax is taking chances in an action Achilles should undertake)

216   *moved* roused, pleaded with

222   *the weak wanton Cupid.* Patroclus refers both to Polyxena and to himself, later called by Thersites, to his face, Achilles' *masculine whore* (V.1.17).

228   *shrewdly gored* severely wounded

231   *Seals a commission to a blank of danger* (that is, opens the door to all kinds of dangers; literally, authorizes a warrant left blank for danger to fill it in. Patroclus does not specify, but seems to be hinting that inactivity generates fear.)

232   *taints* weakens or damages

235   *fool* (another allusion to Thersites as a professional fool; see II.1.85)

237   *a woman's longing* (suggesting the love–hate relationship of the enemy warriors)

239   *weeds* garments

244–5   *asking for himself* (that is, for a jakes, or privy)

251–2   *a stride and a stand* (that is, takes a pace or two, then comes to a stop)

252–3   *an hostess that hath no arithmetic but her brain* (that is, an innkeeper who cannot count, and for whom a great effort is required in reckoning up a bill)

254   *politic regard* appearance of shrewdness

262–3   *a . . . land-fish* (a fish that lives on land, an unnatural creature)

263   *of* on

264   *opinion* (1) conceit (what Ajax thinks of himself); (2) reputation (what others think of him). Ajax, puffed up by the *voices* of the Greek leaders (see I.3.374–83), by

their *opinion*, has become himself overweening. (So the two *sides* of opinion are identical, like a reversible jacket.)

264–5   *a leather jerkin* (a jacket, usually sleeveless, made of unlined leather, and so reversible)

269   *professes* makes a profession of

270   *arms* weapons

put on his presence behave as he does

293   *God buy you* (abbreviating 'God be with you') goodbye

300   *tune* temper, frame of mind

303–4   *fiddler Apollo* (jokingly alluding to Apollo, who, as patron of music, usually was figured as playing a lute – nothing so common as a fiddle)

304   *catlings* strings for musical instruments

307   *capable* able to understand

IV.1   The meeting takes place near the house of Cressida. Both the Trojans and Diomedes are accompanied by servants with torches to show it is a night scene (or rather early morning before dawn).

9   *Witness the process of your speech* as the drift of your account made clear

within indoors (and, in a theatre, behind the stage)

10   *by days* (that is, every day)

12   *question* discussion, negotiation

17   *contention and occasion meet* the chance offers for us to fight

19   *policy* craft

21   *humane gentleness* friendly courtesy

22–3   *Anchises . . . Venus*. Aeneas swears first by his father, then by his mother, perhaps symbolizing the intertwining of love and war here, as in Hector's challenge to the Greeks (I.3.264–83).

26   *sympathize* are in accord

28   *complete* (accented on the first syllable)

29   *emulous* greedy for praise

35   *What business . . . early*. Paris draws Aeneas aside to confer privately with him

41   *constantly* confidently

44	*note* notice
45	*quality whereof* nature of our business or purpose
57	*making any scruple of her soilure* being deterred by the stain (of her adultery)
58	*charge* (load of) trouble or expense
60	*palating* noticing (on your palate)
62	*puling* whining
63	*flat tamed piece* (playing on various meanings: 'flat' or stale beer; 'taming' or tapping a cask; 'piece' as a term for a cask or butt, and as used scornfully of a woman)
66	*poised* balanced
67	*he as you, each heavier.* Q's reading, 'he as he, the heauier', and F's 'he as he, which heauier' fail to complete the equation between the two, and emendation is necessary: each weigh the same, and each is *heavier*, weighed down or afflicted (with distress or guilt).
71	*scruple* minute amount (literally, one twenty-fourth of an ounce)
72	*carrion* corrupt, rotten
76	*chapmen* dealers
79	*We'll . . . sell.* Paris says, in effect, 'we will not praise Helen because we have no intention of selling her'.

IV.2	Troilus and Cressida entered Cressida's or Calchas's 'house' at the end of III.2, and have spent a night together. It is now morning, and at the Globe the lovers probably entered on the main stage; Pandarus enters at line 22 through the same door, which is now open, and the knocking of Aeneas could have been heard at another door, through which he enters at line 43. For this scene the stage, as in III.1, becomes an interior, a room in the house.
3	*unbolt the gates* (so that Troilus can leave the 'house')
5	*attachment* arrest, seizure
9	*ribald* irreverently noisy
12	*venomous wights* embittered persons
19	*What's* why are. (*What* means 'for what'.)
23	*how go* what price

30   *suffer others* allow others to be so

31–2   *capocchia* (an Italian word) simpleton. Pandarus jokingly treats Cressida as if she were a naughty child.

34   *he* (Pandarus; Cressida is speaking to Troilus here)
         knocked i'th'head put to death (but spoken as knocking at the door is heard?)

50   *doth import him much* is of great importance to him

54   *Whoa!* Aeneas brings himself up as if stopping a horse, and switches from blank verse to a style matching Pandarus's prose.

55   *to be* as to be

60   *rash* urgent

66   *concluded* determined

67   *state* council

92   *bane* ruin

96   *consanguinity* kinship, blood-relationship

IV.3   Troilus and Aeneas, who left Cressida's 'house' at IV.2.73, have met with Diomedes outside, and a stage-door now becomes an entry to it (line 5). Paris and Troilus talk apart until the last line, and the others must be grouped separately on stage.

1   *great morning* full day (further marking the passage of time since the night, IV.1.43, when the delegation gathered, and the dawn when Troilus rose, IV.2.1)

3   *Comes fast upon* follows rapidly thereafter

6   *presently* right away

IV.4   The stage becomes again the interior of Cressida's house, and as Troilus and the others walked into it from outside through one door (see IV.3.5 and 12), so now Troilus follows Pandarus and Cressida back on stage through another door; the dialogue itself establishes the locations.

3   *full* absolutely

4   *violenteth* rages. F has 'no lesse', which looks like an attempt to revise the Q reading, but makes no sense and wrecks the metre.

7   *brew it to a weak and colder palate* dilute it to a weak and colder taste, or make myself feel it less strongly. Compare Troilus's use of similar language at III.2.16–19.

8   *allayment* dilution

9   *qualifying dross* impurity lessening the force of it

13   *pair of spectacles* sights (but also implying that Pandarus is looking at them through spectacles)

14   *the goodly saying.* No source has been found for these lines, which Pandarus says or sings as if from a well-known ballad or *rhyme*.

23   *strained* refined (as if filtered through a strainer)

24   *as* as if
       fancy love

32   *suddenly* at once
       injury of chance wrong inflicted by chance events

33   *Puts back* denies

34   *beguiles* deprives

35   *rejoindure* reunion

36   *embrasures* embraces. The word is a coinage, like *rejoindure* in the previous line; 'embrasure' in the modern sense, relating to openings in walls or to windows, is first recorded in 1702.

37   *labouring* (as if in the labour of childbirth)

40   *discharge* (quibbling on the sense 'payment')

42   *Crams his rich thievery up* (that is, presses his stolen property of farewell kisses into too short a time. *Thievery* also suggests Time stealing in the sense of silent movement.)

44   *consigned kisses to them* each confirmed or sealed with a kiss

46   *scants us with* limits us to

47   *Distasted* spoiled, made distasteful
       broken (interrupted by sobs)

49   *the Genius* (the guardian spirit allotted to each person at birth, to guide his fortunes, and lead him at his death out of this world)

52   *lay this wind* lay to rest, moderate, my sighs. Pandarus's absurd hyperbole brings a comic touch to the lovers' parting.

55   *merry Greeks*. See I.2.110 and the note.

56   *see* meet, see each other

58   *deem* thought

59–60   *we must use expostulation kindly, | For it is parting from us*
        (that is, protestation must be treated gently, like a
        parting guest, for shortly we will not be able to talk at
        all)

62   *glove* (that is, in formal challenge)

63   *maculation* stain of impurity

64   *fashion in* introduce the form of

65   *sequent* ensuing

69   *sleeve*. Sleeves were detachable, and still in
        Shakespeare's day could be regarded as separate
        garments and given as tokens; but the suggestion
        came from Chaucer's *Troilus and Criseyde*, V.1043,
        where Criseyde gives a sleeve to Diomed.

75   *quality* accomplishments

77   *arts and exercise* (that is, well-practised in *arts* as both
        acquired skills (such as conversation) and trickery,
        wiles)

78   *parts* natural gifts
        person bodily presence

79   *godly jealousy* (echoing St Paul's words in 2 Corin-
        thians 11.2, 'I am jealous over you with godly
        jealousy; for I have coupled you to one man'. Troilus
        insists on treating Cressida as though she were his
        wife; see the Introduction, page 14.)

84   *mainly* strongly

85   *lavolt* (or lavolta; a dance involving high leaps)

86   *subtle* (1) clever; (2) cunning or crafty

87   *pregnant* receptive

89   *dumb-discoursive* (that communicates without speech)

93   *will not* do not will or intend

96   *changeful potency* strength which proves unreliable

102   *opinion* reputation

104   *crowns* (as coins, and as the crown of the head; for all
        his *plainness*, Troilus skilfully plays with words)

106   *moral* meaning

110   *port* gate (of the city of Troy)

111   *possess* inform

112   *Entreat her fair* deal with her courteously

124   *servant* professed lover. Troilus responds in the language of courtly love to Diomed's submission to Cressida as his *mistress*, line 119.

125   *even for my charge* because I tell you to do so. Diomed ignored Troilus's courteous request, and Troilus resorts to giving orders.

126   *dreadful* awe-inspiring
       Pluto (god of the underworld)

129   *place* office (as ambassador)

131   *answer to my lust* respond (to your challenge) at my pleasure (but also 'pursue my own desire', with reference to Cressida)

133   *but that* but because. Diomedes refuses to value Cressida according to what Troilus says about her.

136   *brave* defiance

145   *address* prepare

147   *chivalry*. See I.2.229, I.3.283 and the notes.

V.5   Diomedes, escorted to the *port* or gate of Troy at IV.4.138, arrives back among the Greeks at line 16 of this scene. The two scenes are linked by the trumpets sounding at IV.4.138 and IV.5.11, and there is no time interval; the Greeks need to sweep on even as Aeneas leaves. It is not clear whether Ajax and Hector fight off-stage or on stage (lines 93 and 112). The Greeks and Trojans group separately to watch, and Aeneas and Diomedes act as marshals; then Agamemnon and the rest of the Greeks join with the Trojans at line 158, where F has the stage direction '*Enter Agamemnon and the rest*'.

1   *appointment* outfit, equipment

2   *starting* bounding (or 'eager to get started')

6   *trumpet* trumpeter

8   *spherèd bias cheek* cheek blown up like a distended sphere

9   *colic of puffed Aquilon*. Aquilon is the name of the north wind, often shown on old maps, with other winds, as faces puffing hard as if griped by colic.

12	*early days* early in the day
14	*ken* recognize
21	*in general* by everyone, and by all the generals of the Greek army
24	*winter* (that is, old age as cold)
28	*popped* came in suddenly
	hardiment boldness. The verse changes into rhyming couplets, suiting the flippancy of the repartee.
31	*horns* (cuckold's horns; see I.2.165 and the note)
33	*trim* fine (ironically)
36	*do you render or receive?* Hitherto silent, Cressida now joins in the ironic and bawdy wordplay, recalling her liveliness in talking with Pandarus in I.2, and rapidly adapting to her new companions; see the Introduction, page 16.
37	*make my match to live* wager my life
40	*boot* odds, the advantage
41–4	*odd ... odd ... odd ... odd* (playing on the senses of odd as (1) strange; (2) single, standing alone; (3) extraneous, odd-man-out; and (4) as variously opposed to *even*)
45	*fillip me o'the head* (that is, remind me I am a cuckold)
46	*your nail against his horn* (that is, the nail with which she fillips or flicks his head, his cuckold's *horn*)
48	*beg then.* This breaks the sequence of couplets, and *then* has sometimes been emended to 'too' or 'two'; but perhaps the discord shows Cressida's recognition that Ulysses is not playing by the same rules as the others.
50	*his* Menelaus's
54	*quick sense* lively feeling. (Nestor may mean no more, but Ulysses brings out the possible implication of sensuality.)
57	*motive* moving limb
59	*give accosting welcome* (that is, give welcome to the addresses of a suitor)
60	*tables* writing-tablets, notebooks
61	*tickling reader* reader who excites or stimulates (making explicit the sexual innuendo in these lines)
62	*sluttish spoils of opportunity* (that is, loose and easy prey

to any man who takes occasion to approach them)

63   *the game* (that is, the game of love or sexual play)

64   *Trojan's trumpet* (that is, Hector's trumpeter, responding to Ajax's, line 11). This could be heard also as 'Trojan strumpet', referring to Cressida.
    (stage direction) *Paris . . . Helenus*. Neither speaks in the scene, but they swell the crowd to watch the fight.

65   *state* council of state

65–6   *What shall be done | To* (that is, how shall we honour)

67   *knights* (here and at lines 75, 86, 88, and 96, associated with medieval chivalry; see I.3.283 and the note)

68   *to the edge of all extremity* (that is, to the death)

70   *voice or order of the field* decision (that is, the judgement of a marshal or umpire) or regulation (as at line 90) of the field of honour

72   *conditions* whatever rules are stipulated

73   *securely* over-confidently

74   *disprizing* undervaluing

77   *whate'er* (that is, no matter what you think)

83   *half made of Hector's blood* (as his first cousin; see line 120)

87   *maiden battle* fight with no blood shed

92   *breath* breather, bout of exercise (as at II.3.111)

94   *opposed* set face to face

95   *heavy* grave, solemn

96   *a true knight*. F adds 'they call him *Troylus*', a phrase repeated at line 108; probably this marks a cut, and lines 97–107 were omitted in performance.

98   *deedless in his tongue* not boasting about his deeds

100   *free* generous (in feeling and in giving)

103   *impair* hurtful, injurious. Shakespeare seems to have made an adjective from the verb 'to impair'.

105–6   *subscribes | To tender objects* gives in, relents at pitiful sights

107   *vindicative* (the usual spelling until the seventeenth century) vindictive

111   *Even to his inches* (that is, thoroughly, from top to toe)
    with private soul (that is, with absolute sincerity in private talk)

112   *translate* explain

112   (stage direction) *Alarum*. Trumpets play throughout the fight between Hector and Ajax, as the direction at line 116 shows.

120   *my father's sister's son*. Various sources, notably Ovid's *Metamorphoses* XI, make Ajax the son of Hesione, Hector's aunt (see also Bullough, VI.198).

121   *cousin-german* first cousin

124   *conmixion* blending

128   *dexter cheek, and this sinister* (terms used in heraldry; Hector turns Ajax's face into a shield, with his cheeks as the right (*dexter*) and left (*sinister*) sides)

129   *multipotent* very powerful (but not quite omnipotent)

131   *impressure* mark, impression

132   *rank* overblown, swollen too great. Compare I.3.318.

136   *him that thunders* (that is, Jupiter)

139   *free* generous (as at line 100)

141   *addition* distinction

142   *Neoptolemus* Achilles. His son was called Pyrrhus Neoptolemus, and Shakespeare seems to have assumed this was a family name; or perhaps he confused the reference to 'cruell Neoptolemus' in Golding's Ovid, XIII.545, with the 'cruell ghost' of Achilles who had just appeared to demand the death of Polyxena (XIII.547).

     mirable marvellous

143   *oyez* hear ye! (the call of the public crier announcing a proclamation)

150   *seld* seldom

     have the chance (that is, to meet with and make requests to Hector)

     desire invite

156   *the expecters of our Trojan part* (that is, those on our Trojan side who await news of the outcome)

157   *Desire them home* ask them to return home

162   *portly* imposing, grand

163   *arms* (that is, the arms of battle, and the arms of embracement: the embracing of the Greek and Trojan soldiers in this scene ironically links with the embracing of the lovers, Paris and Helen, Troilus and Cressida)

165–70   *But that's . . . integrity.* These lines are not in Q. If they were added later, they strengthen the play's concern with time; see III.3.145 ff. and the Introduction, page 26.

169   *hollow bias-drawing* insincere turning from the truth

172   *imperious* imperial, supreme in authority

177,255   *Mars his.* 'His' was frequently used for ''s' by Shakespeare, especially after a proper name.

178   *affect* show preference for
     untraded unfamiliar

179   *quondam* former

184   *Labouring for destiny* doing the work of fate (or more strictly of Atropos, that one of the three Fates responsible for cutting the thread of human life)

186   *Perseus* (who rode the winged horse Pegasus; see I.3.42)
     Phrygian. See the Prologue, line 7 and the note.

187   *forfeits and subduements* (that is, men who have yielded themselves to be killed, or to be subdued and conquered)

189   *decline on the declined* fall on those already vanquished

190   *standers-by* followers (modern 'bystanders')

194   *an Olympian* (1) an athlete in the Olympic games; (2) a god (Mount Olympus was the fabled seat of Jupiter)

195   *still* continually

196   *grandsire* (Laomedon, King of Troy, a famous warrior, and father of Priam)

199   *embrace thee.* See the note to line 163.

213   *favour* face, appearance

216   *Greekish embassy.* According to Caxton's *Recuyell*, when the Greeks reached Troy, they captured the outpost Tenedos, and sent Diomedes and Ulysses on an embassy to offer to withdraw and return home, provided Helen were yielded up and reparations made for her rape by Paris. Ulysses prophesied that if Priam refused the offer (as he did), Troy would fall and be destroyed (see Bullough, VI.195–6).

219   *pertly* boldly

220   *wanton* arrogant
     buss kiss

225   *that old common arbitrator, Time.* Hector's comment is
      proverbial, but the personification of Time relates to
      lines 202–3; see also lines 165–70 and the note.

230   *thee . . . thou.* The use of *thee* and *thou* in this way is
      insulting, and shows Achilles' irritation at being left
      out of account in this scene.

232   *exact* (accented on the first syllable)

233   *quoted joint by joint* scrutinized limb by limb (but with
      hints of the butchery to come in the use of the term
      joint)

235   *fair* in full view

239   *of sport* about hunting

248   *Stand again.* This could mean that Achilles knelt at
      line 242, and now stands; but Hector may merely be
      saying 'stand still and let me look at you again'.

249   *pleasantly* to your satisfaction

250   *prenominate in nice conjecture* name beforehand in
      precise forecast

255   *stithied* wrought (from 'stithy', meaning originally an
      anvil)

260   *chafe thee* get angry

261   *you, Achilles* (distancing him, after the familiar *thee* he
      uses in speaking to Hector)

262   *bring you to 't* (that is, bring you to face him in the field
      of battle)

264   *state* council of war

265   *entreat you to be odd* prevail on you to be at strife

267   *pelting* petty, trivial

269   *fell* ruthless

272   *in the full convive you* let you amply feast together

274   *severally entreat him* individually invite him

275   *taborins* drums

278   *keep* dwell

280   *There Diomed doth feast.* Ulysses has been on stage
      throughout the scene, and could not know this;
      but Shakespeare in this way deftly prepares for
      V.2.

287   *gentle* courteously
      honour standing, reputation

293   *still* now as always

food for fortune's tooth (that is, subject to change and accident)

V.1   After the fight in the morning between Hector and Ajax, the Trojan lords have feasted at Agamemnon's tent, and now night has come; but there is no need to assume a break in the action here, as it moves to the tent of Achilles, the location of III.3. Here the location (perhaps one of the stage-doors draped, or a projecting canopy between the doors) has *lights* (line 64) to show that the scene takes place at night; the group bringing Hector at line 62 act as if they are lost until they notice the lights at Achilles' tent.

5   *botch* tumour or boil. Q and F have 'batch', a number of loaves baked together, an error suggested by *crusty*.

8   *fragment* scrap of leftover food (as at V.2.162)

9   *fool* (quibbling on 'fool' as a dessert)

10   *keeps the tent* stays in the tent (as Achilles has been doing up to this point). Thersites replies by taking *tent* in the sense of a roll of gauze used to clean a wound.

12   *adversity* perverseness
       what need what's the point of

17   *masculine whore.* As so often, Thersites may here be maliciously exaggerating; the play does not clearly define the nature of the affection between Achilles and Patroclus, as expressed notably in III.3.216–25.

18   *diseases of the south* (like the *Neapolitan bone-ache* of II.3.18)

19   *gravel i'th'back* stones in the kidneys (*gravel* properly applies to the crystals that form in the urine)
       lethargies conditions of drowsy torpor

19–20   *and the like.* This phrase of F replaces an extended list of diseases in Q, probably cut for the sake of economy (see the Collations, page 241).

20–21   *preposterous discoveries* revelations of what is contrary to nature

25   *ruinous butt* rotten cask (and hence empty)

26   *indistinguishable* shapeless. This is often taken as alluding to the deformity of Thersites, but probably

belongs in the currency of abuse here, without any special application; see the Introduction, page 22.

27   *exasperate* incensed

28   *sleave-silk* (silk thread used in embroidery)
      sarcenet (soft silky cloth)

29   *tassel of a prodigal's purse* useless ornament on an empty purse (as a prodigal spends all his money)

32   *gall* (as bitter, or perhaps 'gall' as an irritating sore or blister)

33   *Finch-egg* (a term expressing contempt)

38   *taxing me and gaging me* charging me and binding me by promise

42   *trim* make ready

45   *blood* passion, moodiness

49   *quails* (1) birds eaten as a delicacy; (2) courtesans

50–51   *Jupiter there, his brother, the bull* (referring to Menelaus, Agamemnon's brother; Jupiter took the shape of a bull to rape Europa, and the bull's horns suggest the cuckold's horns)

51   *primitive* original

52   *oblique* indirect (as Jupiter was not himself a cuckold)
      thrifty worthy (ironically)
      shoeing-horn hanger-on; someone used as a tool by another

55   *forced* stuffed

56   *ass and ox* fool and cuckold

57   *fitchew* polecat

58   *puttock* kite or buzzard

61   *care not to be* would not object to being
      lazar leper
      so provided that

62   *Spirits and fires.* Those entering carry torches, and look like will o'the wisps or spirits.

64   *lights* (marking the 'tent' of Achilles; perhaps brackets or portable stands in which candles or torches were set)

71   *draught* cesspool
      sink privy

79   *tide* appointed time

81   *Calchas' tent* (where Cressida lodges with her father)

85   *unjust* dishonest

87   *spend his mouth* give tongue or bark like a hunting dog sighting the quarry

87–8   *Brabbler the hound* (a hound that makes a lot of noise but does little; the more usual form is 'babbler', from 'babble', to chatter or give tongue without reason)

89   *prodigious* ominous

89–90   *The sun borrows of the moon when* (that is to say, it will never happen that)

91   *leave to see* give up seeing

91–2   *dog him* follow Diomedes closely

92   *uses* frequents, haunts

V.2   The action now moves to the tent of Calchas (V.1.93), presumably a different location from the tent of Achilles, entered by Hector at V.1.83. Cressida must enter from her father's 'tent', and if this was one of the stage-doors at the Globe, she and Diomedes would have been upstage right or left, with Troilus and Ulysses further downstage on the other side, and Thersites still further downstage behind them. This is guesswork, of course, but the staging of this brilliant scene, in which the audience watches Thersites watching Troilus watching Cressida, is especially interesting.

6   *torch* (probably mounted in a bracket or portable stand to mark the 'tent' of Calchas; see V.1.64 and the note)

      discover reveal

10   *sing any man at first sight* take any man's measure as if sight-reading music

12   *clef* (in music, the sign fixing the pitch of the notes; but also quibbling on 'cleft', the parting of the thighs)

      noted notorious (quibbling on 'notes' of music)

23   *tell a pin!* (that is, 'talk of trivialities!', or 'try to deceive me if you can!')

24   *I cannot* (that is, keep the promise referred to in *remember*, lines 13–14)

25   *open* (that is, sexually available)

33   *fool* dupe

42   *You flow to great distraction* (that is, your rising tide of feeling is leading to violent disturbance of your mind)

47   *truth* loyalty, faith

49   *palter* equivocate

56   *luxury* lust

57   *potato-finger.* Introduced into England in the sixteenth century, potatoes were initially thought of as aphrodisiacs.

        Fry burn with lust

59   *lo* (perhaps merely emphatic (most editors emend to 'la'), but possibly meaning 'behold', 'see if I don't')

63   *will not be myself* (that is, will subdue my feelings and forget my identity)

66   *sleeve* (given to her as a pledge by Troilus at IV.4.69)

76   *sharpens* (that is, intensifies the desire of Diomedes)

83   *memorial dainty kisses* loving kisses of remembrance

94   *Diana's waiting-women* (that is, the stars; Diana, goddess of chastity, was associated with the moon)

104   *starts* causes you to start going

105-6   *Nor I . . . best.* In Q and F this speech is set as prose and given to Thersites; but it makes perfect verse, and is appropriate to Troilus, who twice elsewhere swears by Pluto (IV.4.126 and line 156 of this scene).

105   *likes* suits

107   *plagued* vexed (by memories of Troilus, and by the sense of her own depravity or *turpitude*, line 114)

111   *poor our* our poor

115   *A proof of strength she could not publish more* she could not give out a stronger demonstration

118   *recordation* solemn memorization

120   *co-act* behave together

123   *esperance* hope

124   *attest* testimony

125   *deceptious* (Shakespeare's coinage, displaced by the modern 'deceptive')

127   *conjure* summon spirits

128-9   *She was not, sure | Most sure she was* (printed here as prose, but possibly a short verse line, lacking two

216

syllables; perhaps a word was omitted in the print-shop)

130 *negation* denial

132 *for* out of respect for

134 *stubborn* hostile

134-5 *without a theme | For depravation* lacking any reason for raising the issue of depravity

135 *square* judge, measure

139 *swagger himself out on's own eyes* talk himself by mere bluster out of believing what he saw

140-63 *This she . . . to Diomed.* Troilus seeks emotionally to come to terms with what has happened, but cannot reason away contradictions; this speech conveys his emotion powerfully and painfully, and if the sense of it is not easily grasped, this does not perhaps matter greatly.

142 *sanctimony* (that is, held sacred)

144 *rule in unity* principle or law in the union (of two lovers such as myself and Cressida)

145-7 *O madness . . . revolt.* Reasoning seems to Troilus mad and self-contradictory (*with and against itself*) because he cannot reconcile heart and head, the love he wants to believe in (the *credence in my heart*, line 122), with what he has just seen and heard. Hence reason is a double (*Bifold*) authority, denying the evidence without *perdition*, the loss of reason, or of his *credence* in Cressida, while at the same time demonstrating his own madness, or loss of reason, and loss of Cressida.

150 *conduce* go on, continue

151 *inseparate* united, undividable

154 *orifex* opening
subtle fine

155 *Ariachne's broken woof* (alluding to the story of Arachne, who boasted of her skill in weaving, and was changed to a spider by Athene, who tore asunder the web she had been making (*woof* literally means the cross-threads in weaving). The spelling suggests conflation with Ariadne, who used a thread to enable Theseus to find a way through the labyrinth of Minos

217

in Crete. Both stories are told in Golding's Ovid, VI.162–81 and VIII.231–5.)

156 *Instance* (example adduced to prove a general point)
  Pluto's gates. Pluto was god of the underworld or Hades, the entrance to which was guarded by the three-headed monster Cerberus.

157 *tied with the bonds of heaven.* Troilus thinks of the 'bond' as if he and Cressida were married, though his aim all along had been to seduce her; for the ironies at play in this scene, see the Introduction, pages 15–16.

159 *dissolved* untied

160 *knot, five-finger-tied* (a love-knot formed by joining hands with Diomedes)

161 *fractions* fragments
  orts leavings, refuse

163 *o'er-eaten* eaten away all over

164–5 *attached* | *With that* seized with (such a devotion as) that

167 *Mars his* Mars's (see IV.5.177 and the note)

168 *fancy* love

173 *casque* helmet
  Vulcan (god of fire and of metal-working)

175 *hurricano* water-spout

176 *Constringed* drawn together

177 *dizzy* make dizzy
  Neptune (god of the sea)

178 *prompted* urged on, eager

180 *He'll tickle it for his concupy* (that is, he'll beat Diomed's helmet for the sake of his mistress (concubine) or lust (concupiscence)). Shakespeare coined the term *concupy*, though 'concuby' is recorded earlier as a variant of 'concubine'.

181–2 *false Cressid . . . stainèd name.* Compare III.2.181–94.

184 *passion* passionate outburst

190 *wear a castle on thy head* (that is, protect yourself as strongly as you can)

194 *raven* (a bird of ill omen)
  bode make predictions

195 *intelligence* news

197 *commodious drab* accommodating harlot

still always

198–9 *burning* (associated both with hell and with the effects of venereal disease)

V.3 The night of the previous scene gives way to day as this scene takes us to Troy, where Hector is already armed in the morning for battle. Presumably the torches were at some point put out or taken off stage (perhaps on the entry of Aeneas at V.2.184). This scene, in which nothing can hold Hector or Troilus back from fighting, contrasts with I.1, in which Troilus could hardly be persuaded to arm for battle.

4 *train* induce, lead me on
   offend hurt, annoy

9 *dear* heart-felt

14 *notes of sally* (trumpet-call announcing a warrior's setting forth to do battle)

16 *peevish* headstrong

18 *spotted livers*. In sacrifices of animals to the gods, the entrails were examined, and a tainted or blemished liver was a sign of ill-omen.

20–22 *To hurt . . .* CASSANDRA (not in Q, which gives lines 23–5 to Andromache)

20 *just* true to your oath

21 *For* because

26 *keeps the weather of* stays to windward of (and so is ahead, has the advantage over)

27 *the dear* the truly honourable or worthy (the original meaning of 'dear')

29 *young man.* Troilus is *very young* (I.2.116–18), but Hector's insistence here on his youth (lines 31, 35) seems ironic in relation to Troilus's recent painful experiences.

30 *father* father-in-law (Priam)

31 *harness* armour

32 *chivalry.* See I.3.283 and the note.

34 *brushes* clashes

38 *lion* (as a type of nobility and generosity)

48 *ruthful work* (that is, slaughter that excites others to

pity, as opposed to *ruth* (pity) in Troilus or Hector themselves)

49   *'tis wars*. Troilus means he is determined to fight, and that there is no mercy in war; his term contrasts with Hector's *chivalry* (line 32).

53   *fiery truncheon*. The adjective is transferred: it is Mars, the god of war, who is *fiery*; and in mythology he did not carry a *truncheon* (the baton with which a marshal controlled a formal encounter between knights).

       retire withdrawal

54   *Hecuba*. Priam's queen is named six times in the play (beginning at I.2.1); see lines 63 and 83 in this scene, where her presence is felt, though Shakespeare does not give her a part.

55   *o'ergallèd* swollen and sore

       recourse repeated flow

58   *But by my ruin* (that is, unless you were to kill me; this half-line is not in Q, perhaps inadvertently omitted)

60   *stay* support

65   *enrapt* inspired

69   *the faith of valour* (that is, the trust they put in my courage)

73   *shame respect* (that is, violate the respect due to you by disobeying you)

74   *voice* vote, approval

80   *bodements* forebodings

84   *dolour* lamentations

86   *antics* grotesque clowns

89   *soft* (equivalent to 'wait and listen')

90   *deceive* delude

91   *amazed* alarmed

       exclaim outcry

95–6   *believe* | *I come . . . sleeve*. The rhyme and the implied stage direction in *I come* mark Troilus's attempt to exit here.

101   *tisick* phthisic (consumptive cough)

104   *rheum* discharge

105   *ache in my bones* (suggesting syphilis, the *Neapolitan bone-ache* of II.3.18)

110   *errors* false beliefs

111   *with her deeds.* The text in F continues with the lines repeated at V.10.33–4; see the Account of the Text, page 232.

V.4   The sound of an *Alarum* at V.3.94 anticipated the transition here to the battlefield between the Grecian tents and Troy; the rest of the action is played out with numerous entries and exits by Greeks and Trojans fighting in the next three scenes, marking the ebb and flow of battle.

    (stage direction) *excursions* assaults

1   *clapper-clawing* beating, mauling

8   *luxurious* lecherous

    of a sleeveless errand (1) on a fruitless journey; (2) without the sleeve

9   *policy* crafty plotting (but also 'statecraft', as at line 16)

    crafty-swearing affirming in craft

12   *me.* See I.2.120 and the note.

    in policy by a contrivance

16–17   *proclaim barbarism ... opinion* declare the end of civilization, and statecraft gets a bad reputation

19   *take the river Styx* (that is, try to escape by jumping into the river that bounds the underworld; see III.2.8–9 and the note)

20   *miscall retire* wrongly name withdrawal

21   *advantageous care* timely caution

22   *odds of multitude* disadvantage of being greatly outnumbered

31   *God-a-mercy* (equivalent to 'thank God')

35   *in a sort* in a way

    lechery eats itself (perhaps because the lecher is destroyed by venereal disease, but recalling the more general self-destruction caused by *appetite*; see I.3.121–4)

V.5   Diomedes' capture of Troilus's horse is taken from Caxton's *Recuyell* (Bullough, VI.204), and

Shakespeare uses it to recall the language of courtly love and chivalry, in such terms as *service* and *knight*; see, for example, IV.4.124 and IV.5.96.

5   *by proof* (that is, having stood the test of battle)

6–8   *Polydamas ... Menon ... Margarelon ... Doreus.* These names, like the others mentioned in this scene, are all found in the account of the battles prior to the death of Hector in Caxton's *Recuyell* (Bullough, VI.197 ff.). Polydamas, a bastard son of Priam, and Margarelon (Margareton in the source) were Trojan warriors; Menon, Achilles' cousin, and Doreus, a companion of Ajax, were Greeks.

9   *colossus-wise.* The *colossus*, one of the seven wonders of the world, was a statue of Apollo that stood astride the entrance to the harbour at Rhodes.

       beam (suggesting a huge weapon, a pole or club)

10   *pashèd* smashed

11   *Epistrophus and Cedius* (in Caxton's *Recuyell*, two brothers, both killed by Hector)

       Polyxenes (another Greek warrior slain by Hector in Caxton's *Recuyell*)

12   *Amphimachus and Thoas.* Amphimachus was a companion of Ajax, and Thoas a cousin of Achilles, according to Caxton.

13   *Palamedes.* In Caxton's *Recuyell*, he succeeded Agamemnon as leader of the Greeks, and was killed eventually by Paris.

14   *Sagittary* (a centaur, a famous archer, who fought on the side of the Trojans, according to Caxton)

16   (stage direction) *Enter Nestor with soldiers.* Q and F have simply '*Enter Nestor*', but he must come on with soldiers or attendants who can be sent off to carry out his orders.

20   *Galathe* (the name of Hector's horse in Caxton's *Recuyell*)

22   *scalèd schools* schools of fish covered with scales

23   *belching whale.* Shakespeare did not know that whales spout, and do not *belch*, and that they live on plankton, not on fish.

26   *leaves and takes* spares and kills

29   *proof is called impossibility* (that is, you would hardly think it credible)

39   *Engaging and redeeming of himself* taking on a combat and coming out of it unscathed

40   *careless force and forceless care* casual strength (in *Engaging*) and effortless caution (in defending or *redeeming* himself)

41   *luck* (so F; Q has 'lust' (that is, for revenge), but the line contrasts chance with skill or *cunning*)

44   *we draw together.* Now that Ajax and Achilles enter the battle, the Greeks are at last pulling together.

45   *boy-queller* killer of boys

V.6   The usual scene divisions here are arbitrary; the action on the battlefield continues without a break.

3   *correct* punish, chastise

9   *stand* (that is, stand aside)

10   *look upon* be a mere onlooker

11   *cogging* cheating

14   *Pause, if thou wilt.* Hector allows Achilles to break off the fight, and even though Achilles scorns Hector's *courtesy*, he takes advantage of it.

24   *carry him* take him prisoner, carry him off by force

25   *bring him off* rescue him

26   *reck* care

27   *mark* target

29   *frush* smash

V.7   The action continues without a break, though Achilles has had time since his exit at V.6.19 to gather his Myrmidons, the warrior race he led to fight in the Trojan War. It is uncertain how many actors could be spared to group about Achilles here, but it must have been enough to surround him, and provide a sense of overwhelming Hector by brute force. The death of Hector is based upon Caxton's account of the death of Troilus (Bullough, VI.214).

2   *wheel* turn

5   *Impale* surround, fence in (*not* 'transfix', the more usual modern sense)

6   *execute your arms* (that is, follow out my command in wielding your weapons)

7   *my proceedings eye* watch my course of action

10   *bull . . . dog*. Thersites turns the fight into a bull-baiting, with Menelaus *double-horned* as bull and as cuckold.

     'Loo halloo (a cry to urge on dogs to the chase or to bait the bull)

12   *game* victory

     'ware horns beware, avoid the horns (of the *bull* Menelaus, who has won)

V.8   (stage direction) *Enter Hector, carrying a suit of armour.* Q and F have simply '*Enter Hector*', but the text suggests that Hector carries on the *goodly armour* he hunted at the end of V.6, and that he proceeds to take off the armour he wears.

1   *core* body like a core (and 'corpse'?) inside the armour

7   *vail* setting

13   *amain* with all your might

17   *dragon wing* (unexplained; perhaps associated with the terms 'dragon's head' and 'dragon's tail' used to denote the ascending and descending paths of the moon)

18   *stickler-like* like an umpire (at a tournament)

19   *frankly* freely

20   *bait* morsel

     thus goes to bed. This stage direction in the text for Achilles to sheathe his sword shows the failure of Greek policy; Achilles still goes his own way, and has reason to be prouder than ever. See the Introduction, page 21.

V.9   Again, the action continues without a break; the main body of Greeks marches on at one entrance as the Myrmidons leave by another, shouting that Hector is dead.

4   *bruit* noise, rumour

5   *bragless* without boast

7   *patiently* calmly

.10   The action is still continuous, as the Trojans now enter to claim mastery of the battlefield; this is a night scene (see line 2 and V.8.5), so torches may have been in evidence again, as in V.1 and V.2. Neither F nor Q includes *soldiers with drums* in the opening stage direction, but the text at line 30 calls for drums, and the Trojan army is represented here as the Greek army is in V.9.

2   *starve we out* let us endure in bitter cold

5   *sort* manner

7   *smile* (that is, in scorn)

8   *let your brief plagues be mercy* (that is, be merciful, and put us out of our misery quickly)

9   *linger . . . on* delay

13   *imminence* impending evil

14   *Address* make ready

16   *screech-owl* (a bird of ill omen, hence a bearer of bad news)

19   *Niobes.* In Greek legend Niobe, weeping for her dead children, was turned to stone, from which tears continued to flow.

21–2   *away . . . say.* This rhyming couplet marks a conventional exit-line.

24   *pight* (an old form of this past participle) pitched

25   *Titan* (the sun god Hyperion)

26   *coward* (Achilles; the death of Hector makes Troilus forget Diomedes and Cressida)

27   *sunder* keep apart

28   *still* ever

29   *goblins* (malicious spirits, often associated with haunting)

30   *Strike* beat out on drums

        free (unexplained, but perhaps involving the common
        sense 'unrestrained', or quick, as opposed to the dead
        march appropriate for Hector)

30–31   *go ... woe* (another couplet, suggesting, like lines
        21–2, an exit-point for Troilus)

33   *broker-lackey* pander and hanger-on

        Ignomy (shortened from 'ignominy') dishonour

35   *aching bones* (again suggesting syphilis as the cause;
        see V.3.105 and the note)

37   *traitors* (presumably alluding to Calchas, who took
        over Pandarus's role as bawd to Diomedes in V.2)

46–7   *painted cloths* (commonly used as wall-hangings)

48   *Pandar's hall* (suggesting a guild or fraternity of
        panders)

49   *half out* (because of disease)

52   *the hold-door trade* (bawds who collected a fee for
        guarding the door for their clients)

53   *two months hence* (not a reference to a specific date,
        but rather an indication that Pandarus has had
        enough and sees his death approaching)

55   *gallèd* annoyed (or 'oppressed')

        goose of Winchester prostitute (alluding to the brothels
        in Southwark, licensed by the Bishop of Winchester)

56   *sweat* (alluding to the sweating-tub, a common treat-
        ment for venereal disease)

        eases ways of relieving pain

The Prefatory Letter

2–3   *staled with* made stale by performance on

3   *clapper-clawed* (literally, 'beaten, thrashed'; express-
        ing a scornful attitude to public applause. Thersites
        uses the term *clapper-clawing* at V.4.1.)

4   *passing* very

        palm (symbol of excellence)

5   *your brain* (meaning 'the brain (or "talent") you and
        everyone know'. This colloquial usage of *your* was

common, as in Hamlet's 'Your worm is your only
emperor for diet' (*Hamlet*, IV.3.20–21).)

7   *titles* (playing on the meaning 'legal rights to')
plays. The writer of the epistle seems to distinguish
serious plays (perhaps tragedies) from comedies.

8   *grand censors* (probably alluding to the continuing
hostility of the city authorities and businessmen of
London towards plays and players)

9–10   *main grace of* chief honour or credit to

23   *sea that brought forth Venus*. Venus, goddess of love,
sprang, according to legend, from the froth of the sea
near Cyprus. Love is, of course, the main theme of
Shakespeare's romantic comedies.

26   *testern* sixpence

30   *out of sale* no longer available

31   *inquisition* official investigation (with a joking allusion
to the tribunals of the Roman Catholic Holy Office,
especially identified in Shakespeare's time with the
extremities of the Spanish inquisition)

34   *smoky* (probably alluding to the increasingly popular
habit of smoking tobacco, introduced in the 1580s)

35   *'scape* escape into print

36   *grand possessors* (presumbly the company of actors
who owned the manuscript. It seems to have been
normal practice for a dramatist to sell his plays to a
company.)

37   *prayed for them rather than been prayed* (perhaps
'prayed for them (to release the play for printing)
rather than have been prayed (by publishers to
purchase a copy)')

39   *Vale* (pronounced as two syllables; Latin for
'farewell')

AN ACCOUNT OF THE TEXT

On 7 February 1603 James Roberts entered in the Stationers' Register, 'to print when he hath gotten sufficient aucthority for it', the 'book' of *Troilus and Cressida* as acted by the Lord Chamberlain's Men. Perhaps he never obtained the authority of the company, for he did not print the play. On 28 January 1609 'a booke called the history of Troylus & Cressida' was entered by Richard Bonian and Henry Walley, and it was issued as a quarto in the same year, with a title-page headed 'The Historie of Troylus and Cresseida. *As it was acted by the Kings Maiesties* seruants at the Globe'. While the play was at the press, this first title-page was withdrawn, and another one substituted, reading 'The Famous Historie of Troylus *and* Cresseid. *Excellently expressing the beginning* of their loues, with the conceited wooing of *Pandarus* Prince of *Licia*'. At the same time an epistle was added (see page 161), describing the play as a comedy, asserting it to be 'a new play, neuer staled with the stage', and implying that the 'grand possessors' (the Lord Chamberlain's Men, now the King's Men under James I) had not released it for publication.

The play was next printed in the collected edition of Shakespeare's plays published in 1623, known as the first Folio ('F'). Here the printers began by reprinting from the Quarto of 1609 ('Q'), intending to place it among the tragedies, after *Romeo and Juliet*. When they had set three pages, headed 'The Tragedie of Troylus and Cressida', the printers of the Folio stopped work on the play, and they returned to it only after the rest of the collection was complete. They then reset the first page, and reused the other two previously set up; and they completed printing the play from a copy of the Quarto which they were able to correct and supplement from a manuscript. They did not include the epistle, which suggests that they were using a copy of the Quarto lacking it, and they were able to supply from manuscript a Prologue not in the Quarto. The play was inserted between the Histories and Tragedies in the Folio, too late for it to find a place in the list of contents or 'Catalogue' included among the preliminaries.

The textual history of the play is thus complicated, and unusual in that it involves questions of genre, since in its early printings the play appeared as history, comedy, and tragedy (see the Introduction, page 8). Various explanations have been offered to account for the peculiar features of the publication of *Troilus and Cressida* both in the Quarto and in the Folio, and all involve a good deal of speculation. We do not know why the printers of the Quarto changed the title-page; it may have been to avoid associating the play with the King's Men. We do not know who wrote the epistle, or when. It is often argued that it must have been written in 1602 or 1603 in relation to a private performance of a play written for an Inn of Court, but it could have been composed in 1609, and its claim to be presenting a new play never staged may have been an advertisement to attract readers. We do not know what Shakespeare, whose name appears on the Quarto title-page, thought about it, though he may have retired to Stratford by the time it was published. What can be asserted with more confidence is that the Quarto was printed from a manuscript probably in Shakespeare's hand, his 'foul papers', or final draft of the text. A notable feature of this text is the absence of many essential stage directions, which are supplied in the Folio. The Folio text was printed from the Quarto corrected against and supplemented by a manuscript marked up for stage use, a promptcopy, probably made by a scribe.

With the single exception of the heading to Act I in the Folio, '*Actus Primus. Scœna Prima*', neither text has act or scene divisions, which were first introduced by editors in the eighteenth century. Structurally the play may be seen as falling into two parts (see the Introduction, page 9), and there is no evidence that a division into five acts was relevant to performances at the Globe when this play was written.

Like most early play-texts, the Quarto has a good many errors or misreadings due to carelessness or oversight on the part of compositors, or their inability to make sense of the manuscript. The Folio corrects many of these, but also introduces new errors, perhaps because the manuscript its printers were consulting was not always easy to decipher. Both texts appear to be authoritative, but the Folio incorporates some additions to the Quarto, and also makes some cuts, so that the prompt-copy probably includes Shakespeare's revisions, and therefore should be preferred generally for substantive readings. So, for example, the long speech of Ulysses runs uninterrupted in the Quarto from I.3.54 to 137, but in the Folio is broken by a five-line speech inserted for Agamemnon:

> Speak, Prince of Ithaca; and be't of less expect
> That matter needless, of importless burden,
> Divide thy lips than we are confident
> When rank Thersites opes his mastic jaws
> We shall hear music, wit, and oracle.

No one doubts that these lines are by Shakespeare, and they serve the dramatic purposes not only of breaking up a long speech, but also of introducing the first mention of Thersites, preparing for his appearance in the next scene.

The Folio also corrects simple errors, like 'fame' for 'same' at I.3.236, and changes words and phrases in a way that suggests the dramatist reworking and having second thoughts, as for instance at II.3.129–31, which is changed as follows:

Q: His course, and time, his ebbs and flowes, and if
   The passage, and whole streame of his commencement
   Rode on his tide.

F: His pettish lines, his ebs, his flowes, as if
   The passage and whole carriage of this action
   Rode on his tide.

Here the Folio replaces 'course and time' by the more telling 'pettish lunes' ('lunes' misprinted as 'lines'), or tantrums, and tightens the image in the second line (how can a stream 'ride' on a tide?). A number of changes in the Folio appear to be indifferent variants, more or less equivalent to terms in the Quarto, and such as an author, copying out his own work, might introduce: examples are 'holding' (F) for 'keeping' (Q) at II.2.52; 'old' for 'elders' (II.2.105); 'noble' for 'notable' (III.1.6); 'merits ... most' for 'deserues ... best' (IV.1.54); 'disprizing' for 'misprizing' (IV.5.74); and 'retreat' for 'retire' (V.8.15). Critics may argue over the merits of these, but since the Folio seems to represent the latest Shakespearian version we have of the play, it is the basis of the present edition.

At the same time, any modern editor is bound to end up presenting an eclectic text, including certain words or lines omitted from the Folio and present in the Quarto, like 'tell' in 'I can tell you' at I.2.187. The Folio also has a number of errors that seem to have been introduced from the prompt-copy, or the printer's misreading of it. Examples include 'violenteth' (Q), where F has 'no lesse' (IV.4.4), 'strain'd' for 'strange' (IV.4.23), 'breath' for 'breach' (IV.5.92), and 'Spartan' for 'sparrow' (V.7.11). In these and other instances the Quarto is obviously correct, and no satisfactory explanation has emerged as to why a compositor should have preferred manuscript readings that made no sense to the correct readings he had in front of him in the printed Quarto.

Two further differences between the Quarto and Folio texts are of importance in understanding the nature of the play. When the printer began to set the Folio text, he presumably had in front of him the Quarto in its first state, without the epistle. When he started work again on the play, some time after the first three pages had been set, he was probably setting from a copy of the Quarto that had been corrected and revised against the prompt-book. He also had by him the text of a Prologue not printed in the Quarto. The Prologue promises a play about the Trojan War, not a comedy, but may be taken ironically, especially if it is regarded as a response to Ben Jonson's armed Prologue in his play *Poetaster* (see page 163). The second difference relates to the ending of the play. In both Quarto and Folio, the last scene ends with a kind of epilogue spoken by Pandarus, and introduced by a brief exchange between him and Troilus (V.10.32–4):

Pand. But heare you? heare you?
Troy. Hence broker, lackie, ignomy [Q: ignomyny], and
      shame
      Pursue thy life, and liue aye with thy name.

In the Folio these lines, with minor variants, are to be found also at the end of V.3, after Pandarus brings a letter from Cressida to Troilus. Here they appear to represent an alternative last exit for Pandarus. If then the end of V.10 were cancelled, the play would end on a note of revenge at V.10.31, and could more plausibly be regarded as a tragedy. If Pandarus ends the play with his sourly comic epilogue, the play can more readily be regarded as a comedy. It looks as though both endings were in the prompt-book, since there are variants in the Folio version of Pandarus's epilogue (like 'desired' for 'lou'd' at V.10.39), and if one of them was marked for cancellation, we do not know which, since the Folio printers included both. The printer of the Folio at first intended to place *Troilus and Cressida* among the tragedies, but this is not a secure guide to genre, since he also included *Cymbeline* as a tragedy. In this edition Pandarus's epilogue is retained and the alternative exit for him in V.3 is omitted (see the Introduction, page 9).

The following collation lists, which are selective, show substantive readings taken from F in preference to Q, and from Q in preference to F. They also list omissions and additions, and record points at which the present text departs significantly from both Q and F. Quotations from Q and F are printed as they appear in these early editions, that is, in old spelling (except that 'long s' (ſ) is replaced by 's') and, where appropriate, with speech-prefixes and punctuation also as found in the original texts.

COLLATIONS

I

The following is a list of readings in the present edition which are not in Q, or are taken from F in preference to Q. The Q reading is printed to the right of the bracket. In two cases, at I.1.26 and I.1.77, the F reading is taken from the second setting of the first page in the F text, which shows a number of changes from the first setting (see page 229 above).

Prologue (not in Q)

I.1.   15 must needs] must
           26 heating of] heating
           27 you may . . . to burn] yea may . . . burne
           72 on of you] of you

	77	were not] were
	79	care I] I
I.2.	117	lift] liste
	147	was more] was a more
	180	Ilium] Ilion (*so throughout*)
	191	a man] man
	204	man's] man
	235	ne'er] neuer
	240	come] comes
	247	among] amongst
	254	so forth] such like
	258	another] a
		One] a man
I.3	2	the jaundice on] these Iaundies ore
	8	Infect] Infects
	13	every] euer
	19	think them shame] call them shames
	31	thy] the
	36	patient] ancient
	55	nerve] nerues
	56	spirit] spright
	61	thy] the
	67	the heavens ride, knit all Greeks' ears] heauen rides; knit all the Greekish eares
	70–74	AGAMEMNON Speak . . . oracle] (*not in* Q)
	75	basis] bases
	92	ill aspects of planets evil] influence of euill Planets
	102	to] of
	106	primogenitive] primogenitie
	110	meets] melts
	119	includes] include
	128	in] with
	137	lives] stands
	149	awkward] sillie
	159	unsquared] vnsquare
	164	just] right
	165	hum] hem
	195	and] our
	207	swing] swinge

209 fineness] finesse
219 ears] eyes
236 fame] same
238 Jove's] great *Ioues*
242 he] the
247 affair] affaires
250 whisper] whisper with
252 sense on the] seat on that
256 loud] alowd
262 this] his
263 rusty] restie
265 amongst] among
267 That seeks] And feeds
276 compass] couple
289 or means] a meanes
290 I'll be] I am
293-4 mould | One . . . one] hoste | A . . . no
297 this . . . brawn] my . . . braunes
298 will tell] tell
301 pawn] proue
302 forbid . . . youth] for-fend . . . men
305 first] sir
315 This 'tis] (*not in* Q)
324 even as] as
332 Yes] Why
334 his honour] those honours
336 this] the
352 from hence receives the] receiues from hence a
354-6 Which entertained . . . the limbs] (*not in* Q)
359 show our foulest wares] First shew foule wares
361-2 better yet to show, | Shall show the better] better
      shall exceed, | By shewing the worse first
368 wear] share
370 we] it
373 did] do
377 as the worthier] for the better
388 of it] thereof
391 tarre . . . their] arre . . . a
II.1.   8 there would] would
       17 oration] oration without booke

18 learn a] learne
24 a fool] foole
28 Greece] Greece, when thou art forth in the incursions thou strikest as slow as another
36 AJAX Cobloaf] *Aiax Coblofe*
37–40 THERSITES He . . . AJAX You . . . THERSITES Do] (*speech-prefixes not in* Q)
44 Thou] you
54 do you this?] do yee thus,
61 I do so] so I do
69 I will] It will
73 I'll] I
86 for a] the
100 if he knock out] and knocke at
104 nails on their toes] nails
106 war] wars
121 fifth] first

II.2.
9 touches] toucheth
14–15 surety, | Surety] surely | Surely
27 father] fathers
33 at] of
35 reasons] reason
36 tells] tell
47 Let's] Sets
52 holding] keeping
59 inclinable] attributiue
65 shores] shore
68 chose] choose
71 spoiled] soil'd
75 of] with
80 stale] pale
87 he . . . noble] be . . . worthy
91 fortune never] neuer fortune
105 old] elders
106 can] canst
107 clamour] clamours
211 strike] shrike

II.3.
12 thou] yee
19 dependent] depending
24–5 have . . . wouldst] a . . . couldst

31 art] art not
34 in a] in
36–7 me! ACHILLES] me. *Patro.* Amen. *Achil.*
39 where?] where? O where?
46 thyself] Thersites
49 mayst] must
54–9 PATROCLUS You . . . a fool] (*not in* Q)
62–3 of Agamemnon] (*not in* Q)
64 Patroclus] this *Patroclus*
66 to the Creator] of the Prouer
68 Patroclus] Come *Patroclus*
73–4 Now the dry . . . confound all] (*not in* Q)
79 appertainments] appertainings
83 so say] say so
88–9 the cause] a cause
89 a word, my lord] (*not in* Q)
117 of] on
121 came] come
129 pettish lunes (lines F) . . . his flows, as if] course, and time . . . and flowes, and if
130 carriage of this action] streame of his commencement
140 enter you] entertaine
151 it] pride
152 clearer, Ajax] cleerer
157 I hate] I do hate
185 do] doth
189 Must] Shall
191 titled] liked
199 this] his
201 pash] push
203 An 'a] And he
210 let his humours] tell his humorous
218–19 ULYSSES A . . . | AJAX I] *Aiax.* A . . . I
221 praises] praiers
    in; his] his
224 You] Yon
225 doth] do's
230 thus with us] with vs thus
238 got] gat

240 beyond, beyond all] beyond all thy
246 bourn] boord
247 Thy] This
261 cull] call

III.1.   1 not you] you not
         6 noble] notable
        25 mean, friend] mean
        28 thou art too] thou to
        31 who's] who is
        35 you not] not you
        37 that thou] thou
        38 Cressida] *Cressid*
        87 make] makes
        89 your poor] your
       104 lord] lad
       111 PANDARUS In good troth, it begins so] (*not in Q*)
       115 shaft confounds] shafts confound
       145 They're] Their
           field] the field
       148 these] this
       156 thee] her

III.2.   3 he stays] stayes
         8 Like] Like to
        10 those] these
        36 unawares] vnwares
        79 This is the] This the
        90 merit crown it; no perfection] merit louer part no affection
       108 are] bee
       118 not till now so] till now not so;
       131 My soul of counsel from me] My very soule of councell
    148–9 Where is my wit? | I would be gone; I speak I know not what] I would be gone: | Where is my wit? I know not what I speake
       158 aye] age
       172 truths] trueth
       178 Yet, after] After
       183 and] or

238

191 as wolf] or Wolfe
198 pains] paine
209 and Pandar] Pander

III.3. 1 done you] done
        3 to your mind] to mind
       39 to pass] pass
       81 honoured] honour
      100 shining] ayming
      102 giver] giuers
      116 is] be
      128 abject] obiect
      140 on] one
      141 shrinking] shriking
      155 one] on
      158 hedge] turne
      160 hindmost] him, most
   161–3 Or . . . trampled on] (*not in* Q)
      164 past] passe
      169 O, let] Let
      184 Than] That
      197 every grain of Pluto's gold] euery thing
      198 deeps] depth
      224 a] (*not in* Q)
      233 we sit] they sit
      251 he] a
      255 his] this
   266–7 to him, Thersites] *Thersites*
      271 his demands] demands
      274 the most valorous] the valorous
      278 Grecian] (*not in* Q)
          et cetera] (*not in* Q)
      295 o'clock] of the clock
      299 you] yee
      301 he's out] out
      306 carry] beare

IV.1.   5 you] your
        9 within] wherein
       17 But] Lul'd
       33 despiteful'st] despiteful
       37 it was] twas

239

	41	do think] beleeue
	45	whereof] wherefore
	53	the soul] soule
	54	merits . . . most] deserues . . . best
	57	soilure] soyle
	77	you] they
IV.2.	13	hideously] tediously
	51	'Tis] its
	63	us; and for him] him, and
	66	concluded so] so concluded
	72	nature] neighbor Pandar
	87-8	knees I beseech you] knees
	101	extremity] extreames
	104	I will] Ile
IV.3.	2	Of] for
IV.4.	6	affection] affections
	49-50	Genius so	Cries 'Come!'] *Genius*	Cries so
	53	the root] my throate
	57	my love] loue
	63	there's] there is
	76	Their loving . . . nature] (*not in* Q)
	78	person] portion
	81	afraid] a feard
	131	my lord] you Lord
	134	I'll] I
	141	in] to
	143-7	DEIPHOBUS (*Dio.* F) Let us . . . chivalry] (*not in* Q)
IV.5.	15	toe] too
	43	not] nor
	55	a language] language
	61	tickling] ticklish
	65	all you] all the
	69	shall be] shall they be
	74	disprizing] misprizing
	94-5	They are opposed already.	AGAMEMNON] (*not in* Q)
	98	in deeds] deeds
	132	Of our rank feud] (*not in* Q)
	133	drop] day

161 mine] my
163 of] all
165–70 But that's . . . integrity] (*not in* Q)
178 that I . . . oath] thy . . . earth
187 And seen thee scorning] Despising many
188 thy] th'
190 unto] to some
193 hemmed] shrupd
199 Let] O let
206 As they . . . courtesy] (*not in* Q)
220 Yond] Yon
252 the] an
255 stithied] stichied
272 you] we
275 Beat loud the taborins] To taste your bounties
281 on heaven nor on] vpon the heauen nor
284 thee] you
287 As] But
292 she loved] my Lord

V.1.   4 core] curre
       12 need these] needs this
       14 boy] box
          thought] said
       18 guts-griping] the guts griping
          ruptures, catarrhs] ruptures
  19–20 palsies, and the like] palsies, rawe eies, durtrotte
          liuers, whissing lungs, bladders full of impost-
          ume. Sciaticaes lime-kills ith' palme, incurable
          bone-ach, and the riueled fee simple of the
          tetter
       23 mean'st] meanes
       26 cur] cur, no
       29 tassel] toslell
       51 brother] be
       53 hanging at his brother's] at his bare
       55 forced] faced
  56–7 he is both ox] her's both ox
       57 dog, a mule . . . a fitchew] day, a Moyle . . . a
          Fichooke
       60 Ask me not] Aske me

	62	Hoyday! Spirits] hey-day sprites
	73	both at once] both
	88–9	it, that it] it, it
	93	his tent] tent
V.2.	17	should] shall
	35	one] a
	37	pray you] pray
	41	Nay] now
	42	distraction] distruction
	47	Why, how now] How now my
	49	Foh, foh, adieu] Fo, fo
	57	tickles these] tickles
	58	But will] Will
	62	sweet] my
	69–70	I will be . . . CRESSIDA] (*not in* Q)
	73	have't] ha't
	81	in] on
	94	By] And by
	116	say] said
	120	co-act] Court
	125	had deceptious] were deceptions
	137	soil] spoile
	139	he] a
	142	are sanctimony] be sanctimonies
	145	is] was
	155	Ariachne's] *Ariachna's*
	160	five-finger-tied] finde finger tied
	163	bound] giuen
	172	in] on
V.3.	4	gone] in
	20–23	To hurt . . . CASSANDRA] (*not in* Q)
	45	mothers] Mother
	58	But by my ruin] (*not in* Q)
	84	dolour] dolours
	85	distraction] destruction
	89	yes, soft] yet soft
	93	of] worth
V.4.	3	foolish young] foolish
	26	art thou] art
V.5.	22	scalèd] scaling

	25	the] a
	41	luck] lust
V.6.	26	thou] I
V.7.	16–17	a bastard begot] bastard begot
V.8.	3	good] my
	11	thou: now, Troy] thou next, come Troy
	15	retreat . . . part] retire . . . prat
	16	Trojan trumpets] Troyans trumpet
V.9.	1	shout is that?] is this?
	6	a man as good] as good a man
V.10.	16	screech-owl] scrich-ould
	17	there 'Hector's] their Hectors
	21–2	But march away;	Hector is dead] (*not in* Q)
	23	vile] proud
	24	pight] pitcht
	33	Ignomy and shame] ignomyny, shame
	35	mine] my
	36	world, world, world!] world, world
	39	desired] lou'd
	51	your] my
	52	hold-door] hold-ore

2

The following is a list of readings in the present edition which
are not in F, or are taken from Q in preference to F. The F
reading is printed to the right of the bracket.

I.1.	46	praise her] praise it
I.2.	6	chid] chides
	29	purblind] purblinded
	34	disdain] disdaind
	69	nor] not
	118	Is he] Is he is
	169	for it] For is
	173	do] does
	187	tell] (*not in* F)
	192	judgements] judgement
	194	him] him him
	203	a brave] braue

206–7 there's laying] laying
207 will] ill
217 shall see] shall
231 note] not
239 an eye] money
255 season] seasons
257 date is] dates
263 lie, at] lye at, at
274 house; there he unarms him] house
294 Then] That
    content] Contents

I.3.   27 broad] lowd
31 godlike] godly
67 On] In
118 their] her
127 it is] is it
161 seem] seemes
190 keeps] and keepes
202 calls] call
228 bid] on
324 True] (*not in* F)

II.1.   6 then] (*not in* F)
90 the vile] thee vile
112 Thersites; peace!] *Thersites.*

II.2.   45–6 And fly . . . Jove, | Or like . . . reason] Or like . . .
    Reason, | And flye . . . Ioue
48 hare] hard
50 Make] Makes
57 mad] made
72 sieve] same
186 nations] Nation

II.3.   16 their] the
18 Neapolitan bone-ache] bone-ach
71–2 whore and a cuckold] Cuckold and a whore
72 emulous] emulations,
80 so, lest] of, so
87 if you] if
99 composure] counsell that
105 his legs] His legge
    flexure] flight

	119	like] and like
	125	tend] tends
	159	And yet] Yet
	170	worth] wroth
	174	down himself] gainst it selfe
	239	Famed] Fame
	241	thine] thy
	256	great general] our Generall
	263	boats sail . . . hulks] Botes may saile . . . bulkes
III.1.	17	titles] title
	84	I'll lay my life, with] With
	94	horribly] horrible
	112	still love, still] *still*
	156	PARIS Sweet] Sweete
III.2.	20	thrice-repurèd] thrice reputed
	22	tuned too] and to
	32	as short] so short
	70	safer] safe
	74	Nor] Not
	120	grown] grow
	150	speak so] speakes so
	190	water, wind or] Water, as Winde, as
III.3.	105–6	To others' . . . itself] (*not in* F)
	112	at] it at
	115	man] may
	137	fasting] feasting
	169	farewell] farewels
	183–4	sooner . . . stirs not] begin to . . . not stirs
	184	once] out
	210	our islands] her Iland
	225	air] ayrie ayre
IV.1.	10	a whole] in a whole
	17	meet] meetes
	66	nor less] no lesse
IV.2.	10	joys] eyes
IV.3.	9	his own] his
IV.4.	4	violenteth] no lesse
	9	dross] crosse
	11	ducks] ducke
	23	strained] strange

	40	one] our
	47	Distasted] Distasting
	56	When] *Troy.* When
	78	novelty] nouelties
	118	usage] visage
	121–2	to thee │ In] towards, │ I
IV.5.	13	yond] yong
	29	And parted . . . argument] (*not in* F)
	92	breath] breach
	96–7	knight, │ Not] Knight; they call him *Troylus;* │ Not
	144	could] could'st
	263	may have] may
V.1.	28	sleave-silk] Sleyd silke
	64	lights] light
V.2.	3	your] you
	11–12	sing . . . clef] finde . . . life
	23	forsworn] a forsworne. ——
	28	do] doe not
	44	all hell's] hell
	85	doth take] takes
	92	one's] one
	105	you] me
	124	th'attest] that test
	146–7	itself! │ Bifold] thy selfe │ By foule
	170	Cressid] *Cressida*
	176	sun] Fenne
V.3.	5	By all the] By the
	82	do] doth
	111	deeds.] deedes. │ *Pand.* Why, but heare you? │ *Troy.* Hence brother lackie; ignomie and shame │ Pursue thy life, and liue aye with thy name
V.4.	10	stale] stole
V.5.	24	strawy] straying
V.6.	13	thee, ha?] thee;
V.7.	6	arms] arme
	11	Spartan] sparrow
V.8.	7	dark'ning] darking
	13	and cry] cry
	16	sound] sounds

	20 bait] bed
V.10.	20 Cold] Coole

3

The following readings in the present edition differ from those of both Q and F. Most of these changes were first made by eighteenth-century editors. The reading to the right of the square bracket is common to Q and F unless otherwise indicated.

THE CHARACTERS IN THE PLAY] (*not in Q or F*)

Prologue	12 barks] Barke (F *only*)
	17 Antenorides] Antenonidus (F *only*)
I.1.	33 So, traitor! – 'when she comes'? – when is she] So traitor then she comes when she is
	39 storm] scorne
I.2.	87 wit] will
	130 the] thee
I.3.	51 flee] fled
	54 Returns] Retires
	63 Agamemnon, every hand] *Agamemnon* and the hand
	221 lords] heads
	340 willed] vilde (Q); wilde (F)
	354 are his] are in his (F *only*)
II.1.	14 you vinewd'st] thou vnsalted (Q); you whinid'st (F)
	19 o'thy] ath thy (Q); o'th thy (F)
	104 your grandsires] their grandsiers
II.3.	78 shent] sate (Q); sent (F)
III.1.	33 visible] inuisible
III.2.	19 palate tastes] pallats taste
	21 Swooning] Sounding
	66 fears] teares
	130 Cunning] Comming
	174 Want] Wants
	206 with a bed] (*not in Q or F*)
III.3.	4 come] loue
	110 mirrored] married

	162	abject rear] abiect, neere (F *only*)
	178	give] goe
	200	Does] Doe
IV.1.	67	he as you, each] he as he, the (Q); he as he, which (F)
IV.2.	31–2	capocchia] *Chipochia*
	54	Whoa] Who
IV.4.	76	gifts] guift (F *only*)
	77	flowing] swelling (Q); Flawing and swelling (F)
	121	zeal] seale
IV.5.	37	MENELAUS] *Patr.*
	59	accosting] a coasting
	73	ACHILLES] (*speech-prefix not in* Q *or* F)
	143	oyez] O yes
V.1.	5	botch] batch
	72	sewer] sure
V.2.	84	Nay] *Dio.* Nay
	105	TROILUS] *Ther.*
	170	as much as] as much
V.4.	16	begin] began
V.5.	11	Epistrophus and Cedius] *Epistropus* and *Cedus*
V.7.	11	double-horned] double hen'd
V.10.	47	cloths] cloathes

4

Stage directions

The stage directions in the present edition are based on those of F. Q lacks many essential directions, including a large number of entrances and exits. F appears to incorporate stage directions from a manuscript marked up for use in the theatre.

List A below shows stage directions, or words and phrases in stage directions, found in F but not in Q. Where there is a significant difference between Q and F, the directions in both texts are given, Q first. This list also includes the four stage directions found in Q and omitted, probably by oversight, from F; these are at III.2.207, V.1.75, V.2.199, and V.9.2.

List B shows stage directions added, or significantly

changed, in the present edition, including exits and entrances not marked in either Q or F. This list does not include asides, or directions for one character to address specifically another one on stage, for example, '*to Paris*' at III.1.83, or '*To Aeneas*' at IV.1.35; there are no directions of this kind in the early texts, and all have been added in this edition.

List A

I.2.	38	*Enter Pandarus.*
	239	*Enter common Souldiers.*
	280	*Exit Pand.*
I.3.	0	*Senet.*
	212	*Tucket*
	214	*Enter Æneas*
	309	*Exeunt. Manet Vlysses, and Nestor.*
II.1.	11	*Strikes him.*
	53	*Enter Achilles, and Patroclus.*
	129	*Exit.*
II.2.	101	*Enter Cassandra rauing* (Q); *Enter Cassandra with her haire about her eares.* (F)
II.3.	21	*Enter Patroclus.*
	69	*Exit.*
	102	*Enter Patroclus.*
	140	*Exit Vlisses.*
III.1.	0	*Enter Pandarus* (Q); *Musicke sounds within. Enter Pandarus and a Seruant.* (F)
III.2.	3	*Enter Troylus.*
	27	*Enter Pandarus.*
	32	*Exit Pand.*
	97	*Enter Pandarus.*
	207	*Exeunt* (Q)
III.3.	0	*Enter Vlisses, Diomed, Nestor, Agamem, Chalcas* (Q); *Enter Vlysses, Diomedes, Nestor, Agamemnon, Menelaus, and Chalcas. Florish.* (F)
	37	*Achilles and Patro. stand in their tent* (Q); *Enter Achilles and Patroclus in their Tent.* (F)
IV.1.	0	*Æneas* (Q); *Æneas with a Torch* (F)
	51	*Exit Æneas*
IV.2.	19	*within.*
	22	*Enter Pandarus.*

	57	*Enter Troylus.*
	73	*Enter Pandarus and Cressid.*
	108	*Exeunt.*
IV.4.	96	*Enter Æneas.*
	100	*Exit. (misplaced; omitted from the present edition)*
	107	*Enter the Greekes.*
	138	*Sound Trumpet.*
IV.5.	63	*Exeunt. (misplaced; omitted from the present edition)*
	64	*Flowrish enter all of Troy* (Q); *Enter all of Troy, Hector, Paris, Æneas, Helenus, and Attendants. Florish.* (F)
	158	*Enter Agamemnon and the rest.*
V.1.	44	*Exit.*
	62	*Hector, Ajax,* (Troilus is not named in Q or F)
	65	*Enter Achilles.*
	75	*Exeunt Agam: Menelaus* (Q)
	94	*Exeunt*
V.2.	5	*Enter Troylus and Vlisses.*
	108	*Exit.*
	199	*Exit* (Q)
V.4.	0	*A Larum.*
		Enter Thersites: excursions (Q); *Enter Thersites in excursion.* (F)
	17	*Enter Diomed and Troylus.*
V.6.	11	*Exit Troylus.*
V.8.	22	*Sound Retreat. Shout.*
V.9.	2	*within* (Q)
V.10.	34	*Exeunt all but Pandarus* (Q); *Exeunt.* (F)
	57	*Exeunt.*

List B

Prologue	0	*Enter Prologue in armour*] (not in Q or F)
	31	*Exit* (not in Q or F)
I.2.	0	*Alexander*] (not in Q or F)
	1–40	(speech-prefixes) ALEXANDER] *Man* (Q and F)
	54	*Exit Alexander*] (not in Q or F)
	185	*Aeneas passes across the stage*] *Enter Æneas.* (Q and F)
	188	*Antenor passes across the stage*] *Enter Antenor.* (Q and F)

198 *Hector passes across the stage*] *Enter Hector.* (Q and F)

212 *Paris passes across the stage*] *Enter Paris.* (Q and F)

217 *Helenus passes across the stage*] *Enter Helenus.* (Q and F)

226 *Troilus passes across the stage*] *Enter Troylus.* (Q and F)

239 *Common soldiers pass across the stage*] (not in Q); *Enter common Souldiers.* (F)

275 *Exit Boy*] (not in Q or F)

II.1. 39 *beating him*] (not in Q or F)

51 *beating him*] (not in Q or F)

75 *Ajax threatens to beat him; Achilles intervenes*] (not in Q or F)

II.2. 98, 100 *within*] (not in Q or F)

II.3. 0 *Enter Thersites*] *Enter* Thersites *solus.* (Q and F)

89 *He takes Agamemnon aside*] (not in Q or F)

138 *Exit*] (not in Q or F)

III.1. 42 *Enter Paris and Helen with attendants*] *Enter Paris and Hellen* (Q and F, F reading 'Helena')

144 *Exit*] (not in Q or F)

III.2. 0 *meeting*] (not in Q or F)

5 *Exit Man*] (not in Q or F)

37 *veiled*] (not in Q or F)

58 *Exit*] (not in Q or F)

132 *He kisses her*] (not in Q or F)

III.3. 61 *Exeunt Agamemnon and Nestor*] (not in Q or F)

63 *Exit*] (not in Q or F)

69 *Exit*] *Exeunt.* (Q and F)

215 *Exit*] (not in Q or F)

309 *Exeunt Achilles and Patroclus*] (not in Q or F)

312 *Exit*] (not in Q or F)

IV.1. 0 *and a servant*] (not in Q or F)
and others] (not in Q or F)

51 *with servant*] (not in Q or F)

IV.2. 43 *Enter Aeneas*] (not in Q or F)

57 *Exit Pandarus*] (not in Q or F)

IV.4. 12 *embracing Troilus*] (not in Q or F)

107 *Enter Aeneas, Paris, Antenor, Deiphobus, and Diomedes*] *Enter the Greekes.* (F; not in Q)

138 *Exeunt Troilus, Cressida, and Diomedes*] (*not in Q or F*)

IV.5.　　　0 *and trumpeter*] *&c.* (*Q and F*)

11 *Trumpet sounds*] (*not in Q or F*)

16 *Enter Diomedes with Cressida*] (*not in Q or F*)

18 *kissing her*] (*not in Q or F*)

22, 24, 29 *He kisses her*] (*not in Q or F*)

32 *He kisses her again*] (*not in Q or F*)

87 *Enter Diomedes*] (*not in Q or F*)

93 *Hector and Ajax prepare to fight*] (*not in Q or F*)

112 *Hector and Ajax fight*] (*not in Q or F*)

158 *Agamemnon and the rest come forward*] (*not in Q*); *Enter Agamemnon and the rest.* (F)

276 *all but Troilus and Ulysses*] (*not in Q or F*) *Drums and trumpets sound*] (*not in Q or F*)

V.1.　　　9 *Achilles stands aside to read his letter*] (*not in Q or F*)

62 *Enter Hector, Troilus, Ajax, Agamemnon, Ulysses, Nestor, Menelaus, Diomedes, with lights*] *Enter Agam: Vlisses, Nest: and Diomed with lights* (Q); *Enter Hector, Aiax, Agamemnon, Vlysses, Nestor, Diomed, with Lights.* (F)

82 *Exit Diomedes, Ulysses and Troilus following*] (*not in Q or F*)

83 *Exeunt Achilles, Hector, Ajax, and Nestor*] *Exeunt.* (*Q and F*)

V.2.　　2, 5 *within*] (*not in Q or F*)

5 *Enter Troilus and Ulysses at a distance; after them, Thersites*] (*not in Q*); *Enter Troylus and Vlisses.* (F)

8 *She whispers to him*] (*not in Q or F*)

66 *She gives him the sleeve*] (*not in Q or F*)

71 *She snatches the sleeve*] (*not in Q or F*)

84 *Diomedes takes the sleeve*] (*not in Q or F*)

V.3.　　94 *Exeunt Priam and Hector by different doors*] (*not in Q or F*)

108 *He tears the letter*] (*not in Q or F*)

V.4.　　25 *Exeunt Troilus and Diomedes, fighting*] (*not in Q or F*)

30 *Exit*] (*not in Q or F*)

V.5.　　　5 *Exit*] (*not in Q or F*)

16 *with soldiers*] (*not in Q or F*)

V.6.	11	*Exeunt, fighting*] (*not in* Q); *Exit Troylus.* (F)
	13	*They fight*] (*not in* Q *or* F)
	26	*sumptuous*] (*not in* Q *or* F)
V.7.	8	*Enter Menelaus and Paris, fighting; then Thersites*] *Enter Thersi: Mene: Paris* (Q); *Enter Thersites, Menelaus, and Paris.* (F)
	12	*Enter Margarelon*] *Enter Bastard.* (Q *and* F)
	22	*Exit*] (*not in* Q *or* F)
V.8.	0	*carrying a suit of armour*] (*not in* Q *or* F)
	10	*Hector falls*] (*not in* Q *or* F)
	14	*A retreat sounded*] *Retreat.* (Q *and* F)
V.9.	0	*to drumbeats. Shouts within*] (*not in* Q); *Sound Retreat. Shout.* (F, *after* V.8.22)
V.10.	0	*and soldiers with drums*] (*not in* Q *or* F)

5

Rejected emendations

The following is a list of the more interesting emendations adopted or suggested by earlier editors of *Troilus and Cressida* but rejected in the present edition. The emendations are to the right of the bracket, separated by semi-colons when there is more than one.

Prologue	19	Stir] Sperr
	25	conditions] condition
I.3.	54	Returns] (Retires Q, F); Rechides
II.1.	110	much] much wit
	113	brooch] brach
II.2.	105	old] (elders Q); eld
III.1.	83	HELEN] (*omitted*)
III.2.	175	plantage] planets
III.3.	34	bring word if] bear word that
	168	the welcome] welcome
IV.5.	48	then] too; two; then do

READ MORE IN PENGUIN

In every corner of the world, on every subject under the sun, Penguin represents quality and variety – the very best in publishing today.

For complete information about books available from Penguin – including Puffins, Penguin Classics and Arkana – and how to order them, write to us at the appropriate address below. Please note that for copyright reasons the selection of books varies from country to country.

In the United Kingdom: Please write to *Dept. EP, Penguin Books Ltd, Bath Road, Harmondsworth, West Drayton, Middlesex UB7 0DA*

In the United States: Please write to *Consumer Sales, Penguin Putnam Inc., P.O. Box 999, Dept. 17109, Bergenfield, New Jersey 07621-0120.* VISA and MasterCard holders call 1-800-253-6476 to order Penguin titles

In Canada: Please write to *Penguin Books Canada Ltd, 10 Alcorn Avenue, Suite 300, Toronto, Ontario M4V 3B2*

In Australia: Please write to *Penguin Books Australia Ltd, P.O. Box 257, Ringwood, Victoria 3134*

In New Zealand: Please write to *Penguin Books (NZ) Ltd, Private Bag 102902, North Shore Mail Centre, Auckland 10*

In India: Please write to *Penguin Books India Pvt Ltd, 210 Chiranjiv Tower, 43 Nehru Place, New Delhi 110 019*

In the Netherlands: Please write to *Penguin Books Netherlands bv, Postbus 3507, NL-1001 AH Amsterdam*

In Germany: Please write to *Penguin Books Deutschland GmbH, Metzlerstrasse 26, 60594 Frankfurt am Main*

In Spain: Please write to *Penguin Books S. A., Bravo Murillo 19, 1° B, 28015 Madrid*

In Italy: Please write to *Penguin Italia s.r.l., Via Benedetto Croce 2, 20094 Corsico, Milano*

In France: Please write to *Penguin France, Le Carré Wilson, 62 rue Benjamin Baillaud, 31500 Toulouse*

In Japan: Please write to *Penguin Books Japan Ltd, Kaneko Building, 2-3-25 Koraku, Bunkyo-Ku, Tokyo 112*

In South Africa: Please write to *Penguin Books South Africa (Pty) Ltd, Private Bag X14, Parkview, 2122 Johannesburg*

READ MORE IN PENGUIN

THE NEW PENGUIN SHAKESPEARE

All's Well That Ends Well	Barbara Everett
Antony and Cleopatra	Emrys Jones
As You Like It	H. J. Oliver
The Comedy of Errors	Stanley Wells
Coriolanus	G. R. Hibbard
Hamlet	T. J. B. Spencer
Henry IV, Part 1	P. H. Davison
Henry IV, Part 2	P. H. Davison
Henry V	A. R. Humphreys
Henry VI, Parts 1–3	Norman Sanders
(three volumes)	
Henry VIII	A. R. Humphreys
Julius Caesar	Norman Sanders
King John	R. L. Smallwood
King Lear	G. K. Hunter
Love's Labour's Lost	John Kerrigan
Macbeth	G. K. Hunter
Measure for Measure	J. M. Nosworthy
The Merchant of Venice	W. Moelwyn Merchant
The Merry Wives of Windsor	G. R. Hibbard
A Midsummer Night's Dream	Stanley Wells
Much Ado About Nothing	R. A. Foakes
The Narrative Poems	Maurice Evans
Othello	Kenneth Muir
Pericles	Philip Edwards
Richard II	Stanley Wells
Richard III	E. A. J. Honigmann
Romeo and Juliet	T. J. B. Spencer
The Sonnets *and* **A Lover's Complaint**	John Kerrigan
The Taming of the Shrew	G. R. Hibbard
The Tempest	Anne Barton
Timon of Athens	G. R. Hibbard
Troilus and Cressida	R. A. Foakes
Twelfth Night	M. M. Mahood
The Two Gentlemen of Verona	Norman Sanders
The Two Noble Kinsmen	N. W. Bawcutt
The Winter's Tale	Ernest Schanzer